Education For An Industrial Age explores the relationship between the economic structure and the educational system of the United States. It reveals a growing divergence between the education currently provided for our young people and the requirements of the economy and the worker.

STUDIES OF THE INSTITUTE OF WORLD AFFAIRS

EDUCATION FOR AN

INDUSTRIAL AGE

Alfred Kähler and Ernest Hamburger

6534

Published for

The Institute of World Affairs

CORNELL UNIVERSITY PRESS

ITHACA AND NEW YORK, 1948

Preface

THIS book, which attempts an evaluation of the present state of vocational education and training in the United States, with comparative notes on several European countries, grew out of a research project on "Technological Trends and the Flexibility of Labor," in which the Institute of World Affairs was engaged from 1943 to 1947.

It was in the context of the public discussion on "full employment" that our attention was first drawn to the significance of these issues. As is common knowledge, for the last decade two opposed social philosophies have been at variance over the appropriate means of assuring a high and stable level of employment. But the passion with which each side argues its case should not blind us to their underlying agreement on a fundamental premise. Whether they put their trust in the spontaneous operation of free enterprise, or postulate more or less stringent measures of public intervention, the partners to the dispute seem exclusively preoccupied with stabilizing the *demand* for labor.

To be sure, stability of the aggregate demand for commodities and services, and thus for the labor force that provides them, is a necessary condition for the stability of employment. But common sense makes it quite clear that this condition cannot be sufficient. In a dynamic economy, wherein changes in taste and technology continually alter the qualitative forms and the relative importance of individual commodities and services, even when aggregate demand is quantitatively stable, the level of employment must also be profoundly affected by the *supply* conditions of labor. No market economy, be it free or directed, can guarantee a worker a working place, unless he is willing and able to adjust his technical performance, as well as his place of residence, to such qualitative variations in demand.

The willingness and ability to adjust to change are influenced by many factors, both personal and social. But in the framework of modern industrialism, the occupational skill and the versatility of a large part of the working population play a predominant role in determining the elasticity of the labor supply. In other words, the mobility of the labor force and thus the achievement of employment stability have become largely an educational problem.

In the light of this recognition, vocational education and training gains new significance. But its social importance is even more far-flung. The following pages describe the way in which the investigators were led quite naturally from the economic aspects of the problem to its wider social and cultural implications. Thus the study confirms the methodological principle that no social issue can be fully explored except through a synthesis of the different specialist approaches.

All the work that has gone into the making of this book has been under the direction of Dr. Alfred Kähler, Professor of Economics in the Graduate Faculty of the New School for Social Research. During the last two years Dr. Ernest Hamburger participated in all important aspects of the study. In the early stages of the project much of the research was done by Drs. Josef Berolzheimer, André Lion, and Max Nurnberg. Miss Esther Sussman acted as secretary for the duration of the project and also contributed a great part of the statistical work. Whereas the Institute of World Affairs acknowledges the services of this group with sincere appreciation, it should be noted that, as is the case with all Institute publications, the views expressed in this book are those of the authors alone.

The very extensive and time-consuming investigations, on which the book is based, were made possible by the generous assistance of the Board of Directors of the Hebrew Technical Institute, New York. The lasting gratitude of the Institute of World Affairs, as well as of the authors, is due them, especially Dr. K. George Falk,

William Dubilier, Solon E. Friedeberg, and Charles Mayer. Not only did they grant us unstinting material support; they also showed unflagging interest in the substance of our work, and their expert advice proved of great value in many matters relating to the theory and practice of vocational education.

The Council of Research of the Institute of World Affairs rendered important service by reviewing the progress of the work in all its stages. Special thanks must go to Professors Shepard Clough and Robert MacIver of Columbia University and Professor Frieda Wunderlich of the Graduate Faculty of the New School for Social Research, members of the Council's Special Advisory Committee for the project. The final text owes much to their constructive criticism of earlier versions. The discerning analyses of the manuscript made by David M. Freudenthal and Kurt Porges were also very fruitful.

The Institute, on behalf of the authors and the publishers, wishes to express special gratitude and appreciation to its Associate Editor, Miss Janet Rosenwald. Her understanding, patience, and editorial skill succeeded in transforming a voluminous manuscript into a readable book.

ADOLPH LOWE

Executive Director of Research,
Institute of World Affairs

Introduction

THE objective of the project on "Technological Trends and the Flexibility of Labor" was to analyze the effects of modern technological developments on occupational requirements and to investigate the institutions that could give the labor force an opportunity to acquire the necessary technical knowledge and skills. It was originally intended to lay special emphasis on the work of technical institutes as the main source of training, but early in the course of our study we recognized that the public school system, merely by virtue of its continuous expansion, would have to contribute increasingly to the occupational preparation of youth. The public school, however, has a wider task: its function is to prepare for life—that is, for citizenship and cultural pursuits, as well as for work, and for the development of the individual. A great part of our study, therefore, was necessarily devoted to the problem of how to integrate, especially at the high school level, education for work and these various tasks into a truly general education.

Our technological studies reaffirmed the great importance of mechanization in modern industry and the concomitant need for applied scientific and technical knowledge. At the same time, they demonstrated, contrary to a popular misconception, that manual skills and work experience have remained essential to the effective operation of our industrialized economy. It was also confirmed that the established school system, supplemented by part-time technical education and technical institute courses, can contribute substantially to all required training. Our research, however, revealed the limits to which manual skills and work experience can be acquired in school. We found it necessary, therefore, to investigate apprenticeship and other forms of in-employment training. In view of the fact that this kind of training is not extensively developed in the United States, an inquiry into the educational and training systems of other countries appeared desirable. Germany, Great Britain, Switzerland, and the Soviet Union were chosen for study, each representing a special type of training.

The comparative study underlined the uniqueness of the American educational system, which differs from that of the Old World in scope, aim, and approach to an extent hardly comprehensible or even discernible to the casual observer. Each system is adapted to the technological, social, and political conditions and aspirations of its own nation, yet international comparisons broaden the point of view. It is hoped, therefore, that this portion of the book will increase the understanding of the specifically American problems of occupational training.

Statistical and literary analyses of the economic structure of the country and of our existing educational facilities were extremely revealing in themselves. It was felt, however, that only a broad program of field work in schools and industrial plants could really illuminate our findings. In the course of this investigation we had countless private discussions with key individuals in both areas, which were then supplemented by organized conferences and panel discussions to which leading representatives of education, industry, labor, and various government agencies contributed invaluable information and criticism.

Of the many persons, institutions, and agencies who made it possible for us to achieve our goal we can mention here only a few. Our gratitude to the others, however, is very genuine.

From Dr. J. C. Wright, Assistant United States Commissioner for Vocational Education, United States Office of Education, Washington, D.C., and his associates, we received immeasurable assistance. Dr. Oakley Furney, Assistant Commissioner for Vocational Education, at Albany, gave us the benefit of the wealth of experience accumulated by New York State in the field of vocational education. Our frequent contacts with Dr. Furney and his coworkers were always as productive as they were friendly. To the Board of Education of the City of New York we are indebted for the opportunity to see the school system in operation. We are especially grateful to Dr. George Pigott, Jr., Associate Superintendent, for permitting us to visit classes in vocational high schools, a privilege of which we made extensive use. Dr. Morris Siegel, Assistant Superintendent, was an unfailing source of valuable advice and enlightenment.

Educators and state and municipal authorities in Connecticut, New Jersey, and Pennsylvania cooperated generously in enabling us to study schools outside New York City. In this connection, a special note of thanks is due Girard College in Philadelphia. Other state and municipal agencies and educational institutions throughout the country supplied us liberally with answers to specific queries and with their own publications, thus helping us to round out our documentation.

From the outset of our project, Dr. Franklin J. Keller, Principal of the Metropolitan Vocational High School in New York City, encouraged us with his lively interest and gave us much wise counsel. Dr. Keller read an early draft of our manuscript and contributed substantially to its revision through pertinent suggestions based on his long and untiring devotion to the cause of vocational education.

So many principals, teachers, and advisors in general and vocational high schools gave freely of their time and experience to explain the functioning of their schools that they cannot be listed individually here. It may be recorded, however, that we availed ourselves of this assistance most amply at the East New York Vocational High School, the New York School of Printing, the Machine and Metal Trades High School, the Metropolitan Vocational High School, the Brooklyn Technical High School, the Bronx High School of Science, and the Essex County Vocational and Technical High School in Newark. Dr. Mortimer C. Ritter, Principal of the Central High School of Needle Trades, was also, in his additional capacity of Director of the Fashion Institute of Technology and Design, a reliable and always helpful guide in our approach to the problem of technical institutes.

Extremely valuable aid in our study of in-employment training was extended to us by the Apprentice-Training Service of the United States Department of Labor and that of the New York State Department of Labor. John E. Gallagher of the federal agency, and John F. Marion of the state, gave us both advice and essential data. The United States Employment Service and the Vocational Advisory Service in New York furnished us with valuable material in their respective fields. We were also especially fortunate in securing the cooperation of George F. Fern of the American Vocational Association.

Of the many persons who helped us to integrate the views and requirements of management and labor with our research, we should like to mention particularly M. M. Boring, General Electric Company; Alfred Braunthal, Research Director, United Hatters, Cap and Millinery Workers International Union; Donald Bridgman, American Telephone and Telegraph Company; William H. Friedman, Chairman, Graphic Arts Educational Commission, New York; S. Avery Raube, National Industrial Conference Board; Stanley H. Ruttenberg, Assistant Director of Education and Research, Congress of Industrial Organizations; and Mark Starr, Educational Director, International Ladies' Garment Workers' Union.

ALFRED KÄHLER
ERNEST HAMBURGER

New York, January 13, 1948

Contents

Tables

I

The Problem and Its Background

THE American people stand squarely and hopefully on the threshold of an era in which the average standard of living will reach a new and higher level. Made freshly aware of their country's potential strength by the industrial and technological advances realized during World War II, they envision a future in which the comfort and security that our economy can provide will be the rule and not the exception. A reassuring prospect, to be sure, and yet not beyond the realm of possibility if the widest use of our rich natural resources is supported by the full development of the productive power of the entire population.

EDUCATIONAL GOALS

The United States has long cherished a belief in education as a means of heightening productive power, and conviction on all sides has never been stronger than it is today that in the expansion and improvement of education lies the path to future progress. But at that point agreement ends. The direction of expansion, the content of the adjusted educational program, and the proper participating institutions are subjects of unremitting and heated debate.

The mere extension of our existing academic education is obviously not a solution. However phenomenal its development, and however great its contribution, the traditional system has failed to meet the needs of a vastly augmented school population and of a period in which new social and occupational groups have come forward to claim a significant place in a highly industrialized nation. Academic education as it has evolved in this country is so closely oriented around the occupational needs of the professions and the commercial and clerical groups that it falls far short of providing occupational preparation for the population as a whole. The discrepancy becomes appallingly clear when one considers that approximately 70 per cent of the gainfully employed persons are not included in these groups but are, instead, engaged in work requiring manual skills and technical knowledge.

This situation is wholly incompatible with the industrial progress so earnestly desired, for the full productive power of a nation rests on a proportionate distribution of the labor force among the different occupational branches of the economy at all times. Thus any educational policy designed to serve the country as a whole must aim at increased proficiency in all trades, services, and strata of work, from the professional level to that of unskilled labor. In an effort to determine how the imbalance can be adjusted, this study is primarily concerned with that large group of workers who are not members of the professional and white-collar classes.

It is a curious commentary that for the most part the literature on the role of full employment in attaining a sound and prosperous economy has placed the burden exclusively on the *demand* for commodities, with no reference whatever to the possible effect of what labor can supply. And yet it may well be that the limitations and rigidities of labor itself restrain the productive capacity of the country and thus constitute a persuasive factor in the employment situation. Adopting that premise, the authors regard as the main objective of this study the determination of the means whereby the industry and ingenuity and occupational skills of the great body of the labor force can be developed to the fullest. Although the large manufacturing industries function mainly with semi-skilled and unskilled labor, these workers comprise only a relatively small portion of all the gainfully employed. A substantial section of the labor force must be able to initiate independent production or to perform skilled work of a diversified nature. Without a labor force so trained, any full employment policy, regardless of the amount of government funds devoted to its support, will be more likely to result in price rises and makeshift employment than in a sound increase in useful production and services and the full utilization of the nation's labor force.

The core of this study is, therefore, occupational preparation for work, which at the same time it considers a fundamental principle and an integral part of education, inextricably linked with the economic and moral fiber of our western civilization. Any assumption, however, that only the occupational needs of a country are to be served by education would be, of course, entirely fallacious. If the last war taught us anything besides the value of a more efficient system of occupational training, it was the need for expanded moral, cultural, political, and economic education. Indeed, it is characteristic of all good education to aim at the development of balanced personalities—men who can play as well as work, consume as well as produce, appreciate as well as create. In facing this issue the authors of this study have constantly borne in mind the multiple purposes of education; and they believe that any realignment of the present system should aim at the simultaneous improvement of education for citizenship, for an understanding of human values, and for productive work.

In this connection, the study is not at odds with the views of the proponents of a liberal arts education, as represented by the Harvard report, *General Education in a Free Society*, although the approaches and emphases differ and the opinions on how to attain the educational goals are widely divergent. The Harvard report holds the humanities to be the center of all education that provides unity and direction in life. It finds, nevertheless, 'that the aim of education should be to prepare an individual to become an expert both in some particular vocation or art and in the general art of the free man and the citizen.' [1] Conversely, not even the most ardent advocate of vocational education would deny the value of general education in preparing youth for citizenship and

---

[1] Harvard University Committee on the Objectives of General Education in a Free Society, *General Education in a Free Society* . . . (Cambridge, 1945), p. 45.

participation in cultural life. He would, however, go further by stressing how greatly the experience of working contributes toward building character, stability, and common sense, and heightening an appreciation of democracy. This study holds, therefore, that preparation for work is an indispensable component of an education designed to give unity and direction to life. Approaching the task of education with a different orientation and a somewhat different aim, the participants in this study are no less convinced than the champions of the modern liberal arts education that there are no insurmountable obstacles to the attainment of their common goal.

IMPLICATIONS OF THE AMERICAN SCHOOL SYSTEM FOR OCCUPATIONAL TRAINING

In their historical development, the centers of systematic occupational preparation have undergone considerable change in all countries. As production in separate industrial workshops increased, the home, which for centuries had been the center of occupational training, offered fewer and fewer opportunities, until today, only on farms is there any identity between family life and life in the chosen trade. The industrial workshops developed their own types of training, of which apprenticeship was the most highly organized form, and during the period when handicraft was at its height, apprenticeship constituted a major part of all education. With the widespread growth of factories and the increase in mechanization, however, this system steadily declined. Concurrently, formal education was necessarily extended to larger sections of the population of industrial countries until schools were finally in a position to make a definite contribution to occupational training.

The United States, because of its swift transition from a predominantly agricultural to a large-scale industrial economy, displayed a rather different pattern of occupational training from that of European countries. Owing to its newness and vastness, this country was slow to attain the level of formal schooling that prevailed in Europe, but eventually it outstripped all other countries and has never conceded that there was a limit beyond which it was not willing to go. As shown by the accompanying figures on school attendance between 1910 and 1940, expressed in percentages of specific age groups,[2] the rise in school attendance has been

	14-year-olds	*15-year-olds*	*16 & 17-year-olds*
1910	81.2%	68.3%	43.1%
1920	86.3	72.9	42.9
1930	92.9	84.7	57.3
1940	92.5	87.6	68.7

meteoric in the last three decades. By 1940 virtually all of the fourteen-year-olds and more than 87 per cent of the fifteen-year-olds were attending school full time, while of the sixteen and seventeen-year-olds, nearly 70 per cent were still in school. On the basis of this continuous lengthening of average school attendance and in view of the current trend toward making school virtually compulsory for children up to eighteen, it is reasonable to expect that school attendance for the bulk of American youth will continue to be extended or at least to maintain its exceptionally high level—a factor that has considerable bearing on the problem of occupational preparation of this youth.

This situation is unique, and its implications are even more striking when a comparison is made with conditions in European countries, as in the accompanying figures on school attendance in the United States, England, and Germany.[3] In Germany approximately 80 per cent of the children leave school at fourteen. School attendance for the youngest group in England is comparatively high be-

[2] Computed from Fifteenth Census of the United States, 1930, *Population*, vol. 2 (Washington, 1933), pp. 1096, 1098, and Sixteenth Census . . . 1940, *Population*, vol. 2, *Characteristics of the Population*, Part I, U.S. Summary (Washington, 1943), Tables 11 and 12. Figures for earlier years include part-time and evening school attendance and are therefore not comparable with the figures in Chapter III, which refer only to secondary education; figures for 1940 refer only to full-time attendance.

[3] U.S. figures taken from Sixteenth Census . . . 1940, Population, vol. 2, *Characteristics of the Population* (cited above), Table 11; see Appendix I for sources of English and German figures.

	U.S.	England	Germany
	1940	*1938*	*1931–32*
14-year-olds	92.5%	36.9%	19.4%
15-year-olds	87.6	14.5	16.0
16 & 17-year-olds	68.7	6.8	5.3

cause most children do not complete their elementary education until after they are fourteen, but attendance for the older groups is virtually at the low German level. It is in the sixteen and seventeen-year-old groups that the difference between Europe and the United States is most telling, with the attendance in England and Germany averaging about 6 per cent as opposed to nearly 70 per cent in this country. Thus, in the United States, almost all children are in school full time during their formative years, while in European countries this advantage is enjoyed by only a small minority.

Quite aside from the quantitative variance, there is a vast difference in the basic structure of the American and European school systems.[4] In the United States, primary or elementary school prepares for secondary or high school, and this in turn for college, which in its turn leads to professional school, the whole progression being made within what is essentially a one-line system. In Europe, on the other hand, for the great mass of the population, there is elementary school education, terminal for most children at fourteen and from which they cannot automatically transfer to any other type of free formal schooling. Parallel to this arrangement, yet distinct from it in scope and aim since it involves only a small fraction of the youth, is the program which, after a few years of elementary education, provides eight or nine years of secondary education and extends finally to professional studies at the university level. The separation of students between these two systems usually takes place when they are ten or eleven years old. Enrollments in the secondary schools are small and can in no way be compared with those in the United States.

[4] More detailed accounts of the educational and industrial training structure in Germany, Great Britain, Switzerland, and the Soviet Union are contained in Appendices I–III.

Such a structure implies rigid social, as well as quantitative, limitations, for while most elementary education is tuition-free, secondary and university education are not. This expense, combined with the fact that the more extended course defers wage earning for a considerable number of years, rather rigorously excludes the bulk of European youth from advanced schooling—a strong contrast to the steady democratization that has marked the development of free education in the United States.

It would be unfair, however, to judge European education for work by its formal schooling alone, for the deficiencies in educational opportunities in most of the industrial countries are balanced by an elaborate system of trade training. A wide section of the working population supplements its elementary education with a four-year apprenticeship and finds this combination of schooling with industrial training the best available preparation for economic life. During the apprenticeship, some additional technical instruction is generally obtained in continuation schools, which reach a great number of persons but are limited in scope. There are also the technical institutes, which furnish more extensive technical education but are attended by only a very small proportion of the trained craftsmen.

Thus Europe has absorbed education into the industrial training process. The United States, in contrast, has approached the problem by trying to integrate occupational education into the school system. This specific orientation has marked American education from almost its earliest days, and the persistently recurrent concern with occupational training as a necessary component of general education is one of the most reassuring expressions of democratic thinking.

CHARACTER OF AMERICAN EDUCATIONAL THINKING

In order to understand fully the subsequent analysis of present-day problems of vocational education and training it is necessary to recapitulate briefly their historical origins in this country. During the colonial period, education in America was dominated by

British thought and practice. Instruction of the young was held to be the responsibility of the church, and this view prevailed even after the spread of humanism had caused the classics to replace ecclesiastical dogma as the main content of such instruction. The nine colleges and universities established in this country by 1769 were patterned after English universities; the Latin grammar schools, designed to prepare the well-to-do for college, were almost exact replicas of those in England; and the dame schools, too, drew heavily on their English heritage.

It was not until the middle of the eighteenth century, when Benjamin Franklin and Thomas Jefferson offered the first challenge to the established pedagogical order, that education in this country began to take on a characteristic stamp.[5] Both Franklin and Jefferson were aware of the burgeoning in Europe of new educational theories that stressed the unity of school and everyday living, the value of learning through doing, and the importance of mastering manual skills. As products of the century of enlightenment, both opposed ecclesiastical authority, sectarianism in education, and the tyranny of tradition, and both were keenly conscious of the implications of the increased knowledge of natural science for the individual and society.

To Franklin the formation of useful habits was more important than the mere acquisition of knowledge, though he was devoted to experimental science and the teaching of subjects by which it could be promoted. Advocate of the educational aspirations of the rising middle class, he disliked the 'useless classics' and the institutions in which they were taught, and recommended that the main emphasis be placed on English, mathematics, and science. It was Franklin's ambition to lay the educational foundations for higher proficiency in agriculture, industry, and commerce through the application of science, and for rule by reason, intelligence, and wealth. In every sense Franklin was the initiator of the utilitarian

[5] Merle Curti, *Social Ideas of American Educators*, Report of the American History Association Commission on the Social Studies, Part 10 (New York, 1935), pp. 34–47.

approach which has figured so largely in the educational creed of this country.

Jefferson's contribution, on the other hand, found expression in his 'bill for the more general diffusion of knowledge' (Virginia 1779). Opposed to a class system of education, he antedated the French revolutionaries in contemplating a state school system for all children, although, unlike the French, he was not inclined to make school attendance compulsory. With a deep faith in the reforming power of education, Jefferson believed that equal opportunity for all children to acquire a sense of the values of civilization and to enter the ranks of leadership represented the greatest force for the progress of democracy. Since he placed the emphasis on literary training, the idea of occupational training in elementary and secondary schools was beyond the scope of his planning. Nevertheless, he incorporated in his proposals for a people's university a trade or technical school designed to systematize and to subject to educational methods much of the vocational education of craftsmen.

Thus, ideologically, American educational thinking attained a character of its own. The first practical achievement, however, free of any European influence, was the academy planned and founded by Franklin in 1751. This was the forerunner of the new institutions of secondary education that were to supplant the Latin grammar schools. Although, contrary to Franklin's proposals, the academies took over the traditional college preparatory subjects, they offered additional general subjects and vocational courses designed to fit students for careers in business, commerce, and shipping. An academy opened in Schenectady, New York, in 1771 gave not only a classical but a general course of reading, writing, arithmetic, geography, history, bookkeeping, and merchants' accounts.[6] Early in the nineteenth century, the Woburn (Mass.) Academy listed navigation, surveying, and bookkeeping in its cur-

[6] George F. Miller, *The Academy System of the State of New York* (Albany, 1922), p. 15; Isaac L. Kandel, *History of Secondary Education* (New York, 1930), pp. 397–406.

riculum, and by 1829, the Regents of the State of New York recognized, among the subjects appropriate to an English education, geometry, algebra, advanced arithmetic, trigonometry, chemistry, botany, bookkeeping, surveying, mensuration, navigation, and astronomy. In the academies for girls, courses were offered in embroidery and needlework, practical and fine arts.

This recognition of the value of vocational subjects was not out of line with contemporary European pedagogical thinking, but American practice developed in a different and characteristic direction. European educators, especially the German, took a keen interest in vocational education, but they contested its general educational value and relegated it to special schools, whereas this country, in its unflinching concern for broadening the democratic basis of education and for the integration of school and life, persistently sought to incorporate vocational and vocationally determined subjects into the general school curriculum.

It must be admitted that however progressive American educational thinking and practice may have been, by the end of the eighteenth century only a narrow stratum of society had been touched by the new developments. There was no public school system to provide an indispensable minimum of education and training for the mass of the people, and the few schools that existed for the poor bore all the marks of charity.

With regard to providing education for the poor, European models again served American practice at first. In England, as early as 1601, the apprenticing of all poor children was provided for by law, as a means of reducing unemployment and of giving adequate trade training. This system took on special significance in the American colonies where laws were passed making the care of poor children a public responsibility and requesting parents and masters to teach them 'to read and understand the principles of religion and the capital laws of the country' (Massachusetts 1642) or 'to educate and instruct them . . . in Christian religion and in rudiments of learning' (Virginia 1643; later in North and South

Carolina, Georgia, and other states).[7] Thus a kind of compulsory education for the poor developed in urban centers, serving, in the first place, vocational ends and the supply of skilled labor, and granting educational objectives secondary consideration. But with the importation of Negro slaves into the South, and the development of manufacturing in the North with its progressive division of labor, apprenticeship declined steadily and with it the educational opportunities for the poor. New means of educating the masses had to be devised.

In these circumstances it became apparent to both economic and educational theorists that what was needed was universal education in free public schools, separated from religious authority and economic control, and serving moral and practical purposes. This concept fostered interest in education as a direct function of government, and with the improvement in means of transportation and communication with the growth of cities, realization of the educational ideal moved a long step closer.

ATTITUDE TOWARD SCHOOL TRAINING FOR WORK

Throughout the nineteenth century, public opinion was overwhelmingly concerned with the great issues of general education: free schools, democratization of the class-torn school system in order to bring equal opportunity to all children; and training of competent teachers. Yet even early in the century, short-lived movements in support of manual labor schools and mechanics' institutes foreshadowed later trends in the direction of true vocational education. The work of the Swiss philanthropist and educator, and disciple of Pestalozzi, Philipp Emanuel von Fellenberg, set the example for manual labor schools. Thus the ideas put forth by Rousseau and Pestalozzi on the educational value of manual work found their application in this, as in all other, countries. Between 1819 and 1830, schools combining elementary instruction and farm

[7] Edgar W. Knight, *Education in the United States*, 2nd ed. (New York, 1941), pp. 99–102.

work were founded in several agricultural states, while other manual labor schools, such as those established in New York, laid stress on mechanical work. The mechanics' institutes, based on English models, were, in a sense, adult education institutions designed to give the workingmen members 'instruction in the principles of the art they practice and in the various branches of science and useful knowledge.' [8]

Both the manual labor schools and the mechanics' institutes, however, enjoyed only partial and temporary success mainly because fundamental education was still too deficient. They were, nevertheless, the first materialization of an underlying and ever-recurring idea which reappeared in the middle of the century in a new form and with more fortunate results. In 1850 and again in 1859, the state of Michigan petitioned for a grant of public land to found a college of agriculture. This was the start of a movement that culminated in 1862 in the passage of the Land Grant or Morrill Act granting to the states public land equal in area to half the size of Indiana for colleges of agriculture and the mechanic arts.

Thus the first educational idea to which the federal government extended direct aid was occupational in character. Agriculture and engineering were now accorded legislative recognition as learned professions, and high standards of teaching and research in these fields were put on a par with the traditional subjects of advanced education. The implications of the Morrill Act were especially important for agriculture in the West, where greater knowledge and skill in the farming process were required as the era of free lands drew to a close. In the East, on the other hand, the prospects for engineering had greatly increased with the transformation of a largely agricultural society into one that was mainly industrial. Backed by state and federal aid, agricultural and engineering colleges increased substantially.[9]

[8] Edwin A. Lee, ed., *Objectives and Problems of Vocational Education* (New York, 1938), pp. 10–11; Pittsburgh University, *Report of the Investigation of Engineering Education*, vol. 2 (1934), pp. 27–31.

[9] Knight, op. cit. pp. 396–7; Pittsburgh University, op. cit. pp. 810–16.

In the period following the Civil War, educational developments were largely determined by the social forces set in motion by a rapidly growing population and an enormously expanding industry. Between 1870 and 1890 the population of the country increased from 39 million to 63 million. Immigration soared. New inventions, modern machinery, improved means of communication, the evolution of densely settled cities and the growth of material wealth—all these greatly facilitated the improvement and spread of education. Yet, despite these favorable conditions, even as late as 1890, the 'average length of schooling for each individual in the nation . . . was but four and a half years . . .'[10] It was not until the urgent demands for the abolition of child labor and for the enforcement of compulsory school attendance were heeded that the average term of schooling was gradually extended to an eight-year elementary, and subsequent high school, course. In time the public schools became adequate agencies of education, reflecting in their work the effect of educational theories and of trained teachers upon an ever-growing number of children and age groups, and mirroring in their social composition the entire population of an increasingly industrialized and urbanized nation.

In the light of this situation, educators could not fail to recognize manual training and vocational subjects as necessary components of the school curriculum. As followers of Rousseau and Pestalozzi, Franklin and Jefferson, they were all in general agreement in their devotion to democratic ideals and the principle of learning by doing, and they recognized both the need for vocational education and the reforming power inherent in education itself. There were, however, strong differences of opinion on the precise role to be accorded vocational and manual training by the schools. Whereas some educators supported manual training for its general educational value, others demanded utilitarian vocational training—a stand that implied the need for the inclusion of more science, social studies, and technical, industrial, and household subjects in what was essentially a classical curriculum. They were not unaware,

[10] Curti, op. cit. p. 206.

however, of the dangers inherent in narrow conceptions of vocational education as training in manipulative skills only.

It was John Dewey who, in a remarkable synthesis of conflicting ideas, assigned to vocational education its place in his system of continuous reconstruction of experience for educational purposes.[11] He urged the integration of the basic occupational activities with cultural education, and with progressive methods in the schoolroom, in order to produce a higher type of worker and thus prepare for the democratization of industry itself.

Another group of educators favored the establishment of separate public vocational high schools, regarding this development as indispensable for industrial workmanship in a democratic society, for national industrial efficiency, and for the responsible interest on the part of the worker in the social problems of the day. Precedents for this last plan were furnished by the development of manual training schools and the experiments in technical and industrial training conducted by a few private schools in the closing decades of the last century. Courses and schools in manual training, although conceived as a part of general education, were first established by wealthy businessmen desirous of promoting more practical training for youth. The subject then gradually penetrated public school practice in the form of separate schools or as departments in the regular high schools. This modern manual training movement was supported by the Industrial Education Association, founded in 1884, which aimed '. . . to promote the training of both sexes in such industries as shall enable those trained to become self-supporting . . . and to study and devise methods and systems of industrial training and secure their introduction into schools . . .'[12] The Association thus advocated both manual and industrial training as part of general education without further elaboration.

[11] For the views of earlier educators, especially with regard to vocational education, see Curti, op. cit. pp. 310–498; for a discussion of Dewey's theories, see ibid. pp. 499–541.

[12] Industrial Education Association, New York, *First Annual Report* (New York, 1885), p. 7.

Discussion of the subject persisted in all educational circles, but for about a quarter-century it produced no notable results. Manual training high schools were thinly scattered throughout the traditional school system which by its strength threatened to assimilate and finally absorb them, while the so-called industrial and technical high schools, operated within the system, were hardly more than manual training schools.[13] Manual training and, to some degree, the improved 'practical arts' and 'industrial arts' courses which evolved from it eventually made their way down into the elementary schools where they served as a 'broadening and energizing element of general education.'[14] The fact remains, however, that all such courses served mainly to uncover special talents and in this way to furnish vocational guidance.[15] Neither manual training nor industrial arts has ever functioned effectively in promoting a direct relationship to a future vocation, which is a prerequisite for any genuine vocational education.

As is the case with all new educational work in this country, vocational training in schools was originally the product of private initiative. Interest in the problem was aroused almost simultaneously with the launching of the manual training movement in the 1880's. The first specific trade training at lower than college level was offered by the New York Trade School, which was founded in 1881 and served as a model for a number of other schools. Planned according to the needs of the community or to the theories of their founders, these schools catered either to boys who needed full-time trade training or to older boys and men who required further instruction for advancement. The development of these schools, however, was very gradual. There was no attempt to co-ordinate industrial training on a nationwide basis, and the number of such trade schools never exceeded a very modest figure.

[13] National Education Association, *Report of the Committee on the Place of Industries in Public Education* [Winona, Minn., 1910], p. 5; Charles R. Richards, 'Progress in Industrial Education during the Year 1910–1911,' in *Report of the Commissioner of Education* (Washington, 1912), p. 301.

[14] Charles R. Richards, 'Industrial Education,' in *Cyclopedia of Education*, vol. 3 (New York, 1918), p. 429.

[15] Lee, op. cit. pp. 35–6, 284–304.

Coincident with the growing interest in manual training, the practical arts, and vocational training in schools was the increasing attention given to the need for technical training of below-college grade. Technical schools, defined as 'schools giving training in practical industrial processes and which at the same time offer advanced instruction in the scientific and mathematical principles upon which these processes are based,' [16] also were started by farsighted individuals with a view to filling the gap between the training of skilled mechanics and that of engineers.

As a natural result of the forces that shaped the preceding century, early in the 1900's the trade training idea was taken over by the secondary branch of the public school system. But though the general high school succeeded in integrating commercial subjects into its curriculum, it made no headway in doing the same for other vocational fields, particularly those of interest to the manual labor force. Traditional teacher training and high school curriculums were too remote from the new needs and social demands of the expanding high school population to make easy adjustment possible. It became more and more obvious that in order to solve the problem it would be necessary to establish separate public high schools, contemplated and organized for vocational education as distinct from academic.

With the formation in 1906 of the National Society for the Promotion of Industrial Education,[17] the movement gained momentum. At first, this group campaigned for state-aided vocational high schools but subsequently concentrated its efforts on securing federal support. Scoring the existing school system for assuming that all children would profit by 'bookish' training, the Society held that industrial training in schools was indispensable to the future of the worker and to national industrial efficiency, and urged that separate

[16] Charles R. Richards, 'Progress in Industrial Education . . .' (cited above), p. 302. See also Hebrew Technical Institute, Catalog, 1937, p. 8.

[17] Following the passage of the Smith-Hughes Act in 1917, this organization became the National Society for Vocational Education, which, in December 1926, merged with the Vocational Association of the Middle West to become the American Vocational Association.

vocational high schools provide wage earners with practical skills as a feature of an education that would also include scientific, sociological, and cultural subjects as background for the vocations taught.

The Society soon gained sufficient influence to induce the National Education Association to devote special attention to the problem on industrial education. At the Association's annual meeting in 1908, a symposium on the place of industries in public education heard American education accused of granting equality of opportunity only to those students who were able to attend a college or university, while contributing little to help the average man in the better performance of his life work and in the full realization of his inheritance as an American citizen. Further, the public school was frankly warned that in order to hold its place in the esteem of the American people it would have to grapple with and solve the important problems of vocational education. In its subsequent activity the Association stressed that industry as a controlling factor in social progress had a fundamental and permanent significance for education and that in secondary schools industrial occupations should furnish the central and dominant factor in the education of those who made the final choice of an industrial vocation. The group held that many children should be directed by the school toward industrial life. And it recognized the imperative need for both secondary technical and trade schools.[18]

These exponents of vocational education in both organizations were primarily concerned with a type of school designed to provide wage earners with practical skills. Preparation for efficient industrial workmanship in a democratic society seemed to them more important than industrial experience as a means of cultural education. In taking this stand they were convinced that they were fully aware of the needs of the times and that they remained faith-

[18] Curti, op. cit. pp. 559–60; James E. Russell, 'The Trend in American Education,' in *Educational Review*, vol. 32 (June 1906), pp. 28–41; Charles A. Prosser, 'Education and Preparedness,' in *School and Society*, vol. 3 (3 June 1916), pp. 796–807; National Education Association, *Journal of Proceedings and Addresses of the 46th Annual Meeting* . . . 1908, pp. 155–94.

ful to the democratic ideal, for to their minds industrial education was fully capable of assuming the general function of all education by training the mind through experience related to a future vocation, in a school that would express the needs of the community.[19]

The work of the National Society for the Promotion of Industrial Education was instrumental in securing the passage of laws supporting vocational education and the establishment in several states of public vocational high schools. In 1917 its efforts were crowned by the passage of the Smith-Hughes Act (Federal Vocational Education Law) furnishing federal aid for vocational education. When the law went into effect, eight states already had a system of state-aided vocational education, and others, encouraged by the prospect of federal support, followed suit shortly thereafter. Nationwide application of the Act was soon well under way.

INDENTURE AND APPRENTICESHIP BEFORE 1937

The foregoing résumé of the gradual incorporation of vocational education and training into the public school system must not be allowed to obscure the fact that, until recently, industry carried the main burden of occupational training, however casual and insufficient its effort may be judged. During the period when interest in, and agitation for, in-school preparation for work involving manual skills were developing so steadily, systematic in-employment training was declining, and limited training on the job increasingly furnished practically the sole instruction for the labor force. Nevertheless, the more formal apprenticeship system did exist, but its course was consonant with the peculiar history of the country.

As has already been indicated, apprenticeship in America never acquired the scope or prestige that it enjoyed in Europe. As a means of instructing the poor it was established in most of the colonies by the middle of the seventeenth century. There was a further impetus in the practice of indenture of those persons who,

[19] Arthur D. Dean, *A State Policy of Promoting Industrial Education* (Albany, 1910), p. 68.

unable to pay their passage from England, bound themselves out to masters in the colonies for a specified period as a way of working off the debt incurred by their voyage. The terms of indenture ranged from five to ten years depending on the particular colony in question. The system was most prevalent and most rigid in the South, where it remained in effect until the importation of Negro slaves in the eighteenth century offered a new and cheaper source of labor. In the Northern colonies, the apprentice fared somewhat better, for the increase in population and growth of cities offered him more favorable economic prospects on completion of his indenture.

On the whole, however, the economic and social development of this country did not encourage the continuance of this form of craft training. The economic freedom that became relatively easy to obtain as the country expanded and the rapid spread of modern manufacture were persuasive factors in the gradual decline of the system. In the face of the advancing industrialization, a number of old trades tried to maintain their position in the economy by the extensive use of cheap apprentice labor, with the inevitable result that when organized labor entered the scene early in the nineteenth century, one of its first preoccupations was the limitation of 'apprentice breeding.' In an effort to halt the hiring of apprentices as substitutes for skilled adult workers, labor fought for the enforcement of the age limit and length of term in all apprenticeship agreements, and, after the Civil War, sought legislation to set apprenticeship standards. Some of the manufacturing states actually did enact apprenticeship laws and the labor unions themselves increasingly dealt with the problem by including apprenticeship clauses in their collective agreements.

None of these measures, however, was nearly so decisive for the later development of apprenticeship as the swiftly changing economic conditions throughout the country. As industrial production developed, the training of apprentices became less and less profitable. Neither employers nor American-born workers were eager to enter agreements that would be binding on them for a period of years. Nor was there any pressing economic necessity for large-scale apprentice training so long as immigration provided an ample supply of journeymen.[20] Moreover, the need for skilled labor increased but slowly; to a great extent, industry could make use of semiskilled and unskilled labor, especially since many of the goods that required precision work and high skills were being imported. Labor unions cannot justly be accused of having barred American youth from learning a trade during this period, for the management-labor agreements of apprenticeship allowed for considerably more apprentices than were actually employed.

The general decline in the importance of apprenticeship after 1860 is well exemplified by the accompanying figures on the apprentices and the total labor force in the manufacturing, construction, and mining industries between 1860 and 1940.[21] It is true that

	Number of apprentices	Total labor force	Ratio
1860	55,326	1,850,034	1:33
1880	44,170	3,837,112	1:87
1890	82,057	5,091,293	1:62
1900	81,603	7,112,987	1:88
1910	118,964	11,623,605	1:98
1920	140,400	13,922,102	1:100
1930	77,452	15,094,080	1:196
1940	92,360	16,374,676	1:180

by 1920 the absolute number of apprentices had increased appreciably, but the ratio to total employment in the manufacturing, mining, and construction industries fell rapidly. The stability of the ratio between 1910 and 1920 can be explained by the effort made during World War I to cope with the dearth of skilled labor.

[20] In 1920 as much as 28.3 per cent of the labor force in manufacturing was foreign-born. In the five-year period, 1920–24, the net immigration of skilled labor, excluding farmers, professional, and commercial workers, was about 435,000 or an average of 87,000 a year.

[21] Figures for 1860–1910 are from Paul H. Douglas, *American Apprenticeship and Industrial Education* (New York, 1921), p. 74; figures for 1920 and 1930 compiled on the basis of *Statistical Abstract of the United States*, 1937, p. 56; figures for 1940 compiled from *Statistical Abstract . . .* 1946, p. 183.

The economic crisis of 1929–33 and the resulting mass unemployment temporarily reduced the system to minute proportions.

Not until the period of recovery and increased production in the thirties was the seriousness of the skilled labor shortage felt. Training in all its forms had been at a standstill for some time and immigration with its rich supply of journeymen had ceased.[22] By 1937, although unemployment was still widespread, the scarcity of skilled labor was acute in many trades. Growing public awareness of the situation finally led to the passage of the Fitzgerald Act, the first federal legislation relating to apprenticeship. The formulation of apprenticeship standards and programs under the terms of this Act involves the cooperation of national, state, and regional bodies, as well as of management and labor representatives functioning at national, local, and plant levels. In view of the recency of the legislation and the abnormal wartime conditions under which it has operated, it is not yet possible to evaluate its effectiveness, but the mere enactment signifies an intention on the part of the nation not to discard apprenticeship as a form of vocational training.

Premises and Plan of Discussion

It is against this background of American thinking and practice in the realm of vocational education and training that the present status of such training must be evaluated and its future direction determined. With regard to in-school preparation for work, although clearly there has been a steady preoccupation with both the needs of the nation and the individual, the educational system, in general, has remained far too deeply rooted in the liberal arts tradition to be wholly effective for an overwhelmingly large proportion of the working population. Industry, for its part, has failed to provide adequate systematic occupational training—a situation that may be readily explained though none the less deplored. It is, therefore, the contention of this study that at this particular stage in our history, technological and industrial developments have out-

[22] By 1930, the proportion of foreign-born in the manufacturing labor force had fallen to 23.2 per cent and in 1940 to 15.

run our educational thinking and that stock-taking and decisive action are essential to the maintenance of industrial productivity on a wide scale and a high level.

The survey of technological and economic trends and the occupational distribution of the population, which constitutes the first portion of this study, has been made in the belief that the vocational education system cannot be effective unless it is in harmony with the technological and economic trends of the country. This is not to say that all education of American youth must be strictly governed by these trends, nor to deny that the rapidly changing economic scene makes prediction a somewhat hazardous affair. The pattern of industrial development, however, is such that certain fairly reliable conclusions can be drawn with regard to the future growth or decline of occupational groups. And unless vocational education takes note of the training requirements implied by these trends, American youth will be betrayed into acquiring skills for which the economy has no use.

On the basis of a definition in broad terms of the education and training desirable for our economy, the study makes an analysis of the existing institutions of in-school and in-employment training with a view to determining how effectively they meet the nation's needs. The premise on which this investigation was based is that both in-school and in-employment training are necessary constituents of any adequate system of occupational training, and that they should be well developed, carefully differentiated, and intelligently coordinated, each institution having precedence in the sphere it serves best. Schools perform their most efficient service by teaching technical knowledge and basic skills, while in-employment training is best equipped to offer experience in special and advanced skills and to raise any skill to a level of professional speed and efficiency. It is with these objectives in mind that each of the educational institutions and each form of on-the-job training has been evaluated.

The concluding section of the book is given over to the findings and recommendations. These are offered in the sincere hope and belief that they will not only further the American people's progress toward that earnestly desired era of economic security and well-being, but will also strengthen the educational philosophy and aspirations of a nation that seeks to build the whole man.

II

Industrial Trends and Occupational Distribution

Relation of Industrial Structure to Vocational Education and Training

THE first step toward determining in broad outline what kind of vocational training is required by the nation's youth is an analysis of the industries and jobs that constitute our economy. If, for example, some 30 per cent of the labor force are employed in manufacturing, while 20 per cent are engaged in commercial trades, it may be assumed that corresponding percentages of the high school youth should be trained to enter those fields. Unfortunately the matter is not quite so simple as that—any number of modifying factors immediately challenge the validity of the assumption.

A typical stumbling block is the limitation inherent in any numerical analysis of this sort. Statistics refer to the past, or at best to the present, while occupational education is designed to serve the future. Only if industrial growth involves no change in the distribution of the labor force and in the character of necessary skills will the future demand for new workers be in proportion to established needs. There is, of course, no guarantee that there will be such a consistent development. While some industries are contracting and thus reducing employment, others are simultaneously demanding a greater share of the new labor supply. Fluidity does obtain, and there is no doubt that it greatly complicates the occupational training problem.

Short-term fluctuations in the activity of individual industries, and thus in employment opportunities, are admittedly difficult to forecast. These, however, should not exert too great an influence on the direction of occupational education, which is fundamentally a long-range proposition and would probably always be too late and out of step if it tried to follow the cyclical fluctuations of the economy. But when changes in the industrial structure are long-term shifts, the future is often predictable on the basis of past developments. Education can be adjusted to gradual change. Occupational changes resulting from the establishment of new industries present a different problem, but the difficulties are often overestimated. New industries usually grow slowly and much of the work can be done by the existing labor force without much new training, especially if the workers have had the benefit of broad occupational education. As soon as new industries can be expected to be permanent, occupational education should, of course, be adjusted accordingly.

Thus it is clear that however significant the deviations from past and present conditions may be, the main outlines of our industrial growth are not likely to be radically or suddenly altered. Interpreted qualitatively as well as quantitatively and with careful judgment, the following statistics therefore yield important suggestions for educational planning.

Development of Industrial Distribution of the Labor Force

The development of the industrial distribution of the American labor force in the course of a century, as shown in Table 1, reveals that the percentage employed in agriculture has declined in the United States as sharply as it has in the leading European countries. Whereas in 1840 more than 77 per cent of the gainfully occupied were engaged in farm work, by 1940 the percentage was less than 19. Only to a small degree can this trend be explained by the altered position of the United States in foreign trade and in the international division of labor. The decline is chiefly the result of changes in all production techniques. As the division of labor

TABLE 1. PERCENTAGE DISTRIBUTION OF THE LABOR FORCE, 1840–1940, BY INDUSTRY [a]

Industry	1840	1870	1880	1890	1900	1910	1920	1930	1940
Agriculture, fishing, & forestry	77.6%	53.5%	50.0%	43.4%	38.2%	31.6%	27.6%	21.9%	18.3%
Mining	[b]	1.4	1.7	1.9	2.4	2.6	2.6	2.0	2.1
Manufacturing & mechanical industries	16.8	15.9	18.2	18.8	20.6	23.8	26.2	24.3	23.9
Construction	[b]	4.6	3.9	4.9	4.2	4.7	4.1	4.6	5.3
Trade, transportation, & communications	4.3	11.0	12.7	14.8	17.3	16.8	17.3	20.4	22.9
Clerical occupations		0.6	0.9	2.0	2.5	4.6	7.3	8.2	9.3
Professional service	1.3	2.6	3.2	3.8	4.1	4.6	5.1	6.7	6.8
Public service (n.e.c.)		0.7	0.8	0.9	1.0	1.2	1.7	1.8	2.6
Domestic & personal service		9.7	8.8	9.6	9.7	10.1	8.0	10.1	8.8
TOTAL									
In per cent	100.0	100.0	100.0	100.0	100.0	100.0	100.0	100.0	100.0
In millions		12.9	17.4	23.3	29.1	37.4	42.4	48.8	49.5

a Figures for 1840 were computed from Sixth Census of the United States, 1840, *Population* (Washington, 1841); figures for 1870–1930 were computed from Sixteenth Census of the United States, 1940, Population, *Comparative Occupation Statistics for the United States, 1870–1940* (Washington, 1943), Table XXII, p. 101; figures for 1940 were computed from Sixteenth Census . . . , Population, vol. 3, *The Labor Force*, Part I, U.S. Summary (Washington, 1943), Table 74, and do not include emergency work. Construction figures were separated from those on manufacturing and mechanical industries on the basis of occupational and industrial data in the censuses. Figures for 1870–1930 pertain only to those workers 10 years old and over, while figures for 1940 pertain to those 14 and over.

b Included in manufacturing and mechanical industries.

progressed, much of the work on farms that was not tied directly to the soil was shifted to city workshops. More and more of the actual agricultural work was done with the help of machinery, the production of which augmented the industrial labor force, while the number of laborers required on farms declined as the output per worker increased.

What portion of American labor will be needed in agricultural pursuits in the future is of course a matter of conjecture. It is not probable, however, that the trend of the last hundred years will be drastically changed. Any increase in the use of machinery and in the efficiency of labor in this field leads to a displacement of labor, which cannot easily be reabsorbed by agriculture since the demand for its products increases but slowly even when prices are reduced. A further decline in the portion of labor in agriculture may therefore be expected, although it is likely to be much more gradual than in the past.

Somewhat surprising is the development of the labor force in manufacturing industries. The view that as a result of the industrial revolution an ever-increasing portion of labor has been shifted to industry is only partially supported by the facts. Manufacturing industries did absorb an increasing percentage of the labor force until 1920. But however important their role in the economy may have become, these industries have not yet at any time, except perhaps during the war years, employed more than 26.2 per cent of the labor force. Since 1920 there has been a slight decline in the percentage of labor absorbed by this branch of the economy, but it is too soon to interpret this loss as an established trend.

Technological progress, to be sure, will continue to increase the output per man-hour, but the demand for industrial products is elastic and may increase faster than productivity in factories, especially if new products are developed. Manufacturing industries may also resume their proportional growth by taking over more work from other branches of the economy. The introduction of prefabricated houses, for instance, is fairly sure to create new factory jobs while it reduces the relative employment capacity of the traditional construction industry. Thus it seems too soon to accept the pronouncement that 'we must get used to the notion that our manufacturing needs of the future may quite likely be supplied by a constantly declining percentage of the population' and that 'manufacturing labor should drop to 15 per cent or 10 per cent, or even less of our total available workers.' [1]

On the other hand, the future employment capacity of manufacturing industries, especially that of large-size mass production industries, must not be overestimated. In 1939, although 51.5 per cent of the labor force in manufacturing were employed in establishments with more than 250 workers, only 22.4 per cent were employed in establishments with more than 1,000 workers.[2] The big workshops of the nation produce a considerable portion of the newly manufactured products, but in aggregate employment they cannot compete with the many smaller plants and with the many repair and service industries.

The automobile industry is an outstanding example of the relationship of employment in mass production to that in industries built up around the product of a large-scale industry. Factory employment in the production of automobiles, automobile parts, tires, and tubes in 1940, for instance, was about 644,000. But employment in retailing of motor vehicles and accessories, in filling stations and in repair services, was as high as 1.2 million.[3] It is true that not all mass production generates such a wide range of service industries, but, in general, the latter are more likely to grow than to decline with the expansion of mass production. If ample skills are available, the desire for independent work, which fosters the development of small shops, will persist.

Construction, as an occupational group, has constituted a remarkably regular share of the total labor force. Its further develop-

---

[1] Omar Pancoast, Jr., *Occupational Mobility* (New York, 1941), p. 19.

[2] *Statistical Abstract of the United States, 1944–45* (Washington, 1945), p. 795.

[3] Computed from Sixteenth Census of the United States, 1940, Population, vol. 3, *The Labor Force*, Part I, U.S. Summary (Washington, 1943), pp. 180–81, and *Statistical Abstract . . . 1944–45*, p. 816.

ment, however, is open to wide speculation. Manufacturing industries, as already mentioned, may introduce new building materials and prefabrication, and thereby reduce employment in the traditional building trades. On the other hand, construction, especially in the field of residential building, may witness an expansion far beyond the usual cyclical development. The pent-up demand for new building, in addition to the population increase, and the probable replacement of dwellings now below the standard that a condition of full employment and high and steady national income would find acceptable, make a long period of building activity a virtual certainty.

The data on industrial employment indicate that the traditional producing industries as a whole—agriculture, mining, manufacturing, and construction—have employed a declining percentage of the labor force, dropping from 75.4 per cent in 1870 to 49.6 in 1940. This situation is, of course, due to the sharp decrease in agricultural employment for which the growth of manufacturing never compensated. At the same time, trade, transportation, communications, commercial, clerical, public, and professional services have been growing proportionately faster. In 1940, trade, transportation, and communications alone absorbed 22.9 per cent of all gainfully occupied persons. Obviously, with the division of labor and with an increase in productivity in the traditional producing industries, the other groups must expand their employment unless their efficiency grows at the same rate as the size of their task.

Such an analysis of our industrial structure reveals only in a very general way the economic, technical, and social spheres in which the population moves. Indeed, in some cases, it tends to obscure rather than clarify the nature of the work performed. For example, in the nonproducing industries, manual and technical skills are usually thought to play a secondary role. And yet, transportation, a nonproducing industry, includes railroading and trucking and even air transport, all of which involve a great many jobs requiring well-developed manual and technical skills. The same can be said of the telephone and telegraph services included in communications, while the professional services include engineers, whose occupation is wholly concerned with production techniques and science. Thus, for the purpose of determining the levels of education and training required by the various branches of the economy, a different breakdown is necessary.

OCCUPATIONAL STATUS AND RELEVANT EDUCATION

In Table 2, an attempt is made to classify the labor force of 1940 in direct relation to occupational status and, by inference, to educational background. All occupations have been grouped according to ten broad classifications which will serve our main purpose. Owing to variations in terminology and a lack of precision in job description, a certain amount of overlapping is inevitable, but it is not sufficient to obscure or nullify the major conclusions.

Class 1 contains all the professional occupations with the exception of the technical professions, which constitute Class 2 and comprise engineers, chemists, and architects.[4] Of the 2.2 million persons in Class 1, more than 1 million are teachers, and of these, 788,000 are women. Other large groups in this class are lawyers and judges (179,500), physicians (165,400), and clergymen (138,200). The occupations in Classes 1 and 2 require not only high school but further training on the college or professional level. They constitute, however, only 5.4 per cent of all the gainfully employed or, if distinguished by sex, 4.2 of all male, and 8.8 of all female, gainfully employed.[5]

Less homogeneous is the group of semiprofessional occupations (Class 3) which combines such wide variety as executives in finance and insurance, government officials, trained nurses, and others. An even greater problem is offered by Class 4 which is not really an occupational classification. The group includes, for instance, 427,000 proprietors and managers in manufacturing industry, 121,000 in construction, 142,000 in transportation. Many of

[4] For breakdown of each class into its separate occupations, see Appendix A.

[5] The high percentage of female employment in these groups is due to the overwhelming number of women teachers.

TABLE 2. DISTRIBUTION OF THE LABOR FORCE, 1940, BY OCCUPATIONAL CLASS [a]

Occupational Class	Male		Female		Total	
	Total no. in class	In % of total male labor force	Total no. in class	In % of total fem. labor force	In numbers	In % of total labor force
1. Professional (excl. technical)	1,229,531	3.3	1,044,799	8.8	2,274,330	4.7
2. Technical professional	333,065	.9	2,831	.02	335,896	.7
3. Semiprofessional	885,142	2.4	576,993	4.9	1,462,135	3.0
4. Proprietors, mgrs., officials	696,678	1.9	25,545	.2	722,223	1.5
5. Commercial trades	6,200,090	16.9	3,429,486	29.0	9,629,576	19.8
6. Technical trades	930,927	2.5	85,267	.7	1,016,194	2.1
7. Craft trades	5,303,526	14.4	438,712	3.7	5,742,238	11.8
8. Farmers & farm mgrs.	4,991,715	13.6	151,899	1.3	5,143,614	10.6
9. Operatives	6,063,767	16.5	2,104,907	17.8	8,168,674	16.8
10. Laborers & kindred workers	10,160,817	27.6	3,968,793	33.6	14,129,610	29.0
TOTAL	36,795,258	100.0	11,829,232	100.0	48,624,490	100.0

ᵃ Compiled from Sixteenth Census of the United States, 1940, Population, vol. 3, *The Labor Force*, Part I, U.S. Summary, (Washington, 1943), Table 58. Persons employed on public emergency work and those whose occupations were not reported are excluded.

these would undoubtedly be more accurately classified as craftsmen or as members of the technical trades; others surely belong
to the commercial, professional, or semiprofessional groups.

Classes 1 to 4 account for 9.9 per cent of all gainfully employed,
8.5 per cent of the male and 13.9 per cent of the female. These
classes probably embrace all occupational positions for which education normally extends to college, that is, beyond the level of
employment for which mere high school education, whether of
an academic or vocational character, is usually considered adequate
preparation.

Class 5, embracing the various commercial trades, accounts for
19.8 per cent of the gainfully occupied and is numerically the second largest in the classification. It, too, covers a wide range of
talents, abilities, and learning, nearly all of which are mental in
character. The basic school subjects—reading, writing, spelling,
composition, and arithmetic—are primary occupational requirements for these jobs, while manual skills play only a minor role.
General schooling therefore contributes greatly to vocational education in this field, while commercial high schools and the commercial courses of study in the general high schools offer even
more direct preparation. Even without the specialized subjects,
high school education is sufficiently related to the commercial
trades to be of considerable occupational aid, and to permit an easy
psychological adjustment to this type of work. College education
also is in closer rapport to this occupational group than to the
manual trades.

The remaining five classes—6 (technical trades), 7 (craft
trades), 8 (farmers and farm managers), 9 (operatives), and 10
(laborers and kindred workers)—account for 70 per cent of the
gainfully occupied, 75 per cent of the male, 57 per cent of the
female. The occupations included in these groups vary widely
but they all rotate around manual work, manual skill, and practical, technical knowledge. These jobs, like all participation in a
modern industrial society, constantly require an increasing amount

of formal education. Traditional schooling, however, makes a relatively small contribution to the required *skills* and for the most part only indirectly. Organized occupational education for these jobs, therefore, presupposes either systematic occupational training within the many industries or, if this is insufficiently developed, the absorption of special occupational education into the school system.

In this large group of occupations, farmers—both owners and tenants—constitute 10.6 per cent of the gainfully occupied. Although this study deals mainly with occupational education for industrial workers, it does not consider adequate training for farm work a minor issue. Life on a farm almost automatically involves substantial occupational preparation, but progressive farming has much to gain from well-planned occupational education, especially in view of the increasing mechanization of farm work.

The technical trades account for 1 million jobs, 92 per cent of which are held by males and more than half of which are of foreman grade. It is quite possible that many of the engineers counted in Class 2 and many of the proprietors in the manufacturing and construction industries (Class 4) hold positions that really belong to this group of technical trades. With these inclusions, the total for the group would probably be raised by 200,000 or 300,000. Characteristic of the technical trades is that they require manual skills sufficient to know how the industrial operations ought to be done and, at the same time, enough technical knowledge to plan, arrange, organize, and supervise production within definite limits. Preparation for most of these jobs can therefore be approached from two directions: either engineers may add sufficient knowledge of practical production and workmanship to their education in order to qualify; or craftsmen, trained and reared in the work of the particular industry, may enlarge their technical and engineering knowledge to fit themselves for positions of this kind. It is true that not all jobs in the technical trades bear such a close relation to craftsmanship as do the foremen's. Draftsmen and designers, for instance, are much more closely linked to the junior engineer than to the master craftsman, although they, too, should have a knowledge of the actual production processes.

Class 7, the craft trades, contains the group of manual skills that are in the forefront of any discussion of occupational education and training. In 1940 the census enumerated 5.7 million workers in this group, constituting 11.8 per cent of the total labor force or 14.4 per cent of the male, and 3.7 per cent of the female, gainfully employed. To be sure, not every one of these workers was engaged in fully skilled work at the time. In the automobile industry, for instance, there were 481,470 gainfully employed workers of whom 144,520 were enumerated as craftsmen or foremen. That would mean that nearly 30 per cent of the workers in this industry were craftsmen. But reports on the required length of training for the different jobs in the automobile industry show that a considerably smaller percentage of the jobs demanded training as elaborate as that usually required of craftsmen. In this case the rapidly developing industry absorbed a great many craftsmen without using the full range of their skills. On the other hand, there are industries such as the textile with a total of 1.2 million workers in which the number of craftsmen is much higher than the census indicates. The total figure for craftsmen, therefore, is probably not too high, though it must always be borne in mind that in reality the distinction between skilled, semiskilled, and unskilled work is one of degree rather than essential character.[6] Unquestionably, in-school vo-

[6] The ramifications of this problem are discussed at some length throughout the book. It is necessary to mention here only that the study has used as a general guide the following definitions given by the U.S. Department of Labor and U.S. Employment Service, *Dictionary of Occupational Titles* (Washington, 1939), Part II, pp. 59, 115, 241.

'Skilled Occupations. This group includes craft and manual occupations that require predominantly a thorough and comprehensive knowledge of processes involved in the work, the exercise of considerable independent judgment, usually a high degree of manual dexterity, and, in some instances, extensive responsibility for valuable products or equipment. Workers in these occupations usually become qualified by serving apprenticeships or extensive training periods.'

'Semi-Skilled Occupations. This group includes manual occupations that are characterized by one, or a combination of parts, of the following require-

cational education and apprenticeship are indispensable preparation for jobs in the craft trades.

Classes 9 and 10, composed of operatives and workers of lesser skills, represent as much as 45.8 per cent of all gainfully occupied. The size of this group indicates the extent to which a modern economy can operate with a labor force of narrow or no substantial skills, but the percentage also proves that these jobs continue to be in the minority. The distribution of the labor force between these two classes is necessarily somewhat arbitrary. The 6 million male operatives include almost 1.5 million truck drivers and chauffeurs who could just as well have been included in Class 10, but the group also includes some 650,000 mine operatives many of whom have rather exceptional occupational requirements.

The creation of a large force of machine operatives is occupationally one of the outstanding results of modern mass production. Requirements for this kind of work vary widely. While many of the jobs consist entirely of a few easily learned operations, others involve performance that can be mastered only after several months of experience. In general, the operative's job is characterized not so much by the absence of skill as by narrowness of performance, and the few specialized operations demanded of these semiskilled workers usually have to be done with exceptional accuracy and speed.

In order to determine what the actual occupational requirements of these jobs are, and to what extent occupational education

---

ments: the exercise of manipulative ability of high order, but limited to a fairly well defined work routine; major reliance, not so much upon the worker's judgment or dexterity, but upon vigilance and alertness, in situations in which lapses in performance would cause extensive damage to product or equipment; and the exercise of independent judgment to meet variables in the work situation, which is not based on wide knowledge of the work field and with the nature and extent of the judgments limited either a) by application over a relatively narrow task situation or b) by having important decisions made by others. These occupations may require the performance of part of a craft or skilled occupation, but usually to a relatively limited extent.'

'Unskilled Occupations. Manual occupations that involve the performance of simple duties that may be learned within a short period of time and that require the exercise of little or no independent judgment.'

is implied, further differentiation is an essential preliminary step. It must also be ascertained whether this group of operatives is substantially a fixed group, or whether many of the workers are only temporarily employed in this range of jobs, using them as a springboard to positions demanding greater skill. If such vertical flexibility exists or is to be achieved, it obviously demands occupational training for skilled and technical work for a greater portion of the labor force than is actually employed in these trades at any given time.

That vertical mobility actually exists is proved by an analysis of the occupations according to age groups (Table 3). In 1940, for example, 75.9 per cent of the gainfully employed males eighteen and nineteen years of age were in the classes of operatives and unskilled manual workers. In the group of workers between twenty and twenty-four years old the percentage was 61.9, and of those between fifty-five and sixty-four only 32.6 per cent were working in the jobs requiring least skills.

Class 10 especially, which constitutes the largest single occupational group, comprises many jobs that are held only temporarily. For example, among the 10.1 million male workers in this class are 3 million farm laborers. In the group of eighteen and nineteen-year-olds, farm laborers account for not less than 33 per cent of the gainfully employed, but among persons between thirty-five and forty-four, for only 4 per cent. Their median age in 1940 was only 24.9 years, while that of the farmers was 46.6, from which it may be concluded that many farm laborers change to other occupations, a substantial number of them becoming farmers. Of the 4 million female workers in Class 10, not fewer than 2.1 million are domestic service workers, who not infrequently go on to positions of wider responsibility in their own homes.

The foregoing analysis of the labor force shows its distribution among and within ten major occupational classifications in a specified year. The trends of the major occupational groups between 1910 and 1940 can be seen in Table 4, which employs similar, if not exactly parallel, classifications as a basis.

Occupational Class	18–19	20–24	25–34	35–44	45–54	55–64	65–74	75 & over
Male and Female								
1. Professional	.8%	3.3%	5.8%	5.3%	4.5%	4.4%	4.7%	5.6%
2. Technical professional	b	.3	.7	1.0	.9	.7	.4	.3
3. Semiprofessional	2.2	2.9	3.7	4.1	4.3	4.3	4.5	5.1
4. Proprietors, etc.	.1	.2	.9	2.0	2.5	2.3	2.1	2.2
5. Commercial trades	19.6	22.9	21.5	20.1	17.9	15.9	14.3	14.2
6. Technical trades	.3	.8	2.4	3.9	4.3	4.0	2.5	1.4
7. Craft trades	5.1	7.8	9.9	12.4	13.5	13.0	11.0	7.8
8. Farmers, etc.	2.1	4.2	7.4	10.3	14.3	19.5	29.6	39.6
9. Operatives	18.2	21.2	21.0	17.0	13.4	10.1	6.6	3.9
10. Laborers, etc.	51.7	36.5	26.6	24.0	24.3	25.8	24.4	19.9
TOTAL	100.0	100.0	100.0	100.0	100.0	100.0	100.0	100.0
Male								
1. Professional	.4	1.6	4.1	3.9	3.3	3.4	4.2	5.4
2. Technical professional	b	.5	1.0	1.3	1.1	.8	.5	.4
3. Semiprofessional	.6	1.6	3.0	3.7	3.9	3.7	3.9	4.5
4. Proprietors, etc.	.1	.3	1.2	2.5	3.0	2.7	2.4	2.4
5. Commercial trades	12.3	16.4	17.8	17.9	16.7	15.4	14.9	14.6
6. Technical trades	.3	1.1	3.1	4.9	5.2	4.7	2.9	1.5
7. Craft trades	6.9	10.2	12.3	14.8	15.4	14.5	11.7	8.1
8. Farmers, etc.	3.3	6.3	10.0	12.9	16.9	22.3	32.6	42.6
9. Operatives	17.0	21.3	21.2	16.8	13.4	10.2	6.7	3.9
10. Laborers, etc.	58.9	40.6	26.2	21.6	21.2	22.4	20.8	16.6
TOTAL	100.0	100.0	100.0	100.0	100.0	100.0	100.0	100.0
Female								
1. Professional	1.4	6.3	10.5	10.4	9.9	9.5	7.7	7.0
2. Technical professional	—	—	—	—	—	—	—	—
3. Semiprofessional	4.7	5.2	5.5	5.6	6.6	7.3	8.0	9.9
4. Proprietors, etc.	b	b	.1	.2	.3	.3	.3	.3
5. Commercial trades	31.1	34.7	31.7	28.1	23.2	18.7	14.0	10.9
6. Technical trades	.1	.3	.4	.5	.5	.4	.3	.2
7. Craft trades	2.9	3.3	3.3	4.0	4.7	5.3	6.0	5.9
8. Farmers, etc.	.1	.1	.4	1.3	2.8	4.9	9.0	15.9
9. Operatives	20.2	20.9	20.3	17.7	13.9	9.2	5.9	4.1
10. Laborers, etc.	40.0	29.1	27.7	32.1	38.0	44.4	48.7	45.9
TOTAL	100.0	100.0	100.0	100.0	100.0	100.0	100.0	100.0

[a] Compiled from Sixteenth Census of the United States, 1940, Population, vol. 3, *The Labor Force*, Part I, U.S. Summary (Washington, 1943), Table 65.
[b] Less than 0.5 per cent.

In general, the changes in the occupational pattern over three decades were as follows: a considerable increase in clerical and kindred occupations, which in 1940 accounted for no less than 17.2 per cent of the labor force; an increase in professional groups from 4.4 per cent in 1910 to 6.5 per cent in 1940; a slight percentage increase in the group of proprietors,[7] exclusive of farmers who showed a considerable percentage decline. According to the Census of Manufactures, the absolute number of proprietors and firm members in the manufacturing industries declined during the period under discussion;[8] therefore, the many service and repair industries and small shops beyond the range of the Census of Manufactures must have absorbed a correspondingly larger number.

TABLE 4. PERCENTAGE DISTRIBUTION OF THE LABOR FORCE, 1910–40, BY OCCUPATIONAL GROUP [a]

Occupational Group	1910	1920	1930	1940
Professional	4.4%	5.0%	6.1%	6.5%
Farmers	16.5	15.5	12.4	10.1
Proprietors, etc.	6.5	6.8	7.5	7.6
Clerks, etc.	10.2	13.8	16.3	17.2
Skilled workers & foremen	11.7	13.5	12.9	11.7
Semiskilled workers	14.7	16.1	16.4	21.0
Unskilled workers	36.0	29.4	28.4	25.9
TOTAL				
In per cent	100.0	100.0	100.0	100.0
In millions	37.3	41.2	48.6	52.0

[a] Sixteenth Census of the United States, 1940, Population, *Comparative Occupation Statistics for the United States, 1870–1940* (Washington, 1943), p. 187.

The outstanding shifts in the manual occupations are the decline in unskilled laborers from 36 per cent to 25.9 per cent, and the

[7] This group, however, is not comparable with the classification made in Table 2, since it includes all retailers who were grouped under commercial and clerical trades in Table 2.

[8] Solomon Fabricant, *Employment in Manufacturing, 1899–1939* (New York, 1942), pp. 221–2.

considerable rise in semiskilled workers from 14.7 per cent to 21 per cent. Contrary to common belief, the percentage of skilled workers in the labor force did not decline but was the same in 1940 as in 1910. The peak in 1920 was undoubtedly due to the war production of the immediately preceding years. The 1940 figure, on the other hand, may have been abnormally low because of the long period of unemployment and the lack of activity in the building trades during the thirties.

These statistics give little support to the frequently expressed opinion that the need for occupational skills within the economy is constantly declining. They indicate instead that the group of routine and semiskilled workers has increased at the expense of unskilled, rather than of skilled, labor. Had skilled labor maintained its position within manufacturing industries it would, of course, have grown proportionately with these industries. Manufacturing, however, though it requires skilled labor for key positions, relies heavily on the semiskilled operative. Skilled labor, therefore, has retained its place in the economy mainly because it is so widely distributed among the small shops, repair services, and building industries—and these show no signs of declining.

Development of Individual Occupations

In reviewing the development of the individual occupations between 1870 and 1940, it must be remembered that the total labor force during that period grew from 12.5 million to 52 million workers, or more than quadrupled. Employment in manufacturing and mechanical industries grew about five and a half times. Therefore, any occupation in these industries that did not experience a corresponding rise during this period lost its relative importance in the economy, and any that grew more quickly, gained.

Inasmuch as our chief concern is with the occupations involving technical and manual skills, we have confined our analysis of occupational trends to the main divisions into which this kind of work falls: the technical professions, the metal and allied trades, the building and woodworking trades, the printing, textile, clothing, and shoe industries, and the service trades. The importance to the economy of the clerical and commercial trades, however, is so great that consideration is accorded to this group as well.[9]

The rise of the *technical professions and the allied professional and semiprofessional occupations* (Appendix B.1) within this period was extremely rapid. In 1870, technical engineers, chemists, architects, designers, and draftsmen numbered only 11,200, but by 1940 they had increased more than fortyfold and accounted for 471,700 of the labor force. In 1910, civil engineers and surveyors still made up 58.5 per cent of all technical engineers, but in 1940 they constituted only 38 per cent. Meanwhile, mechanical, electrical, and chemical engineers had increased at a faster rate.

In addition to these professional and semiprofessional groups, the 1940 census enumerated 75,246 technicians and laboratory assistants, raising the total in that year to nearly 547,000. Although this figure may give some idea of the purely engineering and technical positions in the economy, it by no means indicates the large number of other occupations that call for considerable technical education and training. The 100,000 foremen in the metal and machine industries, the 535,000 proprietors, managers, and officials in construction and manufacturing, and the vast number of persons engaged in the trades of aviator, radio operator, electrician, mechanic, toolmaker, and even machinist, would benefit by technical understanding and knowledge in addition to their manual skills. Thus the need for technical education is continuously expanding, in depth as well as in breadth.

The crafts grouped around work with *metal* and in the production of *machinery* (Appendix B.2) have as a common denominator a considerable amount of fundamental skills. Oldest among the metal trades is that of the *blacksmith* which as early as 1870 accounted for 145,000 gainfully employed. The early development of the metal and machine industries was apparently favorable to

[9] *See* Appendix B for tabulations.

this trade, but not beyond 1910 which witnessed a peak employment of 235,800. The particular and personal skill of the blacksmith has become increasingly anachronous in modern factory production, and in 1940, the 87,000 smiths were widely spread throughout the economy, the only concentration occurring in the miscellaneous service industries and hand trades, which accounted for 44 per cent of all blacksmiths.

Machinists achieved a temporary central position in the new system of factory production by increasing from a mere 55,000 in 1870 to 841,400 in 1920. But by 1940 their number had decreased to 521,100. There is little doubt that the 1920 figure was partly inflated by war demands. And in 1940 a more careful census enumeration of the chief occupations in the machinist group—toolmaker, mechanic, and the like—resulted in the lower number for machinists. The decline, however, is too great to be explained merely by changes in statistical classifications. Obviously, the increasing employment of operatives has led to a diminishing need for machinists. This trend is especially apparent in the automobile and electrical industries where mass production and the use of operatives have their widest application.

Most surprising is the rapid increase in *mechanics* from 281,700 in 1920 to 949,700 in 1940, although it may be partly explained by workers' insistence on being so classified when they may have been machinists or only machine tenders. Although somewhat heavily concentrated in the many branches of the machine and electrical industries, mechanics are widely distributed throughout the economy, especially in automobile repair and other services which absorbed some 352,000. Mechanics are usually required to have a fair amount of technical knowledge in addition to manual skills. Automobile repair work, for example, demands an acquaintance with the theory of the automobile and with the construction of various models. This is even more true of airplane mechanics in whose field technical knowledge is continuously changing and expanding.

Toolmakers, diesinkers, and *diesetters* form another group that merits special attention. Their increase from 9,300 in 1900 to 96,-900 in 1940 indicates not only greater specialization and an important distinction between general machinist and toolmaker, but also a wider use of special tools, dies, and fixtures, which is such an important feature of modern production methods.

Plumbers, and *gas and steamfitters* experienced a rapid increase over the whole 1870–1940 period. But inasmuch as two-thirds of the workers in these trades are employed in construction, making them heavily dependent on building activity, their number declined during the 1930's with the long depression in that industry. Conversely, employment may be expected to increase with renewed building; modern housing requires more, rather than less, plumbing and allied equipment.

The *electrician's* trade which developed entirely within the period covered by these statistics could be considered a craft by itself, but from the point of view of education and training there is considerable correlation between this and the other occupations in the metal and related trades group. A knowledge of electricity and electrical apparatus and machinery benefits any worker in the metal trades, while an electrician finds familiarity with metal work, prime power machinery and the like, greatly to his advantage. In addition to manipulative skills, electricians require more technical knowledge particular to the trade than most of the other occupations of the group, with the possible exception of mechanics. Specialization of labor in the electrician's trade has reduced the amount of technical knowledge required for any particular job, but for flexibility within the full range of the trade, technical knowledge of the entire field is essential.

The labor force in the whole *metal trades* group grew from 208,-000 in 1870 to 2.4 million in 1940, and although the figures are not fully comparable for the entire period, they indicate the development of these trades, which, with those of 400,000 engineers, architects, designers, and draftsmen, now hold the central position in modern technology. For purposes of training there should also be considered in this group the 110,000 foremen in the iron and steel, machine and repair industries, and about half the 190,000 proprietors and managers in the same industries. Most of these positions can be filled satisfactorily only by persons with technical as well as craft training. Finally, there are the 272,400 stationary and locomotive engineers and 335,800 cranemen, hoistmen, oilers and firemen, who can be counted with the labor force in metal trades. Most workers in the latter group probably require only a minimum of occupational training; the engineers, however, must be recognized as a bona fide trade group. Although ultimately their work may differ widely from that of the metal trades proper, their occupational preparation usually leads through these trades and allied technical knowledge.

Assuming that these groups, accounting for 3.2 million gainfully employed, command craft skills, it may well be asked how these skills have hitherto been obtained. On the basis of apprenticeship figures it is clear that 90 per cent of these workers did not get their training as apprentices, at least not in the United States. Immigration, of course, contributed largely to the supply of skilled labor, but its drastic decline after the middle twenties eliminates this source as an important contributory factor. Thus the prevailing method of acquiring skills obviously has been ad hoc learning on the job, with organized trade training as the exception.

Workers in all these metal trades must, of course, rely extensively on manual skills, but it is evident that any adequate preparation for these occupations would also include a reasonable amount of technical and scientific instruction. Vertical flexibility even presupposes that craftsmen in these trades have a good technical education and a knowledge of advanced production methods. Without these, their chances of becoming foremen, inspectors, or independent producers are greatly reduced. Granting this premise, the difference in the occupational education for the manual-technical trades and preparation for the strictly technical occupations of designer, draftsman, laboratory assistants, and the like, should be a matter only of degree and not one of fundamental distinction.

A further consideration with regard to the metal trades is the increasing employment of operatives, who in 1940 numbered nearly 1.2 million or 33 per cent of the labor force in this group. Few workers who enter the machine industry by way of routine jobs want to remain at this occupational level permanently, but if they are to be able to gain advancement in the industry, their training must include the fundamentals of science, related manual skills, and experience in the use of a wider range of machine tools than they would use as operatives.

The development of this metal trades group in the future cannot be expected to differ radically from that in the past. In spite of all technological developments in mass production, which were accelerated by the war, the demand for skilled workers in this group will persist. Peacetime industry is highly diversified and the function of the skilled worker is to build the machines used in the many varied branches of production rather than to work at routine operations. Only if the machines used in mass production were also to be produced on a mass basis would the demand for skills in the metal trades be seriously threatened. The metal trades will, therefore, constitute the greatest source of demand for technical knowledge and trade skill.

The development of the *building* and *woodworking* trades (Appendix B.3) has been uneven, with periods of slight expansion followed by periods of considerable growth and then by extremely low activity. Their greatest increase occurred between 1870 and 1910 when they grew about as rapidly as the total labor force of the country. The absolute decrease during the depression of the thirties was extended by the urgent priority of war production, but a sharp and sustained upturn in activity, as discussed in preceding pages, is certain.

The distribution of workers among the trades in this group reveals some interesting aspects of our economy. Cabinetmakers increased very little between 1870 and 1940, at no time reaching the 60,000 mark, although furniture production expanded considerably during this period. Obviously, machine and mass production have steadily displaced cabinetmakers in the furniture industry; in 1940 only about half of the 58,800 cabinetmakers were employed in making furniture though total employment in this industry was 225,600. Large-scale production of furniture is now too well established to be threatened or supplanted by custom work. Indeed, such a development would be highly undesirable since the production of low-priced furniture of comparatively good quality is an essential contribution to the American standard of living. On the other hand, if national income and wealth are sustained at a high level, the production of standard furniture is likely to be supplemented by furniture of special design and quality, suitable to special purposes, homes, and tastes. This demand can be expanded by the increased availability of such furniture. Thus the training of more cabinetmakers than are required to maintain the present working force is indicated, with such training to include the use of all modern machinery and materials.

Among the building trades the carpenter predominates numerically, which is not surprising in view of the fact that 80 per cent of the houses in this country are frame. This explains why in 1930, for instance, there were as many as 933,500 carpenters but only 173,300 brick and stone masons.[10]

The future of the building industry, beyond the present crisis, will depend largely on the product of the building trades and the construction industry, as well as on the previously discussed increase in demand. Relatively few private building projects can afford the services of college-trained architects and engineers, so that the responsibility for much of the quality and style of the building in this country rests with the large number of independent small contractors. Since the ideal American house, from the architectural and practical points of view, is still the rare exception and thus a challenge to the future, the problem of adequate training still lies ahead.

[10] In European countries the opposite is true. In Germany, for example, there were 479,000 brick and stone masons (*Maurer*), but only 190,000 carpenters (*Zimmerleute*) in 1933.

In 1939 the Census of Construction enumerated 226,800 active proprietors and firm members engaged in construction with an employed labor force of 1.1 million, or less than five employees per proprietor or firm member. It is mainly this large body of proprietors who must have creative ability and technical knowledge in addition to manual skills. Modern construction, furthermore, requires more plumbing, more heating and electrical installations, better ventilation, and possibly air conditioning, all of which have to be integrated with the structure of the house. A well-built house therefore presupposes a well-trained labor force working in accordance with the requirements of modern engineering and architecture. The importance of technical knowledge for the skilled workers also in the field of building and construction is therefore greatly increased.

Although technological progress has revolutionized many branches of the *printing* industry (Appendix B.4), employment has grown at about the same rate as in other industries and the need for a comparatively large percentage of highly skilled labor has persisted. To meet these demands the industry has maintained a well-organized system of apprenticeship, but the 10,000 apprentices are by no means sufficient to sustain its force of 250,900 skilled craftsmen. Informal training on the job apparently supplies the deficiency. In addition to the craftsmen in the trade, there are about 50,000 proprietors and 10,000 foremen who also require a knowledge of printing trade skills. It is clear that expanded training for the industry is indicated.

In 1940 the *textile* industry (Appendix B.5), one of the oldest and largest manufacturing industries in the country, had a labor force of 1.3 million workers, including proprietors, and clerical and wage workers. The percentage of women employed is exceptionally large; wages are comparatively low. The census classification of all textile workers, with the exception of dyers, as operatives or laborers fails to indicate the wide range of skills needed by this industry, such as those of the weaver, spinner, or bleacher. The figures therefore show the development of the industry rather than the development of the individual trades within the industry. Employment between 1870 and 1940 grew somewhat faster than total national employment but more slowly than that in manufacturing alone.

In view of international competition, the future growth of the American textile industry depends on increased productivity and higher quality of the product. These in turn require a flexible labor force trained in textile skills. Furthermore, since the textile industry is vulnerable to competition it may be subject to contraction with a resultant displacement of labor. Textile skills, however, are highly specialized and if the workers are to be able to transfer to other industries, a broad program of industrial education is indicated for them.

In the *clothing* industry (Appendix B.6) craftsmen have been increasingly replaced by operatives, although the latter have not increased sufficiently to balance the decline in the number of dressmakers and tailors. The increase in productivity in the making of clothing has been greater than the increase in output, with a resultant drop in total employment. As in the textile industry, the classification of nearly all workers as operatives obscures the fact that many jobs demand wide and diversified skills. In general, the operatives in this industry require greater dexterity and longer periods of training and work experience than in most other industries before top efficiency is reached. Full craft trades in the industry are rare, however, because of the great specialization and narrowness of the functions of individual workers.

What constitutes desirable occupational education in this field is something of a problem. Preparation for factory work in the garment industry is a very different matter from training for tailoring and dressmaking as craft trades. Custom-made clothing, however, is still in demand and there is no reason why it should not continue to supplement the output of the ready-to-wear industry.

Most skills acquired in dressmaking and tailoring are applicable to mass production of clothing and would not be totally lost if a worker so trained entered a mass production industry. Direct training for the latter, however, instead of concentrating on custom work, involves the integration of operational skills into an industrial training program. Technical education in this industry would include designing and patternmaking, and because of the many small shops in the industry, management as well.

The making of *shoes* (Appendix B.7) has undergone developments similar to those in the clothing industry. Small-shop custom production has virtually ceased, while the work in factories has become mechanized, specialized, and routinized, and is performed by operatives who, however, require dexterities that cannot be developed in a few hours or days. Their training requirements are comparable to those of operatives in the clothing industry. The 65,000 shoemakers not in factories, enumerated in 1940, were almost entirely engaged in repair work, for which the necessary skills are limited and can be acquired as part of a broader program of occupational training in skills for related work.

Service occupations have expanded rapidly and with a rise in the standard of living further expansion may be expected. One of the most rapidly growing trades in this group is that of *barber, hairdresser,* and *manicurist* (Appendix B.8), which rose from an employment level of 24,600 in 1870 to 440,100 in 1940. The number of male employees in these trades rose continuously until 1930 but then suffered a decline, owing in part no doubt to their replacement by female workers. The noteworthy expansion of female employment in these trades began about 1920, and by 1940 had reached 218,100. Skills range from simple shampooing to the most demanding operations, such as that of giving a permanent wave. Training for these occupations involves some technical knowledge as well as manual skills and creative ability.

Cooking should be recognized as another service occupation for which organized occupational training is essential. In 1940, *cooks*, except those working for private families, numbered 335,800 of whom 30 per cent were women. To these can be added about 200,-000 in private families, thus raising the total in the group of bona fide cooks to more than 500,000. Needless to say, professional cooking requires a far more specialized program than the cooking course in the home economics curriculum. Closely related to this group are *waiters*, who increased in number from 188,300 in 1910 to 604,900 in 1940; in 1940, 128,300 *bartenders* were also enumerated.

Servants in private families remain the largest group of service workers, numbering more than 2 million in 1940. They have not, however, increased as rapidly as the labor force as a whole. High schools would probably not offer extensive training for this type of work as such, but the average home economics course embraces the occupational requirements for this group as well as providing for the wider duties of the housewife. It is highly improbable that more than a very small fraction of domestic workers have in the past had such training, but the future may witness higher standards and an improved status for such workers, contingent on better preparation.

This review of the service occupations would be incomplete without statistics on *chauffeurs, truck drivers*, and the like (Appendix B.9), a group which in the main belongs to the field of transportation. The figures illustrate impressively what the automobile has done to the old trade of carriage drivers, on the one hand, and how chauffeurs, and truck and tractor drivers have increased, on the other. In 1940 no less than 1.3 million workers earned their living in the latter occupations; this figure is exclusive of the 428,000 deliverymen of whom many are also chauffeurs or truck drivers. The rapid increase in truck and tractor drivers, of course, affected not only carriage drivers, who in 1910 numbered as many as 443,800, but employees in railroads as well, although this section of the labor force has withstood the competition much better.

The tremendous importance of the *clerical* and *commercial* occupations (Appendix B.10) is attested by the fact that in 1940 these groups contained no less than 8.8 million gainfully employed, exclusive of about 0.5 million real estate, insurance, and other agents and brokers, and the self-employed in finance.

Employment in the clerical occupations alone increased sixty-fold between 1870 and 1940. Stenographers and typists, whose number was negligible at the beginning of the period, numbered 1.2 million at its close, while the ranks of clerks and bookkeepers were also greatly expanded. Today these occupations are distributed throughout the economy—in commerce, finance, and public service, as well as in the manufacturing industries, mining, the utilities, and other fields. The incidence of women workers in the clerical occupations is very high; 'stenographer and typist' is an almost exclusively female occupation, and women comprise nearly half the bookkeepers and clerks. The median age of female stenographers, typists, and secretaries in 1940, however, was only 28.2 years, which indicates that although this may be a choice occupation it is abandoned comparatively quickly. Training for these jobs, consequently, should be only a part of a more comprehensive course of study that aims also at preparation for other life pursuits.

Employment in the commercial trades increased almost seven-fold between 1870 and 1940. Wholesale and retail dealers, who are proprietors and not employees as are the members of nearly all the other groups, have shown a steady growth although smaller both relatively and in absolute numbers than in the other categories. According to every reasonable expectation, the future growth of these trades is assured. Occupational preparation for the work involved is directly served by the expansion of high schools, the raising of all educational standards, and the development of commercial courses in high school programs.

RANGE OF OCCUPATIONAL OPPORTUNITIES

From the preceding analysis of the industrial and occupational structure of this country a number of significant facts emerge.

For one thing, it appears that despite the division and routinization of labor in mass production a choice of occupation directed by inclination, rather than by economic necessity alone, is possible over a much wider range of occupations than is generally assumed. It has by no means been unfavorably affected by time; the cleavage between economic necessity and occupational desirability has, on the whole, narrowed rather than spread during the machine age.

Furthermore, with the expansion of the public school system, the shortening of the work week, and the easier access to cultural and adult education for all, even the great number of persons in repetitive work can find the time and the means to develop their personalities and to advance vocationally. Under these conditions, a choice of occupation guided by economic necessity may even be encouraged, for steady work with sufficient income, even if lacking full vocational satisfaction, will afford a good foundation on which to develop the personality.

In the course of the industrial development, agriculture has employed a sharply declining percentage of the labor force, while mining, manufacturing, and construction have shown an over-all increase. The other industries—trade, transportation, communications, commercial, clerical, public and professional services—have shown a phenomenal expansion. It is evident that in relative, as well as absolute, terms modern industry requires a constantly increasing number of organizational and clerical services, more engineering, designing, drafting, and other technical knowledge. The semi-skilled worker is gaining an important position in production lines but at the expense of the unskilled worker. Skilled labor more or less holds its relative position in the economy as a whole, but requires an increasing amount of technical knowledge in addition to manual dexterity. The need for such occupational education and training has therefore been intensified, and, as shown by the occupational classification, it concerns approximately 70 per cent of the gainfully employed.

The existence of vertical mobility within the labor force has been amply demonstrated. Occupational preparation, therefore, must provide for this mobility by furnishing a foundation for the highest skill the worker may reasonably be expected to attain. Thus the occupational requirements demanded by skilled work are applicable to a considerably greater number of workers than is indicated by any statistical picture of the distribution of the labor force at any one time. The task of vocational education and training is therefore challengingly clear.

III

Development of the Academic and Vocational High Schools

IT is evident from the review of the occupational structure of this country that no single institution of occupational training can serve the entire economy. The range of jobs is so great, and the training requirements are so varied in extent and character, that only by utilizing the full resources of both in-school education and in-employment training can the demands of the economy be adequately met.

For various reasons, preparation for most of the professions and for the commercial and clerical trades must be concentrated in schools and special institutions. In these fields, learning on the job can begin only after a considerable degree of proficiency has been attained. There is constant agitation for a closer tie-up between preparation for a profession and the actual job, but it has never been contested that theoretical and classroom instruction must constitute the major portion of the training.

Farmers and industrial workers, on the other hand, have, until fairly recently, acquired most of their skills on the job. But the need for scientific and technical knowledge in addition to manual skills, which has grown with advancing technological developments, has greatly enlarged the potential role of the school even in this field of occupational education. To what extent the schools have recognized this role and with what degree of efficiency they are performing their new task can be determined only by an analysis of the existing institutions and their work. In order to understand the terminology used in such an analysis, a brief survey of the various types of school training is necessary.

Types of Schools Offering Vocational Education

Occupational education and training in schools has a wide range, including in its scope the training of youth of compulsory school age and also that of adults, and providing either elaborate trade and technical education or quick and narrow training for an immediate job. In general, it tends to develop better integrated and broader programs than does in-employment training, but it still retains something of its prevocational character and provides operational skills only to an extent that facilitates later in-employment training but is in no way a substitute for it.

The entry of the public schools into the field of vocational education was a development that went beyond the creation of vocational high schools; in many respects the whole secondary school system felt its influence. Even the traditional academic high schools were not impervious, and in large cities there are now high schools in which the curriculums are systematically differentiated with a view to future professions. New York has its High School of Science and its High School of Music and Art, which remain within the academic high school frame but select their student body and emphasize their special subjects in a way that enables them to attain a standard in their fields unmatched by other schools. Less exceptional, but still by no means widely distributed over the country, are the technical high schools, which tend to become a distinct branch of the academic high school. The technical high schools not only stress the sciences, but also conduct shop classes for demonstrating production methods—a curriculum definitely preparatory to engineering careers or to such technical occupations as those of designer or draftsman. Closely allied to this course is the vocational-technical curriculum which includes a variety of shopwork, not only for the purpose of demonstrating methods of production but also in order to teach manipulative skills.

The vocational high school goes a step further in this direction by preparing for a specific trade and aiming primarily at the development of trade skills, and it includes in the curriculum a certain amount of scientific and related technical instruction. Some vocational high schools may be more aptly called industrial; these center their teaching on the job families found in mass production and performed by operatives, rather than on teaching the trades in the traditional sense.

In addition to the vocational education of secondary grade there is also in-school training of a nonsecondary character, which provides supplementary instruction for those who have left school. It is given in the form of either trade preparatory or trade extension training and mainly in evening courses. Schools that have developed long-term integrated programs of post-secondary training of noncollege grade are usually designated as technical institutes. Their programs generally omit the cultural subjects but are otherwise similar to those of technical high schools; the specific technical subjects, however, are taught more intensively, more practically, and at a more advanced level than in the institutions of secondary training.

DEVELOPMENT OF THE PUBLIC SECONDARY SCHOOL SYSTEM

In appraising the contribution of the vocational schools to occupational education and training, it is necessary to review the extraordinary growth of the public secondary school system in this country and the emergence of the vocational school from the background of academic education. What these more recent schools have retained of their academic heritage, what they have added, and what they have discarded shed considerable light on many of the pressing problems of incorporating true vocational preparation in the school program.

By the middle of the nineteenth century the academies had reached the height of their development, with 6,085 private and publicly controlled units, staffed by 12,260 teachers and attended by 263,096 pupils. From its modest inception in 1830, high school attendance rose little beyond the level of the academies until after

1890, when political, economic, and cultural factors led to an unprecedented increase in enrollments from 357,813 in that year to 7.1 million in 1940. The figures that follow show the growth of secondary school enrollments during this period, and the growth of the fourteen to seventeen-year age group.[1] Although the total

	Sec. school enrollments	% Increase over 1890	% Increase of 14–17-yr.-olds over 1890	Enrollments in % of 14–17-yr.-olds
1890	357,813	—	—	7%
1900	695,903	94.5%	14.9%	11
1910	1,111,393	210.6	34.8	15
1920	2,495,676	597.5	44.5	32
1930	4,799,867	1,291.4	74.5	51
1940	7,113,282	1,888.0	81.5	73

number of persons in this age group less than doubled between 1890 and 1940, the secondary school enrollments of that group in 1940 were almost twenty times those of 1890. The percentage of fourteen to seventeen-year-olds enrolled in secondary schools rose from 7 in 1890 to 73 in 1940.

The number of public high schools rose from 2,526 in 1890 to 25,467 in 1938.[2] With this development of the public high school system the private high school declined in importance, and in 1940 the latter claimed only 451,768 students or 7 per cent of total high school enrollments as opposed to 32 per cent in 1890.[3]

These figures suggest what deep inroads secondary education has made into the mass of the population. Entrance to high school following elementary school has become the normal procedure. This expansion of high school enrollment has put an end to the selective character of secondary education and has resulted in a much more heterogeneous high school student body, with respect to interests, capacities, and vocational aims. A comparison of the annual number of high school and college graduates shows the ex-

[1] *Statistical Abstract of the United States,* 1942 (Washington, 1943), p. 139.
[2] Rudyard K. Bent and Henry H. Kronenberg, *Principles of Secondary Education* (New York, 1941), p. 94.
[3] *Statistical Abstract . . . ,* 1942 (cited above), p. 138.

tent to which the college preparatory function of the high school has lost its importance for an ever-increasing proportion of the students.[4]

The sharp decrease is even more striking in the figures for boys only. In 1870 the proportion of male college graduates to that of male high school graduates was 107 per cent; by 1940 it was only 18 per cent.[5]

	No. of h.s. graduates	No. of college graduates	College grads. in % of h.s. grads.
1870	16,000	9,371	58.5%
1900	94,883	25,324	26.7
1940	1,228,246	186,500	15.2

Inasmuch as the public high school took over from the academy its college preparatory function, just as the academy had taken it from the Latin grammar school, it became an integral part of the educational 'ladder' and eventually the main link between the elementary school and the institutions of higher education. At the same time, it became the terminal education institution for about five-sixths of the youth who continued their schooling beyond the elementary level. This dual function of the high school posed a serious problem for American educators who realized that if the great achievement of a free public high school system was to be maintained, its educational aims would have to be reinterpreted in the light of changed conditions.

The curriculum became the instrument for obtaining this objective, through greater breadth and flexibility and the incorporation of practical pursuits. To a certain extent, these needs had been recognized by the early academies and by the emerging high schools, but with the enormous expansion of the student body, they were intensified and widened. Greater attention was directed to the adaptation and differentiation of the curriculum in order to meet the diverse requirements and interests of the millions of high school students and the growing number of high schools. To be

[4] Ibid. p. 139.
[5] Ibid. p. 139.

sure, for organizational and financial reasons high schools in small communities could not expand their curriculums to any considerable extent. Even in 1938 about one-third of all students were enrolled in high schools whose average enrollment was less than 300 students.[6] But in all other high schools, areas of human experience previously unexploited for educational purposes were included in the curriculums, and it became an acknowledged principle that all subjects taught for the same length of time were of equal value and were to be offered according to the individual needs of the students and the re-evaluated demands of a modern democratic society. Vocational subjects thus found their theoretical justification.

The adjustment of the American high school to the new conditions, which developed so rapidly, was a notable achievement. In so far as the high schools were not too small to permit specialization, their curriculums were classified in two main divisions: the academic and the general. The first was designed to meet college entrance requirements, the second to lead simply to high school graduation.

Because of the variations in college entrance requirements in accordance with the times and local conditions, the academic curriculum had to be continuously revised.[7] Latin, Greek, and arithmetic were the traditional requirements for admission to college, but during the nineteenth century many new subjects were introduced—geography and English grammar, algebra and geometry, ancient and modern history, physical science and physiology, rhetoric and modern languages. Lack of uniformity in the matter of entrance requirements finally caused so much confusion that college associations and state boards of education were forced to establish some order. An accrediting system was introduced and widely accepted, standard requirements were set, and certifica-

---

[6] J. B. Edmonson, Joseph Roemer, Francis L. Bacon, *The Administration of the Modern Secondary School* (New York, 1941), p. 564; Bent and Kronenberg, op. cit. p. 29.

[7] U.S. Office of Education, *Handbook of College Entrance Requirements,* ed. by W. W. Hinckley, Bulletin No. 13 (Washington, 1941), pp. 2–4.

tion was extended to high schools that established and maintained these standards. The 'unit' was adopted as the standard of credit for a course meeting five times a week for one school year, and the minimum entrance credit for liberal arts colleges was set at 15 or 16 units. Currently, 94 per cent of the colleges require these minimums, 77 per cent stipulating 15 units, 17 per cent, 16.[8]

The units are distributed mainly among the major required subjects—English, social sciences, mathematics, science, and foreign languages. The number of units required in each subject, however, has shown a downward trend—a development favorable to the recognition of untraditional subjects. A typical pattern is as follows: English, 3 units; mathematics, 2; science, 2; social sciences, 1; foreign languages, 2; electives, 6. Electives are, for the most part, ramifications of the core curriculum,[9] or vocational subjects, or art, music, and the like.

In the East the adherence to the traditional principles is more pronounced than in the West, a tendency extending to liberal arts as well as to engineering colleges; the unit requirements in specific subjects for admission to two-thirds of the engineering colleges in the New England and Middle Atlantic states vary between 10 and 16, whereas in the Middlewestern and Southern states half or more of the institutions require only 7 units or less. The decline of the importance of a specific number of units has been balanced

[8] More than 92 per cent of the engineering colleges require 15 units, the small remainder, either 14½ or 16. These and all subsequent statistical data on admission to the study of engineering in American collegiate institutions have been taken from Society for the Promotion of Engineering Education, *Report of the Investigation of Engineering Education*, 1923–29, 2 vols. (Pittsburgh, 1930–34). *See especially* Walton C. John, 'A Study of Engineering Curricula,' vol. 1, pp. 427–53. The figures refer to 1924–25 and have been checked for 1929–30.

[9] For instance, in mathematics a choice may be made among elementary, intermediate, and advanced algebra, plane and solid geometry, and trigonometry for the required units. Interested students may choose one or more electives in this group. The same is true of general science, physics, chemistry, and biology, and of the four languages—Latin, French, Spanish, and German. In English, which is required in every curriculum, the electives include journalism, dramatics, public speaking, and the like.

by the introduction of more flexible factors, such as the student's rank in his high school class, his rating on standardized aptitude, intelligence and achievement tests, his health and character.

Although these changes permit more flexibility in the high school curriculum, they are not sufficiently pronounced to allow high school educators to consider integrating the academic with the general course of study. Adherence to a rigid core curriculum is still necessary for entrance to many colleges. The elimination by some colleges of all specific subjects, other than English, as entrance requirements is an interesting experiment, which may gain admission for especially promising students whose preparation has been unorthodox. But as a rule, a certain amount of specific subject requirements will probably be maintained and will therefore continue to exercise some standardizing influence on the high school curriculums.

With regard to the general course, the heterogeneity of the student body has necessitated the inclusion of hundreds of unrelated subjects in order to satisfy cultural and vocational needs. In many instances, there emerged business preparation programs, either incorporated into the general curriculum or organized as independent curriculums.[10] In others, programs are even designed to fit the special interests of individual students.

To be sure, 91 per cent of the students in rural, and 56 per cent in urban, high schools still pursue academic courses of study,[11] but the high proportion in rural schools can be attributed to the limited personnel and scant opportunities for flexibility, which restrict them mainly to one course of study, with at best a few electives. The lower but still considerable percentage in urban schools is mainly due to the large number of students who start with the college preparatory course and later change to the general course.

There is nevertheless a marked shift toward the practical. A survey of high school curriculums, conducted by Leonard V. Koos

[10] John Minor Gwynn, *Curriculum Principles and Social Trends* (New York, 1943), pp. 386-91.
[11] Edmonson, et al., op. cit. p. 549.

in 1927, listed 26 types among 702 curriculums in 150 high schools.[12] Each of the major types appeared with the following frequency: commercial, 142 times; college preparatory, 73; general, 72; scientific, 66; industrial or manual arts, 63; household arts, 55. Of these six types, three were predominantly vocational or prevocational. Some years earlier, Koos had made an analysis of twenty high schools in Connecticut and had found 20 curriculums in physics and physical geography, 12 in English grammar, 10 in Latin, 7 each in Greek and German, while bookkeeping appeared only 3 times, and business forms, once. Any comparison of these two tabulations must take into account the widely different scope of the surveys. But the general trend suggested by this and other findings is indisputable.

Spectacular in Koos's analysis is the frequency of the commercial curriculum, which heads the list. Indeed, the traditional high school's most important contribution to vocational education is in the field of the commercial course of study. A few mercantile courses like bookkeeping were scattered through high schools of Massachusetts and California early in their history, but the commercial course as such began to emerge in the seventies, developing gradually until it finally became specialized. In the eighties 'commercial English' was offered, in the nineties 'business,' 'commercial,' 'complete commercial,' and 'shorter commercial' courses. At the end of the century, although the rapid development of the public high school was already under way, the private commercial schools still held the field, and the ratio of attendance in private commercial schools to that in commercial courses in the public high schools was 8:1. From then on, however, the enormous progress in industrial and commercial expansion led to a conspicuous development of these courses in the public high schools. Currently the principal subjects of study are bookkeeping, stenography and typewriting, merchandising and salesmanship.

There is hardly a high school today that does not have at least a

[12] Leonard V. Koos, *The American Secondary School* (New York, 1927), pp. 523-4.

commercial course; in most instances, there is an entire department for these studies. Even in junior high schools, provision is made for a commercial course in the ninth year. Basically the course is patterned on the general course, requiring the same number of units as for the academic or general diploma, except that the electives are chosen from, and concentrated in, the commercial subjects. In New York and many other large cities the programs are planned to enable students to enter colleges and universities having departments or schools of business.[13]

In stressing commercial subjects the general high school did not inspire the social demand; it followed it. This is demonstrated more conclusively by the following figures, which show what percentages of all high school students were enrolled in commercial subjects, in languages, and in science in 1928 and 1934.[14]

	1928	*1934*
Typewriting	15.2%	16.7%
Shorthand	8.7	9.0
Bookkeeping	10.7	9.9
Elementary business training	3.0	6.1
Latin	22.0	16.0
French	14.0	10.9
Spanish	9.4	6.2
German	1.8	2.4
General science	17.5	17.8
Biology	13.6	14.6
Chemistry	7.1	7.6
Physics	6.9	6.3

During this period of a rapidly growing high school population, enrollments in commercial subjects increased 11 per cent—a greater increase than in any other group. Science course enrollments increased by 5 per cent; registration for foreign language courses took a sharp drop. While it cannot be assumed that all of those enrolled for shorthand and typewriting were preparing for a

[13] New York City Board of Education, *The Public High Schools of the City of New York* (New York, 1942), p. 4.
[14] Computed from Bent and Kronenberg, op. cit. p. 378.

commercial or a clerical career, the registrations for both commercial and science subjects imply that the orientation of the high school students is in the direction of practical pursuits and future occupational needs.

The commercial course is the latest development in the general high school curriculum and has remained within its framework. This is desirable, since the academic high schools provide favorable conditions for the broad and purposeful planning of this course of study. But in some cities, the vocational high school system has also leaned toward incorporation of the commercial course.

The combined benefits of the prolongation of school attendance to the age of seventeen and beyond, and the expansion of the commercial and clerical course, have contributed to the educational and training needs of white collar workers, enlarging both their general knowledge and their vocational preparation. Since the members of this occupational group, especially the women, frequently shift to other occupations, in-school preparation for their careers should be as broad as possible, academically as well as vocationally.

EMERGENCE OF THE VOCATIONAL HIGH SCHOOL

Unlike the business preparation curriculum, a trade preparation curriculum, although frequently attempted, did not develop successfully within the structure of the academic high school for a number of reasons. Business preparation had always been the concern of high school educators, whereas trade preparation had not. In-school preparation for a trade required shop and manual work as the center of training and therefore entailed the reconstruction of the entire curriculum. In the academic high school the shop, if present at all, was at best an adjunct to the regular course, and the practical arts courses, which represented the culmination of manual activities, never reached the stage of vocational training. One and the same organization could hardly function successfully for two types of education so divergent in aims and methods. Moreover, neither the training for high school teaching nor the prime interests of the teachers were conducive to trade education.

Thus, as the millions of prospective manual workers streamed into the high school, discrimination of one kind gave way to another. The high school catered to boys and girls preparing for professions, commercial, or clerical work by offering an educational and training program that combined the traditional cultural and scientific subjects with what was directly useful for, or appropriate to, their careers. But the future manual workers were denied an equally useful education.

In these circumstances the creation of the vocational high school was not an arbitrary act, but rather the inevitable result of democratic thinking. The vocational high school is the institutional embodiment of the idea that an overwhelmingly large part of its students will engage in agricultural or industrial pursuits or in home economics; that the social environment has been transformed and determined by the industrial revolution and new labor relations; that certain modern occupations have developed on a large scale, and that equality of opportunity requires that general education include training for such pursuits. The creation of the vocational high school is, therefore, the final acknowledgment of the equal value of physical, technical, and mental activity necessary for the maintenance and progressive development of modern society.

The evolution of the vocational high school cannot be compared with that of the older forms which developed within the secondary school system. It is not the fourth type of secondary school, succeeding in its turn the Latin grammar school, the academy, and the academic high school, but is, instead, a variety of high school designed to serve the special needs of a great part of the heterogeneous student body. It will not absorb an increasing part of the potential school population still out of school as did the earlier, newly established types; the potential high school population has, to a great extent, already been absorbed during the last two decades, and would have been even without the vocational high school. Nor will the vocational replace the academic high school, for it has its own well-defined tasks and concentrates on educational functions which in no way interfere with or even threaten to supersede those of the academic high school. Neither does it necessarily endanger the standards of achievement set by the high school in general; indeed, it has the potentialities for maintaining them by being a free public school determined to increase the attractiveness of, and thus prolong, school attendance.

The existence of the vocational high school does, however, pose several major problems that have not yet been satisfactorily solved. Among these are the maintenance of academic standards on a level with those of the general high school, and the avoidance of the premature imposition of a choice of vocation on fourteen-year-old children. The vocational high school, moreover, is not legally a part of the educational 'ladder' and its curriculum is usually incompatible with the college preparatory function; in other words, it is a terminal institution and therefore the top rung of an adjacent ladder. Rigid adherence to this terminal character of the vocational high school divides the secondary school student body into two groups—those who can look forward to continuing their studies at the college level and those who at an early age must renounce this prospect. These conditions imply a sharp cleavage between the academic and vocational high school that cannot be considered in the interest of American democracy or of the American worker.

A quick glance at the development of the vocational high schools [15] shows that they made rather slow progress both before the passage of the Smith-Hughes Act in 1917, and in the first decade of its application, but expanded rapidly in the thirties. They have become a recognized institution growing along with the general high schools, although until World War II they never attained comparable prestige. Proof of their importance to education, however, may be found in the following figures on enrollments in vocational courses in federally aided all-day vocational schools or classes between 1924 and 1942.[16]

[15] This subject is treated at greater length in Ch. VIII.
[16] U.S. Office of Education, *Digest of Annual Reports of State Boards for Vocational Education* . . . 1940 (Washington, 1941), Table 5, and *Digest of Annual Reports* . . . 1944 (Washington, 1945), p. 64.

1924	134,873
1930	241,486
1936	546,014
1940	1,025,271
1942	1,197,213

From 1930 to 1940 the annual increase in enrollments was between 80,000 and 100,000. In 1930, the proportion of students of high school age in vocational high schools was 5 per cent; in 1940, it was 16. That one decade witnessed a 48 per cent increase in general high school enrollments and a 426 per cent increase in those of vocational high schools. During World War II, vocational high school enrollments declined along with the general decrease in high school attendance. By 1943, they had been reduced to 1,025,-582, and by 1944 to 936,627, a level of enrollment that was maintained in the following year.

Closer examination of the figures on attendance in the three different types of all-day vocational high schools—trade and industry, agriculture, and home economics—reveals a less pronounced trend with reference to the first of these types. In 1941, enrollments in trade and industrial schools totaled 231,239; in agriculture schools, 332,612; in home economics, 545,408.[17] Nearly half the enrollments were in home economics, with 31 per cent in agriculture, and only 20 per cent in trade and industrial classes—that is, only 20 per cent of the vocational high school students were preparing for the vocations that absorb the largest part of the industrial labor force. The average ratio of vocational high school to general high school students is 1:5, but it is by no means applicable to the students destined for work involving industrial skills. For this group the ratio is 1:29. The present contribution, therefore, of the vocational high school to industrial manpower, although rising, is still far from adequate.

[17] U.S. Office of Education, *Digest of Annual Reports* . . . 1944 (Washington, 1945), p. 64.

IV

Types and Aims of In-School Vocational Education and Training

DEFINITION OF TERMS

IN the broadest sense, in-school vocational education and training includes any education and training pattern directed toward the preparation for occupational life. Thus conceived it embraces nearly all secondary and college education, much of which is motivated by occupational considerations. Even the liberal arts studies can be included, especially if they are pursued with a view to a professional career. Since, however, it is general practice to rule out preparation for the professions from any definition of vocational education, this study will observe the usual procedure.

In-school vocational education, in a narrower sense, excludes college education and a large part of secondary education, confining itself entirely to schooling with predominantly vocational objectives. Secondary vocational education is often referred to as terminal, but this is only a partly accurate description since such education is often followed by other in-school and out-of-school vocational education and training in the form of apprenticeship, technical institute training, or attendance at any of the adult education part-time or evening classes; in rare instances, it is followed by college.

Since the passage of the Smith-Hughes Act in 1917, in-school vocational education has in many quarters acquired an even narrower meaning. Under the provisions of the Act it is limited to education and training for agriculture, trades, industry, and home economics, given in schools or classes of less than college grade, under public supervision or control, and designed to meet the needs of, and fit for useful employment, persons over fourteen years of age who are to enter the work of the farm, a trade or industrial pursuit, or who have entered upon such work.[1] This definition excludes technical education, as offered by technical high schools and technical institutes, and also the training given in private trade schools.[2] It does, however, include training programs offered by junior colleges, in so far as they meet the provisions and standards of state plans for vocational education.

The confusion resulting from this conflicting terminology is widespread. New York State education legislation referring to 'vocational schools and classes' includes not only federally aided vocational high schools but also technical schools and all-day commercial vocational schools of secondary grade;[3] but a report issued by the Board of Education of New York City classifies technical high schools among the academic high schools.[4]

[1] Sections 10 and 11 of the Smith-Hughes Act, reprinted in U.S. Office of Education, *Statement of Policies for the Administration of Vocational Education*, revised ed. (Washington, 1937), pp. 75–82; the George-Deen Act of June 8, 1936, reprinted ibid. pp. 91–3. The latter has since been amended by the 'Vocational Education Act of 1946' (Public Law 586, Ch. 725, 79th Congress, 2nd Session).

[2] Efforts have been made in a number of states to establish public control of privately operated trade schools. Under the state laws governing the operation of trade schools, each school is required to apply for an operating license to the state department of education. The school must submit a detailed statement showing the program of instruction and the facilities and equipment at its disposal for carrying on the instruction. The schools are visited by officials of the state department of education before being approved and licensed. In Pennsylvania, several private trade schools have voluntarily met the state requirements; in New Jersey, numerous questionable schools have closed rather than face investigation. See U.S. Office of Education, *Digest of Annual Reports of the State Boards for Vocational Education . . . 1943* (Washington, 1944), pp. 39–40.

[3] *Laws of the State of New York*, 1935, Ch. 250, Law of March 26. All-day commercial high schools and commercial courses in vocational high schools are not federally aided. In the George-Deen Act (and also in its amended form, Section 7), appropriations are made for teacher training, and the like, in distributive occupational subjects, but they are limited to part-time and evening courses. See U.S. Office of Education, *Statement of Policies . . .* (cited above), p. 93.

[4] New York City Board of Education, *Vocational and Practical Arts Education in New York City Schools* (New York, 1942), p. 17.

In order to avoid further confusion, a definition of terms is necessary. For the purposes of this study, therefore, in-school vocational education and training is considered to include all education and training below college grade that aims primarily at preparation for work, as offered mainly by technical high schools, vocational high schools, junior colleges, and technical institutes, regardless of whether such education and training is federally aided. Preparation for the strictly professional occupations is excluded.

At the secondary level, this training is given primarily in vocational and technical high schools, full time in school or, in some cases, on a cooperative basis. At the nonsecondary level there are the trade preparatory or pre-employment courses and trade extension courses intended for adults, the continuation courses, and trade apprentice classes. Nonsecondary vocational training has a primarily economic function and is narrowly utilitarian, being aimed directly at specific jobs in given industries; it is, for the most part, occupational training rather than education. Such courses are offered mainly by vocational and technical high schools, but also by technical institutes, junior colleges, and private trade schools, on a full- or part-time basis, in day or evening classes.[5]

Institutions of secondary vocational education vary greatly in character and quality, but all of them have certain goals in common. Their main emphasis is on the educational process, and the curriculum therefore includes many cultural subjects. The schools aim to familiarize the student with the important aspects of technology and skill, through study and performance under the direction of trained teachers who are required to know not only shopwork techniques but also pedagogical methods of presentation.

Shopwork in school is intended to furnish practical experience. It is not concerned with immediate commercial goals or remuneration and is therefore not subject to periodic changes in commercial requirements. These conditions make possible the long-range planning of programs, answerable only to the demands of teaching

[5] Technical institute training will be discussed separately in Ch. VII.

and learning. By the same token, however, the atmosphere of the
school, the composition of the curriculum, and the freedom from
concern for the job or the costs of production prevent this in-
school training from attaining full occupational efficiency or the
standards of achievement set by training in industry. Such schools,
therefore, do not claim to produce full-fledged technicians, craftsmen, or operatives. But if they are well staffed and well equipped,
they are in a better position than are industrial plants to prepare
students for the complex technical and industrial world, by providing a broad educational background and by teaching fundamental
skills and trade knowledge together with related technical subjects.
Private trade schools, technical institutes, and part-time evening
courses for adults, all of which are more closely allied to specific
jobs or industries and directly supplement on-the-job training,
lack one or another of these characteristics of secondary vocational
education entirely, or have them to a lesser degree.

TECHNICAL HIGH SCHOOLS

The technical high school is designed to prepare students for
work in engineering or other technical pursuits. The need for such
training has been felt most keenly in those localities where the industries offer wide opportunities to technically minded and technically trained young men. But the response to these needs by state
and local governments has been far from uniform. The technical
high schools are for the most part sparsely scattered throughout
the country, with the highest concentration in New York State.[6]

The origin, growth, and vocational-technical character of these
schools, which receive no federal financial aid, present a highly
variegated pattern. The designation, 'technical high school,' ap-

---

[6] New York has created a special office of supervisor of technical education. Technical high school enrollments in the state increased from 309 in
1920–21 to 12,487 in 1934–35, and to 15,399 in 1940–41. See University of the
State of New York, The Organization and Administration of Technical
Courses in Secondary Schools, Bulletin No. 1086 (Albany, 1937), p. 6; U.S.
Office of Education, Vocational-Technical Training for Industrial Occupations, Vocational Division Bulletin No. 228 (Washington, 1944), p. 153.

pears to mean different things in different places. On the one hand, we find highly developed institutions such as Brooklyn Technical High School, with extensive shop and laboratory facilities and well-organized curriculums, offering programs of study that prepare young men for employment of a definitely technical character or prepare them for admission to engineering schools, sometimes with advanced standing. On the other hand, there are institutions which claim the title but which appear to offer little more than a general high school curriculum with a few scattered courses in practical arts.

There is, however, a trend toward more bona fide technical high schools. Academic high schools have been transformed into technical high schools or have set up technical departments. In some communities the technical high school is operated under the same roof as the vocational high school, as a separate unit but with the same administration. In others, technical high school departments have been added to vocational high schools.

In recent years there have been indications of keener federal interest in technical high schools, especially since their number began to increase with the expansion and importance of technical occupations. In March 1943, the United States Commissioner of Education appointed a Consulting Committee on Vocational-Technical Training, thereby conferring upon this type of training an official title which has rapidly gained currency. In the following year, this Committee, whose twenty-six members represented management, labor, and education, submitted an extremely valuable report, *Vocational-Technical Training for Industrial Occupations*. It is significant that the Assistant Commissioner for Vocational Education was entrusted with the over-all planning and supervision of the study and that the Vocational Division of the Office of Education published the report as the first volume of a 'Vocational-Technical Training Series.' Thus, with the consent of the Commissioner of Education, the Division has expanded its field of activity beyond the limits set by the Smith-Hughes Act almost thirty years ago, when the present urgent need for technical education and training could not have been fully foreseen. This action may foreshadow a movement toward closer coordination of all technical education at the secondary level and of the administration and teaching methods of the vocational and the technical high schools—an orientation that should be regarded favorably and given active encouragement.

Pedagogically, the content of technical high school instruction is ideally suited to in-school occupational education. Its main emphasis is on the acquisition and use of technical information; shopwork, although essential to the program as a whole, does not constitute its center, and the amount of manipulative and machine-operating skills acquired varies with the course of study. Thus, the industrial design course may involve only a minimum of shopwork, offered mainly to illustrate industrial processes but having no direct bearing on the course as a whole. A chemical course may call for a moderate amount of shopwork for direct demonstrational purposes, while an electrical course is likely to require, in addition, the learning of certain basic skills. In a mechanical course, technical knowledge and understanding must be supplemented by the acquisition of a considerable amount of manipulative skills, but even in these courses shopwork may receive only minor emphasis.

The most elaborate list of approved technical subjects is that offered in New York State, where they are taught in the seventeen registered technical high schools or in the technical departments of registered high schools, and for which Regents diplomas may be earned. Courses are now being offered in the following fields: applied and advertising arts, architectural drawing and building construction, aviation, electricity, industrial chemistry, mechanical design and construction, power generation, and structural drafting and design.[7]

In New Jersey, the Essex County technical high schools offer advertising art, aeronautics, industrial chemistry, manufacturing

---

[7] In addition, the Straubenmuller Textile High School in New York City offers courses in applied design, applied science, costume draping and design, textile maintenance, textile manufacturing. *See* University of the State of New York, *Syllabus in Technical Subjects* (Albany, 1941), pp. 5–6.

techniques, mechanical drafting and elements of machine design, photographic techniques, printing techniques, radio and principles of television, refrigeration and air conditioning, and technical industrial electricity. The programs offered in the vocational-technical field at the Technical and Vocational High School in Bayonne include engine testing, electrical testing, radio and electrical communication, metal trades and drafting, laboratory techniques, heating and ventilating.

In Detroit, the Cass Technical High School offers separate curriculums in machine tool operation, mechanical drafting, architectural drafting, and building, and in the electrical, automotive, and aeronautical fields.

The variety of the courses offered demonstrates that the field of technical instruction is impressively wide and steadily expanding. Moreover, the nature of the subjects is such that they can be taught more effectively in the technical high school than elsewhere.

Vocational High Schools

The vocational high schools, although they originated as state projects, owe their phenomenal development to the Smith-Hughes Act from which they derive inspiration for their teaching standards and methods, as well as financial aid. They operate as all-day secondary education institutions designed to prepare students for agriculture, the trades, industry, and home economics, and admission is granted only to those students who have selected one of these fields for future work.

The Smith-Hughes Act defines certain conditions under which federal money is made available 'for the purpose of cooperating with the States' in vocational education, but much of the actual work of the schools is left entirely to state control. Federal aid is intended to contribute to the training and salaries of teachers of agricultural, trade and industrial, and home economics subjects. It is further intended to help defray expenses for studies, investigations, and reports of the Federal Bureau for Vocational Education (now the Vocational Division of the United States Office of Education) and for office expenses and the salaries of the staff.[8]

Federally aided vocational high schools are required to devote at least 50 per cent of the instruction time to shopwork, 25 per cent to related subjects, and not more than 25 per cent to cultural subjects. The Smith-Hughes Act stipulates that 'at least half of the time . . . be given to practical work on a useful or productive basis, such instruction to extend over not less than nine months per year and not less than thirty hours a week.'[9] Among the cultural subjects offered are English, social science, and health education, while related subjects include mathematics and science (general science, physics, and chemistry), sketching, blueprint making, or applied art.

Shopwork in the vocational high schools usually includes the basic elements of one broadly conceived trade or of a closely related job family, or it provides training in general industrial processes. The first type of training is offered in the 'unit trade school' which is either a general vocational high school or a central vocational high school. Both kinds of schools are found in large cities or industrial areas. The former serves a particular city school zone and offers programs in diverse fields; the latter serves an entire city or industrial area, and training is given in only one trade or a very closely related job family.

In areas where there is less demand for industrial training and where the placement possibilities are restricted, there are general industrial schools which teach the basic elements of several trades. Similar training is offered by federally aided vocational departments of high schools in smaller towns and communities. The general industrial schools and vocational departments do not have unit trade classes; instead, the basic elements of several trades are offered.

[8] U.S. Office of Education, *Statement of Policies* . . . (cited above), pp. 75–82. According to Section 6 of the Smith-Hughes Act, studies, investigations, and reports may also cover commerce, commercial pursuits, and requirements of commercial workers.

[9] Section 11 of the Smith-Hughes Act, ibid. pp. 80–81.

The number of trades taught in the trade and industrial high schools is less than the 120 listed as apprenticeable by the Apprentice Training Service of the War Manpower Commission.[10] But in general, vocational high school instruction in many trades is broader than apprentice training. The trades most commonly found in vocational high school programs are machinist, sheet metal, carpentry, electrical, bricklaying, plastering, auto mechanic, cabinetmaking, instrument making, foundry, patternmaking, upholstering, tailoring, printing, beauty culture, and photography. The number and variety of others depend on local needs. New trades and job families are added as the scope of the vocational high school increases and as its educational value to craftsmen as well as operatives becomes more apparent. A four-year vocational high school course gives the graduate 2,250 to 2,400 clock hours of shopwork or the equivalent of about 56 to 60 forty-hour weeks, and about 1,200 hours of related instruction.

Although vocational high schools vary greatly in character and quality, they have a common goal. They are bound by federal legislation to prepare youth for useful employment—as was the case with earlier state legislation. The teaching is largely prescribed, and instruction in manual skills is the center of all programs.

The transformation of schools into productive workshops, however, has been effected variously. Where the vocational high schools have been absorbed into the traditional system of secondary education they have usually been required to observe educational methods and standards similar to those of the general high schools. This is particularly true with regard to the cultural subjects. In many instances, the quality of technical instruction related to the respective trades is raised beyond the practical needs of the average industrial worker; and in the workshops, extensive demonstration rather than production is commonly emphasized. The latter situation may result from conditions beyond the control of the school, such as the inability to secure an adequate work project;

[10] U.S. Apprentice-Training Service, *The National Apprenticeship Program* (Washington, 1943), p. 6.

nevertheless, it characterizes the pedagogical approach of these schools.

Some vocational high school systems, on the other hand, have developed more independently of traditional public education. Training in manual skills is more highly concentrated and approaches actual working conditions, while cultural subjects are not given at all or are restricted to very few hours, and technical instruction is reduced to a minimum. Vocational schools of this type are to be found in Connecticut, where they are characteristically called trade schools.

For the country as a whole, however, the prevailing vocational education is an integral part of the secondary system. Its purpose is occupational education and training, built largely around a chosen trade or industrial pursuit. The schools do not claim to meet business standards of efficiency. Their primary purpose is to convey to the students a broad understanding of their future work and its relation to their trade or occupation as a whole; and to familiarize them with basic operations, tools, and machinery, the properties of materials, the use of measuring devices, and the like. In general, the attempt is made to introduce students to the discipline of work; to teach them to follow technical directions, both written and in blueprints, and to observe safety rules; and finally, to induct them into economic and industrial life.

COOPERATIVE EDUCATION

Under the system of cooperative education the student alternates school work with work in industry, usually as one of a pair of students performing the same work and spending two weeks at a time in school or on the job. In contrast to purely vocational high school education, in which the entire time is spent in school and all work is on a strictly educational basis, the cooperative system embraces both school education and experience in employment, and the participants are referred to as student-learners.[11]

[11] For a comprehensive definition, see U.S. Office of Education, *Digest of Annual Reports* . . . 1940 (Washington, 1941), pp. 82, 83, 84.

The instruction time schedule in cooperative vocational high schools is the same as in full-time vocational high schools: of the 30 clock hours required per week, half are spent in the study of related and academic subjects, and the other half in practical trade training in industrial shops. At least 2,000 hours or more of 'organized instruction and organized work experience on the job as determined by occupational committees' are required for graduation.[12] State, local, and craft advisory committees are appointed to supervise this work.[13]

The agreements protecting student-learners are very similar to apprentice agreements and indentures, containing provisions for wages, hours, length of training, responsibility of supervision, and the like. Such contracts are required wherever the cooperative system is in operation. In order to encourage this type of occupational preparation the Wage and Hours Division of the United States Department of Labor grants special permits for student-learners. Furthermore, there are definite rules for the selection of the student-learners, their ratio to workers, schedule of processes, high school credit, and other considerations. In other words, every effort is exerted to make the training program as comprehensive as possible and to give the student-learner adequate occupational preparation.

Since the student-learners are brought into contact with real work and working conditions, they may be best described as junior apprentices. But cooperative training can by no means be considered a real apprenticeship, because the time spent on the job is much too short for the acquisition of comprehensive skills. For the student it has the added attraction of earning while learning, while the employer who has any misgivings about the preparation given in vocational high schools gets an opportunity to judge the

[12] C. E. Rakestraw, 'Cooperative Part-Time Diversified Occupations Program,' in *Occupations* (March 1940), p. 2.
[13] The committees and their functions are described in *Standards for Cooperative Part-Time Programs in Diversified Occupations* (State Supervisors of Trade and Industrial Education in the Southern Region, Regional Conference, Little Rock, Ark., April 1939), quoted in Rakestraw, op. cit. p. 2.

quality of the teaching from his contacts with cooperative students. As a result, student-learners have a better chance for permanent employment by the plants in which they have received shop training.

The advantages of student-learnership, however, are individual and practical, rather than collective and educational. For one thing, students who have been holding a job and earning money lose interest in their school work and, in consequence, their general education suffers. Employers, for their part, are reluctant to hire boys of sixteen on a part-time basis and to try to adjust the work in their plants to school work. Even at best, work in plant shops and technical instruction in school can be coordinated only with great difficulty because of the divergence between the economic and educational orientation.[14]

In any case, the number of students trained under student-learnership programs has remained relatively small, and their ratio to other vocational high school students is only 1:10 or even lower. In 1943, the enrollment of boys was 12,831, that of girls, 7,765. The general increase in the number of students in all-day vocational high school classes before and during the first year of the war was not reflected in cooperative class enrollments. With the exception of Massachusetts and Ohio, most of the remaining cooperative students are not in the industrial states, where enrollments in vocational high schools are greatest, but in southern states and others with large rural populations.

SELECTED VOCATIONAL HIGH SCHOOL SYSTEMS

The range and diversity of the vocational high school may best be illustrated by examples of various systems throughout the country.

In New York City, for example, the system is widely expanded and its integration with the secondary school has been carefully

14 U.S. Office of Education, *Vocational-Technical Training* . . . (cited above), p. 232.

studied. There are, at present, twenty-six vocational high schools in Greater New York, forty-eight academic, and eight special high schools (technical, scientific, music and art). Most vocational high schools admit graduates of elementary school (8B graduates) as well as graduates of junior high schools and those students who have successfully completed one year of academic high school (9B). In the main, the vocational high school course is of three years' duration beginning with the tenth school year; in some cases the ninth year is also included.

Typical of the central vocational high schools are the Brooklyn High School of Automotive Trades, the Machine and Metal Trades High School, and the Central High School of Needle Trades, in each of which the curriculum concentrates on a particular field.

The general vocational schools offer various unrelated curriculums. Thus, in the East New York Vocational High School, courses are offered in auto mechanics, electrical installation, woodworking, machine shop, general commercial subjects, trade dressmaking, and beauty culture. The Metropolitan Vocational High School also teaches a great number of trades but concentrates mainly on maritime occupations, which gives the school a unique position in the system. The course is unified in so far as 'it trains for the sea, yet it is coordinated with a number of other standard mechanical operations in such a way as to provide a diversity of skills and to train for a versatility that may be applied to a number of land operations, such as stationary engineer and building maintenance. Boys may choose any one of the major departments—deck, engine, radio, or steward . . . But, whatever the major course, some work must be taken in each of the other departments. All the boys get some machine shop practice, woodworking, electrical work, plumbing . . . all in terms of activity aboard ship.' [15]

The New York City vocational high schools teach 89 different

[15] New York City Board of Education, *All the Children*, 41st Report of the Superintendent of Schools, City of New York 1938–39 (New York, 1940), p. 73.

trades in 288 courses, 170 of which are designed exclusively for boys, 90 for girls, and 28 are intended for both. Of the trades, 15 (including beauty culture, office machine operation, doctor's assistant, trade millinery, and others) are planned for girls only, 24 for boys and girls, and 50 for boys only. All courses have recently been brought up to date, given more precise definitions, and organized for a greater degree of correlation and integration of shop, academic, and related subjects.[16] Virtually all the vocational high schools are provided with the necessary machines and equipment of the respective trades, and many of the school buildings have been newly erected for specific uses.

Among the city systems, that of Cincinnati is remarkable for its gradual approach to vocational aspects of education and its cooperative plan for the twelfth year. The program of instruction in each of the four public vocational high schools prepares the pupil for work in an occupation of his own choice from among several trades and, at the same time, provides him with the essentials of a standard four-year course leading to a high school diploma. In the first two years, the schools operate according to usual high school plans, with required mathematics and science and beginning shopwork. The last two years provide specialized instruction in chosen industrial fields as preparation for profitable employment.

Students may choose to take their senior year on a cooperative basis if jobs are available in their chosen trade. As of February 1943, the following courses were being given in the Central Vocational School: aeronautics, air conditioning, allied construction (woodworking), locomotive, communications, Diesel engines, electrical, machine, machine design, patternmaking, refrigeration. All vocational high school programs include technical drafting, mathematics, and science related to the trade; many include servicing.

The Connecticut 'trade schools' show the strongest tendency toward serving as a substitute for the traditional apprenticeship

[16] Ibid. p. 66.

system. Indeed, it is expressly stated that 'the purpose of the Connecticut Trade Schools is to provide organized apprenticeship under public supervision and control . . .'[17] Through its State Board of Education the program is conducted by a state director of vocational education and a supervisor of trade and industrial education. The system currently includes eleven schools located in New Britain, Bridgeport, Putnam, Torrington, Manchester, Danbury, Meriden, Stamford, Middletown, Willimantic, and Hartford.

All features of the program—instruction time, curriculum, vacations, graduation—show striking deviations from the usual secondary vocational schools. The schools are in continuous operation throughout the year except for a two-week vacation period during the summer. Sessions are held for eight hours, five days a week, and for four hours on Saturday. While the state provides equipment, machinery, tools, materials, supplies, and the salaries of directors, instructors, and office personnel, the city or town school committee furnishes housing, heat, light, maintenance, and similar services.

Admission is granted to students who have completed the eighth grade, reached the age of sixteen, and are 'natively fitted to profit by the instruction.'[18] The usual length of time required to complete a course in the boys' trades is 4,800 hours (about 2⅔ years), and for girls it averages 3,600 hours (about 2 years). In all, 27 trades—24 for boys and 3 for girls—are offered.

The usual types of all-day training are provided in all-day trade preparatory courses for those who wish to attend full time for the purpose of learning a complete trade. This kind of course requires a total of 2,600 to 7,000 hours (approximately 1½ to 4 years) of attendance, depending upon the trade selected. Training is also provided by the high school trade cooperative course, arranged in collaboration with local high schools to enable a student to secure both a trade school and a high school education in approximately

[17] Connecticut Education Department, *Connecticut State Trade Schools* (Hartford, 1941).
[18] Ibid.

four years. Outlines of the various trades in which instruction is given specify in detail the experience and knowledge necessary for complete training. The specifications originate in, and are kept up to date by, committees of instructors who determine through careful analysis all items of learning to be covered.

A unique feature of the Connecticut system is the opportunity offered to students in the building trades. In New Britain, Danbury, Middletown, Willimantic, and Hartford, it is possible for the trade schools to build complete houses. The trades taught include masonry, carpentry, electrical work, plumbing and heating, painting.[19] 'Houses built . . . stand as ample proof of the ability of apprentices under proper instruction to carry out a complete job.'[20] In Meriden, the center of the silver industry, the trade school students learn to fashion and fabricate objects in sterling and nickel silver according to the standards of the trade. Many of the students are absorbed by the local industries.

The Essex County (New Jersey) vocational high schools, located in Bloomfield, Newark, and Irvington, are representatives of a county system of vocational education. They prepare for profitable and efficient employment of many types and levels, ranging from the operative or semiskilled to the highly technical and artistic. Students may enter at any time of the year, since the instruction and progress are individualized. Graduation takes place not at a stated time but after satisfactory completion of all assignments, which are very specifically outlined units of work.

The schools offer several identical courses: automotive repair and service, carpentry, electrical construction, maintenance and repair, machine shop practice. The Newark vocational high school supplements these programs with others adapted to the needs of the community, such as bricklaying, plastering and concrete work, cabinetwork, commercial art, commercial photography, manufacturing, patternmaking, printing, and restaurant

[19] Ibid. The course in house painting is given in Hartford only.
[20] Ibid.

and cafeteria work. The Irvington school gives courses in manufacturing, industrial clerk training, and sheet metal work, in addition to the group common to all three cities.

In Massachusetts there were, in 1940, 30 all-day industrial schools for boys, 4 for girls, 7 industrial departments, and 29 general vocational departments. Some of the day industrial schools offer a choice of several courses of study; others, such as the Independent Industrial Homemaking School, the Attleboro Jewelry School, and the Vineyard Haven Carpentry School, specialize in a single trade.

In the general vocational departments, no unit trade is taught, but shop offerings are developed in line with dominant local industries. Thus, in Gloucester, a general department has been set up for separate courses in carpentry, auto repair, electrical wiring and appliances, sheet metal work, and printing. A skilled craftsman serves as teacher in charge of each shop. The plan provides for rotation between courses or for work in only one course.

The Boston Trade School offers thirteen trades, including airplane mechanics, automobile mechanics, cabinetmaking, carpentry, drafting, electrical work, machine shop practice, painting and decorating, plumbing, printing, radio, sheet metal, and welding. Of the 30-hour school week, 55 per cent is devoted to shopwork, and 45 per cent, amounting to 20 forty-minute periods, to related and theoretical subjects. The school is not a cooperative school.

In Wisconsin the vocational schools are more like a substitute for employment than regular vocational schools. 'They are particularly organized for people who are not attending the regular public schools, as grade schools, high schools, colleges.' [21] 'Any person who is not indentured as an apprentice, who has not completed the equivalent of four years of high school work, who resides in a district which maintains a vocational and adult education school, and who is not required (by law) to attend school full

[21] Letter to authors from T. S. Rees, Director of Vocational and Adult Education, Racine, Wisconsin, 11 June 1943.

time, must attend in the daytime, for at least eight months in the year . . . some public, private, parochial or vocational and adult education school, half-time from the end of the period of full time compulsory education to the end of the school year in which he is 16 years of age.' [22] Following this he has to attend continuation school for at least eight hours a week if he is regularly, lawfully, and gainfully employed at home, and if unemployed, full time until the end of the division of the school year in which he is eighteen years of age.

CONTINUATION, TRADE PREPARATORY, AND TRADE EXTENSION SCHOOLS

Public part-time and evening in-school vocational training is offered in the general continuation school, the trade preparatory school, and the trade extension school. Attendance in the continuation school is compulsory and its purpose is general education; attendance in the trade preparatory and trade extension schools is on a voluntary basis and the objective is trade and industrial education. The general continuation school is intended only for boys and girls who have left school for employment at the end of the compulsory full-time education period. The other institutions are open to the entire out-of-school population and have no age limits.[23]

The development of the general continuation school, youngest of the three types of part-time education, can be traced to the compulsory attendance laws of the various states. These laws were designed to complete the standard education for young workers between the ages of fourteen and sixteen (in a few states, between fourteen and eighteen), who had left full-time school and were engaged in trade- and industrial pursuits.[24] The system

[22] Wisconsin State Board of Vocational and Adult Education, *Wisconsin Laws Relating to Vocational and Adult Education*, Bulletin No. 27 (Madison, 1941), p. 23.

[23] The so-called part-time cooperative schools and classes are regarded as part of all-day vocational education, and have therefore been treated in that context.

[24] Agricultural and domestic service occupations were usually not in-

met with only slight initial success. The early legislation which provided for attendance at evening schools aroused objections on the grounds that the health of the young people would be endangered; laws calling for instruction during working hours were therefore substituted.

The Smith-Hughes Act drew the continuation school into its orbit by providing 'that at least one-third of the sum appropriated to any State for the salaries of teachers of trade, home economics, and industrial subjects shall, if expended, be applied to part-time schools or classes for workers over fourteen years of age who have entered upon employment, and such subjects in a part-time school or class may mean any subject given to enlarge the civic or vocational intelligence of such workers over fourteen and less than eighteen years of age.' [25] In general, attendance in continuation school is required for from four to eight hours a week. For the non-employed, especially during the 1930's, the continuation school took on the character of full-time vocational schools, offering a 20-hour weekly program of shop and related work.

The phrase, 'civic and vocational intelligence,' in the Smith-Hughes Act allowed for the reorganization of general continuation education. The result has been a shift in emphasis from the academic and cultural subjects to such matters as civics, vocational guidance, and the educational opportunities related to the student's job and choice of trade. In other words, an attempt is being made to build the curriculum around the individual needs of the adolescent whose education has been prematurely ended by withdrawal from school. By interpreting the law somewhat generously it has also been possible to include commercial subjects in continuation school programs.

In many states there are no continuation school students, at least not in federally aided schools; in others there are only a few hun-

cluded. For material on continuation work prior to World War I *see* David Snedden, 'Continuation Schools,' in *Cyclopedia of Education*, vol. 2 (New York, 1919), p. 195.

[25] Section 11 of the Smith-Hughes Act. *See* U.S. Office of Education, *Statement of Policies . . .* (cited above), pp. 80–81.

dred. About half the total enrollments are concentrated in three states—California (with about 25 per cent), New York, and Michigan. From a peak attendance in 1930 of 168,807 male and 167,490 female pupils, the number decreased as shown in the following figures.[26]

	Male	Female		Male	Female
1930	168,807	167,490	1938	69,948	84,743
1932	127,931	143,301	1940	77,634	64,847
1934	80,591	94,027	1942	47,467	58,316
1936	67,039	78,304	1943	52,981	56,939

The sharp decline in continuation school attendance is chiefly due to prolonged compulsory full-time school attendance. This trend, together with the reluctance of employers, under normal labor market conditions, to hire youth below the age of eighteen and with safety regulations which bar young workers from certain occupations, may lead to a further contraction of this type of school.

Trade preparatory and trade extension courses offer opportunities not easily provided by industry to improve old skills or acquire new ones. This does not mean that such skills cannot be acquired on the job at all. But any training on the job for these purposes is greatly aided by intensive and systematic in-school training. This is especially true of trade extension training which, qualitatively and quantitatively, plays a more important role than in-school trade preparatory training. Many employed workers are aware of the advantages of the demonstrational methods, which can be so much more conveniently applied in schools than in commercial shops, and they are eager to utilize the schools' greater facilities for augmenting practical or special skills with theoretical or general knowledge of the field.

These part-time or evening training institutions are not only helpful for, but often indispensable to, the transfer from one job to another unrelated occupation requiring very different manipula-

[26] U.S. Office of Education, *Digest of Annual Reports* . . . 1943 (cited above), p. 80.

tive skills, technical knowledge, and mental aptitudes. Such training also eases the friction caused by sudden shifts in the labor market and contributes to that quick flexibility of labor without which the needs of production and the labor supply would follow divergent lines with disastrous effect. The practical aspects of part-time vocational education are stressed in the George-Deen Act, which extended financial aid to part-time training opportunities in 'public and other service occupations' and to business education. As a result, federally aided part-time business education expanded rapidly from the time of its inception in 1938. In 1943, distributive education programs were in operation in 46 states and the District of Columbia. Enrollments in all types of federally aided distributive occupational classes increased from 215,049 in 1942 to 297,534 in 1943,[27] a period in which all other federally aided vocational education was contracting.

Students in pre-employment trade preparatory courses are drawn from widely different backgrounds, and are either unemployed, or employed and seeking a change in occupation. The courses are for the most part restricted to instruction in one or a few machine operations like welding, wiring, or drilling, and do not offer complete preparation for an entire trade. The basic requirements of the new occupation, the character of the materials, the handling of tools and machines, the safety regulations, shop setup, and the like, comprise the instruction.

Trade extension training serves adult workers, including those already employed and those seeking work in specific trades, as a means of increasing their skill or trade knowledge. The student body comprises apprentices, workers who have been upgraded, foremen, all-around craftsmen, many of whom have had high school education, and some with college training. The three major fields covered by trade extension courses are specialties, new inventions and developments, and related subjects. The specialties generally belong to a trade other than that practiced by a worker

[27] U.S. Office of Education, *Digest of Annual Reports* . . . 1944 (Washington, 1945), p. 64.

but essential to the efficient performance of his own job. They include such courses as drawing and drafting, forging, heat treating, and certain electrical or mechanical subjects. With regard to the second group, systematic knowledge of the changes in production methods and in market and training conditions, created by new products and new materials, can best be obtained in school either before or after employment. Generally included in the related subjects are mathematics, science, chemistry, and technical courses, indispensable to the knowledge of any trade and often prerequisite to advanced skilled work.

Part-time and evening training courses differ entirely from the all-day courses of study since they are geared to the immediate and direct objectives of the student. Instruction is based on job requirements and is specific rather than general, concrete rather than abstract. Academic subjects are not included in trade extension training, whereas related subjects form an integral part and often constitute the exclusive content. In trade preparatory courses shopwork is more heavily stressed, since their primary purpose is to train operatives rather than highly skilled workers.

The courses are relatively short. At first, in order to be eligible for federal aid the minimum course was 144 hours a year, but the George-Deen Act did not sustain the time requirement.[28] Actually, some of the courses are longer, amounting to as much as 200 hours a year, depending on the subject and the curriculum; most are one-year courses; others, especially those for apprentices, are for two, three, or even four years. In any event, the in-school training must be supplemented by working on the job in order to reach results that are satisfactory from the standpoint of business requirements.

GOVERNMENT PROJECTS

This account of the various types of vocational education and training institutions would be incomplete without some reference to the federally aided projects born of the economic depression of the thirties and of World War II. Established for specific tem-

[28] Nor did the Vocational Education Act of 1946.

porary purposes, these programs are no longer in effect, but their experience may serve in part some future need.

During the depression, the federal government organized the National Youth Administration (NYA) in an effort to aid youth through occupational education and training. The purpose of the program was to provide the unemployed and needy with useful work in such a way as to achieve educational ends as well.

The NYA training and education program was probably the first entirely federal undertaking in the field. Not only was it financed by the government but it was also controlled and operated by it, thereby evoking considerable opposition from the states and municipalities. Another unusual aspect of this program was that the student-learners received remuneration while in training. Since the dissolution of NYA, the army and navy have maintained many members of the armed forces in engineering and medical schools, and the GI Bill of Rights provides financial support for veterans who wish to complete their education. Traditionally, however, public support for the education of youth has not been extended beyond tuition-free instruction.

The instruction itself had rather special characteristics. As the defense program got under way, NYA set up training centers in schools for a number of specific occupations in which the demand was expected to exceed the available labor supply. The courses lasted from a few weeks to a few months, and prepared for definite jobs rather than for entire trades. Related technical instruction was offered on a very limited scale, but in all other respects these courses paralleled the work of the vocational high schools. But whereas vocational high schools are usually equipped with small, easily handled machinery, many NYA centers employed full-size production machinery of all kinds. Moreover, because of its federal status, NYA was able to secure production work in quantity from the army, navy, and other federal agencies. Thus production in many of the centers more closely resembled actual factory production than that of any other kind of in-school training.

The desirability of such a setup, of course, is another question.

NYA, especially in its later stages, concentrated on training for defense industries rather than on vocational education in the broad sense, and the ways and means therefore had to be different. And, as a whole, the program's primary function was to train unemployed youth for useful employment while education as such was always a secondary consideration.

This country's participation in World War II required rapid training of huge masses of inexperienced persons for war production. The urgency of this task called for training on a large scale within the shortest possible time. The program was carried through by the federal government in close cooperation with the vocational high schools. According to the U.S. Office of Education, as many as 12 million men and women were trained for essential war jobs. Under various federal acts a considerable sum was appropriated and allocated to various programs, the greatest part of which was in support of courses supplementary to employment in occupations essential to the national defense, and pre-employment and refresher courses for workers preparing for such occupations.[29]

The contribution of the vocational high schools to this program was outstanding. Persons who had had no previous factory experience were trained for specific occupations in war plants; workers already employed were enabled to change from one phase of work to another, or to take jobs requiring higher skill or involving greater responsibility; training for plant foremen and supervisors was provided. In addition, the vocational schools assisted employers in analyzing and organizing various training activities. Under the supervision of the State Boards for Vocational Education public vocational schools also provided training for army and navy personnel and civilians attached to the services.[30]

[29] Another large sum was appropriated by Congress to provide brief courses of college grade to meet the shortage of engineers, chemists, physicists, and production supervisors in fields essential to national defense and war production.

[30] For regular surveys of war production training programs, *see* the volumes of U.S. Office of Education, *Digest of Annual Reports* . . . (cited above), published during the war.

The experience in vocational education and training, gained during the war, and the institutions established for training purposes may yield valuable data for any other emergency involving training on a large scale. Such training, however, was largely confined to teaching the worker a few simple operations which, although adequate for mass production in the particular circumstances, would not be satisfactory for peacetime industrial output. On the whole, normal training in the postwar period, although it has adopted some of the wartime shortcuts, has resumed its more extensive character.

V

Technical and Vocational
High School Curriculums

General Content and Time Distribution

ALL high school curriculums have the common objective of training students to work both independently and cooperatively, to develop their personalities freely, and to take their places as intelligent citizens in a democratic society. But within the system the various types of high schools follow different lines of approach toward this threefold goal. In general, the traditional high school curriculum reflects the organization of experience that only indirectly serves practical ends. The vocational high school curriculum, on the other hand, is closely determined by strictly vocational objectives. It bases its content on the assumption that the student has decided on a future occupation and it attempts to create a realistic atmosphere of work so that the student may more clearly understand, and find a better adjustment to, the world in which he will live.

In the vocational high school, differentiation and specialization are introduced at an early stage. Courses of study are designed to meet the individual needs and abilities of the student, and once the choice of a course of study has been made, it must be adhered to. By and large, the curriculum is composed almost entirely of constants, with the content of shopwork and related subjects determined by the requirements of the chosen trade. The academic work that fills the remaining time covers only the essentials and admits of little variation. For example, only a few of the New York State vocational high schools allow for any electives at all and these are fairly restricted. In the Central High School of Needle Trades in New York City, for instance, the only electives offered are typewriting, business practice, and the science of living.[1]

In general, these conditions prevail in the technical high schools as well. Thus, for its seven terminal courses of study,[2] Brooklyn Technical High School has organized rigid curriculums with no allowance for electives. And among the curriculums listed in the report of the Consulting Committee on Vocational-Technical Training,[3] only the general technical course at the Lane Technical High School in Chicago makes provision for any electives.

The rigidity of the vocational high school curriculum is a consequence not only of the necessary content of the courses of study, but also, largely, of the stipulations of the Smith-Hughes Act, particularly with regard to distribution of instruction time. In vocational high schools, instruction time amounts to 30 clock hours or 40 forty-five-minute periods weekly, whereas in academic high schools it totals 25 clock hours or 30 fifty-minute periods. The greater amount of time spent in vocational high schools does not imply that greater effort is required of the vocational high school student than of the academic. Manual skills must be acquired through shopwork instruction and practice in school but do not require preparation in advance or homework. The vocational high school student effects a balance, therefore, by spending less time on his work out of school than does the academic high school student.

At least 15 clock hours or 50 per cent of the instruction time in the vocational high school must be devoted to shopwork, 7½ clock hours or 25 per cent to related subjects, and the remaining 7½ to general education or cultural subjects. The allocation of 25 per cent of the time to subjects directly related to a trade has been

---

[1] Central High School of Needle Trades, New York, *Needlecrafter*, 1942.

[2] Aeronautics, architecture and building construction, art (industrial design), industrial chemistry, electrical science, mechanical, structural. *See* Brooklyn Technical High School, *Course of Study*, p. 2.

[3] U.S. Office of Education, *Vocational-Technical Training for Industrial Occupations*, Bulletin No. 228 (Washington, 1944), pp. 239–42.

established by the Office of Education as a minimum requirement for federally aided schools.[4]

No such fixed standards have been elaborated for the technical high schools. In several New Jersey schools of this type the time-table is identical with that of the vocational high schools. For the most part, however, the division of instruction time is different in the technical high schools from that in vocational high schools. In conformance with the emphasis on technical work, a minimum of 50 per cent of the time is devoted to the vocational-technical subjects and the immediately related subjects. No general rule exists for the remaining time. It is often equally divided between shop-work and general education, but whenever the purely technical prevails over the vocational-technical character of a program, shop-work is more limited. In a number of schools outside New York, more than 25 per cent of the time is allowed for shopwork in vocational-technical programs.

The wide variation in the amount of shopwork time stipulated by different courses in a technical high school is well exemplified by the aeronautics course and the mechanical drafting and elements of machine design course given by the Essex County technical high schools.[5] In the aeronautics course, which is a three-year vocational-technical program, $42\frac{1}{2}$ per cent of the total instruction periods are allotted to shopwork.[6] The other, which is entirely technical, accords only $11\frac{2}{3}$ per cent of the total instruction periods to shop-work.[7]

---

[4] U.S. Office of Education, *Statement of Policies for the Administration of Vocational Education* (Washington, 1937), pp. 52–3.

[5] Essex County Vocational and Technical High Schools, *Bulletin 6*, Part II, pp. 12–13, 25–6.

[6] The distribution of periods per week is as follows: machine shop and manufacturing shop practice, 16 (10th year, 1st term); aircraft construction, 4 (10th year, 2nd term) and 12 (11th year, 1st term); aircraft sheet metal shop, 8 (10th year, 2nd term); electrical shop and laboratory, 4 (10th year, 2nd term); aircraft rigging, 8 (11th year, 1st term); aircraft engines, 16 (11th year, 2nd term); aircraft electricity, 4 (11th year, 2nd term); aircraft engine accessories, 10 (12th year, 1st term); advanced plane and engine work, 10 (12th year, 2nd term); aircraft instruments, 6 (12th year, 2nd term); aircraft welding, 4 (12th year, 2nd term).

[7] The distribution of weekly periods is as follows: electrical shop, 4 (10th

The usual distribution of instruction time in the three broad types of curriculums is as follows: [8]

Academic: general education subjects, 66⅔ to 80 per cent (required); electives, 33⅓ to 20 per cent.

Technical: vocational-technical and immediately related subjects, at least 50 per cent; shopwork, 25 per cent (average); general education subjects, about 25 per cent.

Vocational: shopwork, at least 50 per cent; related subjects, at least 25 per cent; general education subjects, not more than 25 per cent.

A comparative analysis of three-year courses of study in three types of schools serves to point up the distinctive features of typical curriculums. In Table 5, we see not only the time distribution for academic, technical, and vocational programs, but also the major differences between the college preparatory course in the general high school and in the technical high school, and the difference between technical high school college preparatory and terminal courses.

GENERAL EDUCATION SUBJECTS

The general education subjects in the vocational and technical high schools are English, social studies, health education and hygiene, and music, all of which are standard subjects in the curriculum of the academic high school as well.[9] In a school week of 30 hours, more time is available for general education and related

---

year, 1st term); automotive shop, 4 (10th year, 1st term); manufacturing shop, 4 (10th year, 2nd term); machine shop, 4 (10th year, 2nd term); carpentry shop, 4 (11th year, 1st term); pattern, sheet metal or airplane shop, 4 (11th year, 2nd term); manufacturing shop (automotive machines), 4 (12th year, 1st term).

[8] Among the electives taken by the average pupil in four years of academic high school there is usually one year of general shop for boys and one of home economics for girls. *See* Rudyard K. Bent and Henry H. Kronenberg, *Principles of Secondary Education* (New York, 1941), p. 379. Neither the role of this subject matter nor the equipment of the shop justifies a special subdivision for it.

[9] In rare instances, English is considered a related subject in the vocational curriculum.

TABLE 5. AVERAGE NUMBER OF INSTRUCTION PERIODS PER WEEK IN THREE-YEAR COLLEGE PREPARATORY AND TERMINAL COURSES IN THREE TYPES OF HIGH SCHOOL, BY SUBJECT [a]

Subject	*General High School*	*Technical High School*		*Vocational High School*
	College preparatory	College preparatory [b]	Terminal [c]	Terminal [d]
English	5	5	6⅔ [e]	4
Social studies	3	2½	2⅔	3
Health education; hygiene	2	2⅔	2⅓	2⅔
Foreign languages	5–6⅔	3⅓ [f]	—	—
Mathematics [g]	5	—	—	—
Mathematics (technical, applied)	—	5	4⅔	4
Science [g]	3⅓	—	—	—
Science (applied)	—	5	3	2⅔
Drawing, art	1⅓	3⅓	—	—
Mechanical or applied drafting	—	—	5⅓	1⅓
Applied technical subjects	—	—	2	2⅓
Shopwork	2	6⅔	13⅓	20
Commercial subjects	1⅔–3⅓	—	—	—
TOTAL	28⅓–31⅔	33½	40	40

[a] Periods last 50 minutes in academic high schools, 45 minutes in other schools; average school year is 38 weeks.
[b] Brooklyn Technical High School.
[c] Course in manufacturing techniques.
[d] Course in machine shop practice.
[e] Including a weekly average of 2 periods of applied English and 1⅔ of library and study.
[f] If in preparation for a college requiring 3 years of a foreign language, a weekly average of 5 periods; in that case, a weekly average of only 3⅓ periods is spent on science.
[g] Instruction time in mathematics and science is generally adjustable between the two subjects in academic high schools; this

subjects than would be possible if the vocational high school were limited to the 25-hour week of the academic high school. Even so, the vocational high school has only 13½ hours a week for these subjects as compared with the 20½ hours accorded them by the academic high school.[10]

English is given throughout the four-year course, usually for five periods a week. In some New York City vocational high schools 'related English' or 'related trade English' is given in addition to the regular program: for example, in the course for printers, this includes the study of punctuation, symbols, and proofreading. In other schools, 'practical English' replaces English composition or literature, as is the case in the 11th and 12th grades of the Central Vocational High School in Cincinnati. In New Jersey, 12th-year English in the automotive repair and service course includes selling service.

Technical courses frequently allot three periods to selected readings and the remaining two to 'applied English,' in which the 'student is taught to write letters of application and fill out application blanks and to write shop and technical reports, specifications, business letters, and technical articles. He is taught, also, how to give oral directions, state his qualifications for a job, describe tools and machines, explain how a job is done and meet and introduce people. Those preparing for certain occupations are given some instruction in sales English.' [11]

'Social studies' is the inclusive term for the integration of courses generally comprising one term of civics, one of economics, two of American, and two of modern world history. Ancient and medieval history are not offered in vocational high schools, and world history rarely so, although the last-named is frequently included in

[10] Health education and music, which are given equal instruction time in both types of school, are not included in these figures. The remaining instruction time in the academic high school is devoted to general shop (1 clock hour) and commercial subjects (2 clock hours). The greater part of the discrepancy in the time accorded by the two types of schools to general education subjects is accounted for by the academic high school's emphasis on foreign languages.

[11] Essex County Technical and Vocational High Schools, op. cit. pp. 53-4.

the study of American history or of modern problems of American democracy. Sometimes a course in general social studies is given as a concise survey of the entire field. Part of the economics course may be integrated with the history courses, particularly those phases that may be related to industrial history, while such topics as the discovery, exploitation, and use of raw materials may be linked to shopwork instruction. Business management often supplements the social studies course. In the vocational high schools of Philadelphia, social studies is classified among related subjects, except in the printing course where it is regarded as a general education subject.[12] On the whole, social studies, although treated as a general education subject, includes more practical subject matter in the vocational, than in the general, high school.

Health education and physical training courses are identical in all types of schools and are offered two or three periods weekly. Technical and vocational high schools frequently add discussion of occupational hazards and their relation to health as part of shop and technical instruction.

With rare exceptions, foreign languages are not offered by the vocational high school curriculum or the technical high school terminal unit courses. They are, however, included in the college preparatory courses of some technical high schools.

RELATED SUBJECTS

Mathematics and science, both of which are general education subjects in the traditional high school, and the large group of technical studies are related subjects in vocational high schools. Mathematics, for example, generally 'consists of a selection of a few special items from arithmetic, algebra, geometry and trigonometry which are used in the occupation being taught. They are taught by repeated application to practical occupational problems.'[13]

[12] Philadelphia, Pa., Public Education Board, *Program of Studies of Senior High and Vocational Schools* (1942), pp. 41-4. This classification may be motivated by the desire to comply with conditions prerequisite for federal financial aid, which is admissible for preparation and salaries of teachers of related, but not of cultural, subjects.

[13] Essex County Technical and Vocational High Schools, op. cit. p. 54.

The shortcuts actually used in the trade, empirical formulas, rule-of-thumb methods, and the like, are usually included in the related shop mathematics course.[14] Other related subjects are similarly treated.

Related (or applied) trade mathematics is usually given five periods weekly for three years, and applied science for two years, or vice versa, an arrangement that corresponds to the total time devoted to mathematics and science in traditional high schools. Whereas in the latter these minimum requirements may be rounded out by electives, in the vocational high school they are supplemented by other prescribed related subjects.

Thus the mathematics course in the automotive repair and service trade course in the Brooklyn High School of Automotive Trades includes the study of tables, formulas, measuring instruments, selected items from plane geometry, and business mathematics and practice. Ignition and lighting system is included in applied science. The rest of the time is given to other related subjects—trade drawing, radio code, Diesel theory and car driving, each occupying from half a term to a term and a half. A course in machine shop practice in the Essex County vocational high schools includes blueprint reading and shop sketching (one term); electrical laboratory and theory (two terms); applied drafting, applied metallurgy, applied mechanics, and strength of materials (two terms). In the field of bricklaying the same schools offer applied drafting (shop sketching); building construction details; plan reading; and quantity estimating. Related subjects in a printing course include estimating (costs and paper requirements); English for printers; art in printing, such as the layout of a newspaper, proper margins and title pages; science as related to printing; and the hygiene of the trade.[15]

What standards can be achieved in the teaching of these related subjects is a controversial issue. According to one official appraisal,

[14] U.S. Federal Board for Vocational Education, *The Training of Teachers for Trade and Industrial Education*, Bulletin No. 150 (Trade and Industrial Series, No. 42) (Washington, 1930), p. 25.
[15] U.S. Office of Education. *Statement of Policies* . . . (cited above) (Washington, 1937), p. 52.

'a related mathematics course extending over two years can be a real bona fide course in mathematics which will develop a much larger degree of actual ability to use mathematics in solving specific problems than the traditional theoretical courses are able to do . . . The study of related trade science should have a world of meaning to a trade school student and develop a real comprehension of scientific principles in a way that no amount of formal study of traditional high school physics, elementary mechanics or chemistry will ordinarily develop . . .' [16]

It is further pointed out that in the teaching of mathematics and science general experience has shown that no principle should be taught in advance of application and no application drawn from fields with which no previous experience is connected. The related subjects as offered in vocational high schools are therefore considered to be richer in educational possibilities from the standpoint of both practical application and general educational objectives.

But notwithstanding the praise given to this kind of teaching, neither this nor any other statement on the subject claims that in the field of mathematics and science are vocational high schools able to approach the academic standards of the general high school. The prescribed way to teach related subjects may be a valuable supplement to the training of a future worker, but it may be doubted—and actually it has never been claimed—that it imparts sufficient fundamental knowledge of mathematics and science, or adequately develops the ability to think independently or to draw logical conclusions in these fields. It may even be doubted that the student grasps the principles underlying the work methods he has mastered.

The teaching of mathematics in technical high schools is far less narrowly conceived. In fact, in some schools both mathematics and science are taught on a higher level than in most academic high schools, and are considered general subjects to be adjusted to the content of each course rather than related subjects. At Brooklyn

[16] U.S. Federal Board for Vocational Education, op. cit. pp. 53-7.

Technical High School, for example, the program in mathematics (three years in the terminal course, four years in the technical college preparatory course) is fundamentally theoretical even in those courses designated as 'technical mathematics' and 'technical trigonometry.' The terminal three-year course of 'pure and applied mathematics' includes elementary and intermediate algebra, plane geometry, some solid geometry, and technical trigonometry.[17]

Suggestions for shaping the technical portion of a technical high school curriculum are offered by the Supervisor of Technical and Cooperative Education of the State of New York.[18] These show how vocational-technical and related subjects other than mathematics and science can be combined in well-rounded programs.

For example, for a course in architectural drawing and building construction the following distribution of periods is recommended: 1st and 2nd terms—industrial processes, 5, and technical drawing, 6 (mechanical, 4, and freehand, 2); 3rd and 4th terms—industrial chemistry, 5, and technical drawing, 6 (mechanical, 4, and freehand, 2); 5th and 6th terms—applied mechanics and strength of materials, 5, and architectural drawing and design, 4; 7th term—architectural drawing and design, 14; 8th term—architectural drawing and design, 20.

The suggested program for a technical mechanical course is the same in the first two years as above. The remaining time is divided into periods as follows: 5th and 6th terms—applied mechanics and strength of materials, 5, and machine drawing and design, 4; 7th term—steam and gas engines, 5, heat treatment of metals and shop management, 5, and machine drawing and design, 4; 8th term—power generation and distribution, 5, and machine drawing and design, 4.

Describing the content and goals of such a subject as industrial processes, one school states that it 'includes the study of sources, processes, characteristics, and uses of the basic materials of indus-

[17] Brooklyn Technical High School, *Handbook*, vol. 11 (1944), pp. 27–30.
[18] University of the State of New York, *The Organization and Administration of Technical Courses in Secondary Schools*, Bulletin No. 1086 (Albany, 1937), pp. 28–9.

try and engineering. The topics are selected to give the pupils a background of experience for future work in the sciences, a knowledge of the materials used in the shops, an appreciation of the work of the men who helped in the development of industry, as well as an understanding of the qualifications and abilities demanded by industry of those aspiring to fill technical positions.' [19] Such a course as the strength of materials requires the student to make computations involving the simple stresses, modulus of elasticity, moment of inertia, deflection, design of simple and overhanging beams, safe loads on columns, riveted and welded joints; perform mechanical tests with a variety of testing machines, and write a report on each test; study the mechanical properties of materials of construction.

SHOPWORK

Occupying, as it does, at least half the instruction time, shopwork is the hub of the vocational high school curriculum. Its basic principle is to introduce the student to the fundamental operations, manipulations, and characteristics of a trade, and to produce intelligent and manually well-prepared candidates for jobs in industry. In unit trade schools the shopwork is centered in one trade, but it is adjusted to the educational and training needs of the student and therefore embraces the elements of other trades as well, thus affording better opportunities to test the student's abilities, to broaden his background and develop flexibility, and to encourage the development of wider skills. Such extensiveness does not, of course, permit intensity of training comparable to that given in apprenticeship. Neither can it provide the speed and accuracy achieved by on-the-job training.

A few examples may serve to clarify the nature of a shopwork curriculum in the vocational high schools. For instance, the Machine and Metal Trades High School of New York City prepares students for the following trades: machine shop, sheet metal, patternmaking, mechanical drafting, foundry. Shopwork subjects in-

[19] Brooklyn Technical High School, op. cit. p. 34.

clude the heat treatment of metals, and welding. Instruction in the latter is part of most metal trades curriculums, though welding is also regarded as an independent trade. Sheet metal shopwork comprises general sheet metal practice, layouts, duct construction, and complementary shop training in electric and acetylene welding. Students of mechanical drafting learn general drafting, technical sketching, patent office standards, sheet metal drafting, piping details, layouts and mechanisms, machine details and assembly, and tool design; in addition they receive complementary shop training in patternmaking, machine shop, and sheet metal.

The nine courses offered in the Central High School of Needle Trades of New York are organized on a similar basis: fur manufacturing, shoe manufacturing and design, patternmaking, tailoring, dressmaking, dress manufacturing, millinery, interior decorating and novelty, and draping costume design. The course in shoe manufacturing and design includes design, cutting, fitting, stitching, lasting, stock fitting, heeling, finishing, cleaning and packing, practice in shoe manufacturing. The student of costume design learns fashion design, women's patternmaking and design, power machine operation, draping, grading, textile design, art appreciation, history of costume, and museum. It is significant that most of the courses include designing and allied work, subjects usually considered a trade in themselves and of a semiprofessional nature.

In the automotive trades high schools the students are given instruction in motor, electrical equipment, and body and fender work, subjects that cover what are in actual practice two or even three different trades. In the Essex County vocational high schools the course includes the study of auto chassis and machine shop in the first year, internal combustion engines in the second year, and auto testing and service in the third year. At the East New York Vocational High School shopwork in grades 10 to 12 of the electrical installation and practice course comprises low tension work—signal and alarm systems, and lighting (domestic and commercial); wiring for heat and power; radio (transmission and receiving); code practice; photoelectric application; motors and generators; installations and control, operating characteristics and maintenance. Students in the commercial photography course of the Essex County schools learn the fundamental processes, and elementary and advanced techniques in the photography laboratory and studio, while in the course for industrial clerk training the students operate the tool cribs and material bins of five different shops and study the tools, materials, and procedures in each.

In general, the curriculums list the subjects but do not indicate the operations to be taught. It is assumed that standard operations and manipulations for any given trade constitute the core of shopwork. Beyond that, the school staff or even the individual teacher often determines what other operations and performances are to be included in the instruction.

In the technical high schools 'shopwork, though essential, is organized to supplement, illustrate and clarify the instruction in technical subjects. The shop teacher serves the technical teacher. The pupil works on as large a variety of projects in the shop as possible, but the degree of skill required is not so great as in the industrial high school . . .' [20] Shopwork, in addition to teaching skills, is in itself considered a means of familiarizing the student with a wide range of technical problems in different phases of production. In each of the first two years at Brooklyn Technical High School, for instance, shop courses in patternmaking, foundry practice, sheet metal, and elementary machine shop are required of all students for ten periods a week. Patternmaking and elementary machine shop are 20-week courses; foundry practice and sheet metal, 10-week courses. The amount and nature of shop work in the last two years depend on the course of study.

The aim and method of teaching shopwork are well illustrated by the sheet metal shopwork course in Brooklyn Technical High School which is 'planned to acquaint the student with the fundamentals of sheet metal work, and to give him a limited amount of practice in the use of the various machines and tools used in the

[20] University of the State of New York, op. cit. p. 18.

industry. The course, organized according to the difficulties of learning, consists of a series of problems involving parallel line developments, radial line developments, and triangulation. These problems in turn lead up to the design and layout of a project in sheet metal, into which are incorporated the three styles of pattern development and many of the operations of the trade. Included in this work are marking, cutting, punching, forming, riveting, seaming, soldering, etc. In conjunction with the work mentioned above, information is introduced concerning various sheet metals and their properties, and other scientific and chemical information as applied to the trade.' [21]

Ninth Grade or the 'Exploratory' Year

In studying the curriculums of vocational and technical high schools, special attention must be given to the 9th grade, or first high school year, which has come to be known in the high school system as the 'exploratory' year. This adjustment of the 9th grade was the logical outcome of the vast qualitative and quantitative expansion of the high school, which demanded that some means be devised to screen the huge student body and direct it into proper educational channels. Since the average 8th grade graduate is unaware of the varied opportunities offered by the different high schools and their many courses of study, and is therefore unable to choose the one best suited to his particular needs, some provision had to be made for guiding him according to his individual abilities, capacities, interests, and aims. An exploratory 9th grade, in which these abilities and aims could be brought to light, has furnished the most satisfactory answer to the problem.

The vocational high school has accepted the idea of the exploratory year in shaping its program and making the curriculum much more flexible than that of the 10th to 12th grades. The Essex County vocational high schools, for example, offer three basic courses for the 9th grade. The students are sent through several shops or departments related to the field in which they are interested and

[21] Brooklyn Technical High School, op. cit. p. 54.

stay in each of them for six or eight weeks. Those who prepare for occupations in carpentry, cabinetwork, or patternmaking, work consecutively in the general shop, carpentry shop, cabinet shop, patternmaking shop, and mechanical drafting department. After satisfactory completion of the basic course, students are eligible to choose any one of the occupational courses.

A similar practice is observed in New York City where all students who enter vocational high schools directly from elementary school are obliged to spend the first year in exploratory work and are given shop experience in several trade subjects. In general, no more than 15 weekly periods or less than 12 clock hours of shopwork (out of 35 weekly periods for all subjects) are required, thus remaining somewhat below the 50 per cent required by the Smith-Hughes Act for shopwork. An important aspect of the exploratory year in New York is that mathematics and science are taught as fundamental, rather than as related, subjects; they take on a related character only at the beginning of the 10th grade.

In other parts of the country, some vocational as well as technical schools expand this scheme into a graduated vocational curriculum for the 10th grade. In the Cincinnati vocational high schools, as has already been noted, the 9th and 10th grades are academic in emphasis but include beginning shopwork, while during the 11th and 12th grades the state requirements for secondary vocational education and training are met; in addition the 12th year may be spent on a cooperative basis if jobs are available.

A system that is not quite comparable but is also characterized by the graduated vocational approach has been adopted by the Brooklyn Technical High School. The differentiation of the curriculums of eight courses does not start until the 11th grade; during the 9th and 10th grades all students take the same basic course. No general policy for technical high schools elsewhere has been elaborated thus far; their programs are still in the experimental stage.

VI

Vocational High School Teachers, Guidance Counselors, and Advisory Committees

TEACHER TRAINING

WITH the establishment of vocational high schools there arose the need for a new type of teacher and new methods of teacher training. The traditional academic teacher is not equipped to teach shopwork; nor can he, without additional training, comply with the requirements for teaching related subjects. Thus, recognizing the necessity for developing shop teachers, the federal government, through the Smith-Hughes and George-Deen acts, appropriates to the states funds for teacher training to be matched by equal sums appropriated by the state governments.

For 1942, the peak year in vocational education, government statistics with regard to teachers of vocational courses in federally aided schools or classes showed a total of 27,830 vocational teachers in all-day classes,[1] 16,588 in evening classes, and 16,275 in part-time classes.[2] These figures, however, only suggest the actual situation, not merely because they are restricted to federally aided classes but because they take no account of trade teachers in private schools and shop teachers in technical schools. On the other hand, the enumeration may contain duplications since the same teachers are likely to have been members of more than one group.

With reference to the problem with which this study is mainly concerned—vocational education in secondary schools—a break-

---

[1] Including 403 in agricultural day-unit classes.
[2] Computed from U.S. Office of Education, *Digest of Annual Reports of State Boards for Vocational Education . . . 1943* (Washington, 1944), p. 78.

down shows the following picture: 9,457 teachers in all-day agricultural classes, 7,651 in trade and industrial classes, and 10,722 in home economics classes.[3] Considering that the number of students in home economics classes was almost twice that in trade and industrial classes, the number of teachers for trade and industrial training compares favorably. To what extent this refers to shop instruction alone is difficult to determine since in some schools shop teachers give the instruction in related subjects as well, while in others these subjects are covered by the teachers of academic subjects.

The teachers of English and social sciences in the vocational high schools are not included in the above statistics since they are not among those for whom the state is entitled to receive federal aid. They are the same type of teachers as those in the general high school and may be shifted from one kind of school to another without making any save minor adjustments. The statistics refer exclusively to shop teachers and to some of the teachers of related subjects. Their number increased from 2,300 in 1928 to about 8,000 in 1943, but the number of vocational high school students increased at an even greater rate within that period. From 1928 to 1932 the teacher-student ratio was 1:24; between 1934 and 1942 it averaged about 1:30. In 1942, which was not a normal year because of the war, the ratio stood at 1:38, but in 1943, when high school classes declined in number, the ratio reverted to 1:24.5.

The failure of teacher training to keep pace with the rapid increase in the number of students is regrettable. It may be partly attributed to the fact that, as the economic depression of the thirties abated, craftsmen, whose replacement had become increasingly difficult, were urgently needed in industry and found conditions there which made them little inclined to give up their jobs to become shop teachers. Inasmuch as good trade teachers usually have the opportunity to find industrial employment in times of accelerated business activity, their replacement rate is accordingly high. From 10 to 12 newly qualified teachers are needed annually

[3] Ibid. p. 78. The figure on agricultural classes includes day-unit classes.

for every 100 employed teachers in all-day trade and industrial education; the rate rises to 50 per 100 for trade extension programs. Expansion of the vocational education system will not be possible unless the vocational teaching staff is stabilized by being made more attractive financially and by being granted greater prestige.

The three sources of teachers of shopwork and of related subjects, in so far as the latter are not drawn from the ranks of academic teachers, are journeymen, former engineers and technicians, and teachers of industrial arts in the elementary and junior high school systems. The Smith-Hughes Act, in appropriating funds for teacher training, specifies that such training 'shall be given only to persons who have had adequate vocational experience or contact in the line of work for which they are preparing themselves as teachers or who are acquiring such experience or contact as a part of their training.' But the federal legislation makes no stipulations with regard to the educational background and work experience of those who are to do the training or with regard to the methods of training. The determination of qualifications for these teachers of teachers and the establishment of training institutions, programs, and methods are left to the states, subject to the approval of the Office of Education.

In 1942, there were 198 federally aided training institutions or agencies, a substantial part of which offered training in several fields: teachers of agricultural subjects were trained in 118 institutions, of trade and industry in 107, of home economics in 158, and of distributive education in 61.[4] Additional teacher-training classes were conducted without federal aid in substantial numbers in Texas (26), North Carolina (20), Massachusetts (13), Pennsylvania (10), California (9), Iowa (5), and Virginia (5). Total allotments made under the Smith-Hughes Act for teacher training in the fiscal year 1943–44 amounted to approximately 1.1 million dollars, of which only a little more than $300,000 went to training teachers of trade and industrial subjects.[5]

[4] Ibid. p. 81.
[5] U.S. Office of Education, *Digest of Annual Reports* . . . 1944 (Washing-

The fact that state teaching programs require federal approval insures certain minimum standards, but even without it there would be a number of common requirements for teacher candidates, such as good character, good health, and American citizenship, a minimum age limit of twenty-one to twenty-five years, and favorable references. The professional and educational requirements for part-time and evening teachers are less strict than those for all-day teachers. Shop teachers, other than engineers and with the exception of those in continuation schools, must be recognized trade experts, who have completed an apprenticeship and worked as journeymen for two or three years. There are many more journeymen among shop teachers than there are engineers and industrial arts teachers—a favorable situation, on the whole, because actual experience and knowledge gained on the job are a definite asset in teaching.

All teacher-training programs are divided into two complementary parts—pre-service training and in-service training; the latter is also referred to as professional improvement.

A typical state program for training teachers of vocational education is that formulated by the Washington State Board for Vocational Education, which stipulates detailed requirements ranging all the way from trade and educational background to the necessary amount of in-service training.[6] This program discloses that the all-day vocational high school teachers usually start out as evening school trade extension teachers, most of whom have had no previous teaching experience. They generally obtain their first teacher training from the local supervisor of trade and industrial education, in the form of a few hours devoted to trade analysis, simple teaching methods, and regulations of the school in which the candidate is to teach. After the candidate takes over a class, the

---

ton, 1945), p. 72. The sums spent for training teachers of agricultural subjects was approximately $353,000 and teachers of home economics about $355,000.

[6] U.S. Office of Education, *The State and the Preservice Preparation of Teachers of Vocational Education*, Vocational Division Bulletin No. 219 (Washington, 1941), p. 121.

supervisor follows up the pre-service training by assisting him as need arises. Evening school trade extension teachers are often employed as journeymen during the day and divide their evenings between teaching and preparation for teacher training.

The Pennsylvania program offers another interesting example of teacher training requirements.[7] Candidates are subjected to a thorough oral and written test, the purpose of which is to check the quality of trade knowledge and skill. But before they can become candidates they must have spent at least six years in the trade, of which two have been on a proven journeyman's level. Minimum certification requirements for shop teachers in all-day classes include, in addition to trade experience, twenty-four semester hours of approved professional courses in trade and industrial education, of which six were devoted to observation and practice teaching; additional hours must have been spent on professional courses in general education. Teachers of related subjects must have had at least two years of industrial experience coupled with much higher academic qualifications than are demanded of shop teachers.

Pre-service training of teachers may be the direct function of the state board of education or it may be delegated to a teacher-training institution; it is usually at the college level and under the constant supervision of the state board. These institutions offer either resident or extension courses given by itinerant teachers or by local supervisors. To enable craftsmen to take the courses without relinquishing their jobs, the instruction is being given increasingly on an extension basis after working hours; thus it involves prolonged periods of study. Courses are given in all the large cities and in some small ones; summer courses often attract the largest number of students. Several weeks of full-time practice teaching, carefully supervised by the local authorities, are frequently required. In general, 'students have contact with day and evening classes, attend teachers' meetings, help out with extra-curricular activities. In short, they get as many practical experiences as can be secured in the time available. They make sketches of shop lay-

[7] Ibid. p. 121.

outs, make records of text and reference books used, secure sample copies of instruction sheets and record forms of many kinds that are in use. They also get cost data on equipment and supplies and learn where these are obtained. Students are required to prepare notebooks in which much of this information is recorded for future use.' [8]

In addition to providing general, comprehensive pre-service teacher training, the same institutions serve as in-service training centers, giving short inclusive courses for employed teachers. They also furnish many of the itinerant teacher trainers who conduct extension courses for new and employed teachers. In-service training is given, for the most part, in evening and summer courses, and is regarded as probably the most successful method of training.

The 100 federally aided trade and industrial courses given in 1943 employed 547 teacher trainers, the highest number in the history of vocational education in this country. The trainers of trade and industrial teachers constituted less than a third of the total of 1,779 in all branches; if, however, one deducts the number of female trainers, most of whom instruct home economics teachers, the 493 male trainers of trade and industrial teachers constituted almost half the remaining total of 1,022.[9] The number varies from state to state; in some, teacher-training activity under state auspices has not yet attained substantial proportions.

Requirements for trainers of trade and industrial teachers show a remarkable similarity in most states. All but two stipulate that these trainers have experience as wage earners in a trade or industrial occupation over a period ranging from 1 to 8 years; 42 plans specify 3 years. Furthermore, '41 state plans require trade and industrial class teaching experience, with 36 plans specifying 3 years of such experience and the range from 2 to 5 years. 45 plans require a specified number of clock-hours of trade and industrial courses with a range from 180 to 640 clock hours. 26 plans specify

[8] Ibid. p. 125.
[9] U.S. Office of Education, *Digest of Annual Reports* . . . 1943 (cited above), p. 81.

4 years of college training or its equivalent, while others range downward to a plan which stipulates approved high school courses. 15 state plans specify varying degrees of technical training with the highest requirement being that of graduation from a technical college or equivalent.' [10]

Among the subjects most commonly offered to vocational teachers for pre-service and in-service training are the following: job, operation, trade, or occupational analysis; the organization of subject matter from a teaching standpoint or from the angle of learning difficulties; methods of teaching, both specifically and generally, applied to individual shop and related subjects; the use of auxiliary teaching material, such as educational films and working models and the various types of job or operation sheets; courses in vocational guidance; informational courses, such as administration and organization of trade and industrial education or the history of industrial education; shop organization for instructional purposes; courses in mental testing; various types of subject matter courses to round out a teacher's experience or training; research, and foremanship work.[11]

From this list it is apparent that the teacher-training subjects are eminently practical. For the most part they do not pertain directly to the specific trade, but outline the methods by which this trade knowledge and skill can best be imparted; in other words, the courses concentrate on how to teach the subjects that are usually learned through practical experience. This choice of the subjects of instruction is based on the fact that the teacher candidate has acquired his knowledge and his skill before entering upon his training as a teacher; no extension of this knowledge is considered necessary. But by virtue of his work experience the candidate is so steeped in his subject that he performs most operations almost unconsciously, taking for granted the ease of certain procedures that students may find difficult to master. He has, therefore, to be

[10] U.S. Office of Education, *The State* . . . (cited above), p. 48.
[11] U.S. Federal Board for Vocational Education, *The Training of Teachers for Trade and Industrial Education*, Bulletin No. 150 (Trade and Industrial Series, No. 42) (Washington, 1930), pp. 19–20.

trained to rediscover all the elements of his trade so that he may teach them thoroughly and precisely. He has also to be familiarized with the breadth of the economy and of the trades and occupations of which the various jobs are only a part. And furthermore, he must recognize the basic difference between shop practice in a vocational high school and industrial production—that the main purpose of the school shop is not actual production but the learning of the methods of producing goods. All these major aspects of teacher training are covered by the subjects of instruction listed above.

Either when he starts teaching or when he applies for a certificate, the vocational teacher takes an examination, which in many cases includes a performance test but usually deals mainly with pedagogy, informational subjects, and even administrative matters in the vocational field. The employed teacher is also observed periodically and rated on his qualities and development by the principal or local supervisor. An essential point, in addition to the usual standards for rating teachers, is whether the trade projects and operations which the teacher assigns to the class and the methods employed in their execution are up to date. It is for this reason that vocational teachers, on their own initiative and with the encouragement of vocational education authorities, repeatedly spend a summer as industrial workers in their own fields.

Under wartime pressures certain changes had to be made in order to expand and accelerate the training of vocational teachers. There were a number of excellent war training programs, but many of the measures they employed would not be feasible in times of normal industrial production. The few features that constitute genuine improvements in training techniques rather than mere emergency expedients stand a good chance of incorporation in permanent training programs. Among them is the trend toward decentralization through extension services and the wider inclusion of technical material in the teacher-training curriculum—further evidence of the ever-increasing importance of technical education, so frequently emphasized in this study.

OCCUPATIONAL GUIDANCE SERVICES

In the field of vocational guidance there are two general areas. One is concerned chiefly with the abilities and interests of the individual; the other area is related to factors aside from the individual, such as occupational information, training opportunities, community relationships, and social activities.[12] Unless counseling grants due consideration to both sides of the picture, it cannot be either intelligent or effective.

The emergence of vocational education at the secondary level did not alter the basic principles of determining individual characteristics, though more precise reference to the future vocation was made possible by the organization and methods of in-school vocational education and training. Guidance based on occupational information, however, began to require redefinition when, in an increasing number of cases, a curriculum closely related to a future vocation was substituted for a curriculum designed to prepare for all the professions but indifferent to the future occupational needs of the majority of high school students. That something new had to be devised in this field of guidance was recognized at the top level by the creation of the Occupational Information and Guidance Service in the Vocational Division of the United States Office of Education. The chief of this Service bluntly asserted in 1945 that 'the occupational information and guidance aspects of vocational education are in about the same state as training in trade and industry or agriculture was in 1920.'[13]

With regard to discovering and evaluating the characteristics of the individual, undeniable progress has been made in recent years. The establishment of individual records; administration of appropriate aptitude, interest, personality, trade and scholastic

[12] Eugenie A. Leonard and Anthony C. Tucker, *The Individual Inventory in Guidance Programs in Secondary Schools*, U.S. Office of Education Vocational Division Bulletin No. 215 (Washington, 1941), p. 1.

[13] Harry A. Jager, 'Vocational Guidance Is Needed,' Science Research Associates, *Guidance Reprints*, No. 192. (Reprinted from *Illinois Vocational Progress*, vol. 2, no. 4, May 1945.)

achievement tests; preparation of scores for such tests; gathering of information on hobbies, special interests, personality traits and aptitudes, on financial status, social background, family or personal responsibilities—all these have been developed and refined.[14]

Actually, however, until very recently, counseling was in no position to utilize these modern methods advantageously. In the first place, only a small number of schools had established guidance services. Of approximately 25,000 public high schools, only some 1,300 or hardly more than 5 per cent were listed by the 1938 Biennial Survey of the United States Office of Education as having one or more persons each—a total of 2,273 for all together—who devoted at least half time to counseling.[15] Answers to an Office of Education questionnaire, however, revealed that even those schools that employed counselors operated under great handicaps, chief among them the lack of interest and adequate training on the part of those engaged in guidance work.[16] No less than 40 per cent of the small number of schools maintaining guidance services reported that their counselors were deficient in industrial experience, in the ability to interpret test results, or in some other equally vital qualification. This shortage of trained guidance counselors is a consequence not only of a lag in entering a newly opened area of educational activity, but also of the currently noticeable decline in the number of those persons willing to join the teaching profession in any capacity.

With regard to the availability of guidance counselors, present conditions in vocational high schools are hardly better than in general high schools. In 1944, of 43 vocational high schools in 35 states, named by state authorities as outstanding, only 13 had full-time counselors; of 114 high schools with vocational departments, located in 35 states and cited by the Vocational Division of the Office of Education as outstanding, only 33 had full-time counselors. It can be assumed, therefore, that in vocational high schools, as in the

[14] U.S. War Manpower Commission, *The Training of Vocational Guidance Counselors* (Washington, 1944), pp. 1–2.
[15] Leonard and Tucker, op. cit. p. 2.
[16] Ibid. p. 59.

general high schools, about 75 per cent of all students were being deprived of the benefits of systematic guidance services.[17] Since 1944 the states have striven to improve the situation. Full-time and part-time counselors have been added to school personnel in many communities; local schools have been granted state funds for the support of guidance programs, and publications in the educational field have devoted attention to guidance counseling and testing for the purpose of encouraging new counselors to use approved methods and to improve their techniques.[18]

In vocational high schools, guidance in the 9th grade is extremely important because the results of the exploratory work in this year weigh heavily in the choice of the vocation. The student's performance in the basic courses or in the manifold types of shopwork offered in the 9th grade influences his program for the next three years, the content of which is directed toward his chosen vocation. The abilities and interests of the individual are thus classified early in the vocational high school period, though good schools make it possible to reverse a decision and to transfer to another course if the original choice proves faulty or if the development of new aptitudes calls for reconsideration.

For those students who spend their exploratory year in junior high schools and then transfer to the 10th grade of a vocational high school, other provision has to be made. As has already been mentioned, shop equipment in junior high schools is often insufficient for the detection of the individual capacities of that great body of students who will engage in manual work. This imposes upon the vocational high schools the task of combining regular 10th-grade instruction with some exploratory work. The wisdom of the student's choice of a course has to be checked and the guidance counselor must be provided with data essential for his work in the individual area.

The other area—that of occupational guidance—has been served

[17] Jager, op. cit.
[18] U.S. Office of Education, *Digest of Annual Reports* . . . 1944 (Washington, 1945), pp. 34-6.

by the creation of the previously mentioned Occupational Information and Guidance Service, with the necessary cooperation of the United States Employment Service. In 1934, a systematic program of occupational research was inaugurated by the USES. Subsequently designated as the Occupational Analysis Section of the USES, and conducted after 1943 as the Division of Occupational Analysis and Manning Tables in the Bureau of Manpower Utilization of the War Manpower Commission, this program was designed to develop authoritative information concerning industries and jobs and to discover the qualifications required for success in various occupations. The work of the Division was, from the first, cooperative in nature and was supported not only by both federal and state funds but also by grants from private foundations. Employers, workers, schools and colleges, and persons in government services and all branches of the armed services 'cooperated in the job studies and in the adaptation and use of research materials as aids in improving occupational adjustment in this and other countries.' [19] Job analysis, definition, and classification in a systematic manner, the establishment of families of occupations, the determination of physical demands for jobs, and measurement of occupational aptitudes were among the main subjects of investigation.

In the course of the vast armament program, the USES assembled considerable data on labor supply, demand, and shortages, and on turnover, training, and utilization of labor. Currently, through special programs for veterans, effective employment counseling is being provided by state employment offices for applicants who seek satisfactory placement. The value of this program is not limited to veterans, since in the future the collaboration of public officers with vocational high school advisory boards will extend its benefits to school-leaving applicants for jobs.

At the local level, a series of surveys conducted to obtain information for use in vocational guidance have been adopted as a basis for curriculum planning, and are comprehensively analyzed in a

[19] *Occupations*, vol. 22, no. 7 (April 1944), p. 389.

publication of the Vocational Division of the Office of Education.[20] These are classified as youth surveys and consist of the
following types: follow-up surveys which are usually inquiries
into the circumstances of individuals who have had a common experience, such as graduates of a particular high school or university;
surveys of particular occupations and industries, usually known as
occupational outlines, occupational descriptions, or occupational
studies; surveys of job opportunities or openings for beginning
workers; surveys of unemployment; local labor market studies
which, of course, are focused on fluctuations in the local situation
rather than on the distribution of the entire labor supply. Joint
studies by the United States Department of Labor and the Office
of Education, such as that on occupational data for counselors,[21]
also demonstrate an increasing inclination to combine all efforts
for intelligent vocational counseling.

STRUCTURE AND FUNCTIONS OF ADVISORY COMMITTEES

In the field of in-school vocational education and training, numerous advisory committees constitute a firmly entrenched element. Their prototype is the Federal Board for Vocational
Education, created in 1917 to administer the Smith-Hughes Act
and granted broader powers than have been given to any of the
lesser committees. The Board has six members, three of whom—
the Secretary of Agriculture, the Secretary of Commerce, and the
Secretary of Labor—are members ex officio; the other three are
lay members representing the interests of agriculture, manufacturers and commerce, and labor, respectively, and are appointed
by the President with the advice and consent of the Senate.[22]

One of the most important developments in the administration

[20] Marguerite Wykoff Zapoleon, *Community Occupational Surveys*, U.S.
Office of Education Vocational Division Bulletin No. 223 (Occupational
Information and Guidance Series, No. 10) (Washington, 1942).

[21] U.S. Labor Statistics Bureau and Office of Education, *Occupational Data
for Counselors*, U.S. Office of Education Bulletin No. 817 (Washington,
1945).

[22] U.S. Office of Education, *Digest of Annual Reports . . . 1944* (cited
above), pp. 54-5.

of the Smith-Hughes Act was the transfer of the functions of the Board to the Commissioner of Education, a move that established that vocational education and training is above all an educational, not an economic, task. But in order to insure the future cooperation of all interested governmental agencies and representatives of economic groups that would profit by the progress of vocational education, the Federal Board was retained as a Federal Advisory Board for Vocational Education. Composed of the same elements as its predecessor, the Board is designed to advise the Commissioner of Education on various phases of vocational education and to aid him in formulating and implementing policies in keeping with the needs and desires of the groups represented by the Board members. This scheme of organization leaves to the educational authorities the predominant position that they should retain in all educational matters, and does not permit narrow vocational or private economic interests to prevail. At the same time, it opens the way to systematic cooperation between representatives of education and those of the national economy. This method is indispensable for any practical planning of vocational education and might well be considered a precedent for similar collaboration in other educational fields.

In order to become really workable the advisory boards had to be developed at regional and local levels, as well as national, and had also to be extended to special fields of vocational education. At the federal level, industrial and technical education is served by a technical advisory committee on trade and industrial education, established by the Commissioner of Education in 1936. The committee, consisting of nine members representing vocational educators, employers, and labor equally, advises the Office of Education on policies and practices in setting up and operating training programs in the entire field of trade and industrial education. In addition, since October 1940 there has been the Joint AFL-CIO Consulting Committee which, with the consultant in employee-employer relations of the Office of Education, advises the Commissioner of Education on employee-employer problems.

Also at the federal level is the recently organized Consulting Committee on Vocational-Technical Education, which has been engaged in studying vocational-technical training programs, facilities, and needs. This Committee, whose work is repeatedly cited by this study, is composed of twenty-six members, including a working committee of twelve which meets with the chairman of the Consulting Committee from time to time.[23] Similar advisory committees have been established in the nonindustrial fields of vocational education.

State and local advisory committees have been created in numerous instances with the encouragement of the Office of Education. These committees are set up to advise school authorities 'in matters concerning the program and to make suggestions and recommendations for the guidance of the state and local authorities in whom authority is vested.' The Office of Education views this method as the 'democratic means of group participation in the administrative process' and as the expression of 'the fact that vocational education is a cooperative enterprise among public schools, management and labor.'[24]

Such advisory committees are in operation in each of the 48 states, the District of Columbia, and Puerto Rico, and in every school district in which federally aided vocational education is established; the number reporting to the Office of Education is about 1,500.[25] The employer-employee balance is equal, and care has been taken to have the various organizations of management and labor adequately represented. Occasionally, and especially in the field of trade and industrial education, additional representatives have been appointed in order to cover the manifold trades and branches of industry.

Beyond the observance of certain fundamental principles in

[23] U.S. Office of Education, *Digest of Annual Reports . . .* 1943 (cited above), pp. 37-9.
[24] U.S. Office of Education, *Representative Advisory Committees* (Washington, 1943), p. 7.
[25] F. Theodore Struck, *Foundations of Industrial Education* (New York, 1930), p. 123.

setting up these committees there is a good bit of variety among them. State advisory committees, for example, have usually been established to deal with general policies of vocational education of more than local concern, but in a few instances they have been created to assist with training problems of single industries or even with special phases of training. In some states, regional committees handle the training problems of single industries or training problems common to a particular part of the state. The same variations exist among local committees. In certain communities, general local advisory committees have been appointed to advise on problems relating to all types of trade and industrial education; in others, several committees are in operation, one for each industry or craft represented in the training program.[26] In the large towns and cities, each of the vocational high schools has its own advisory committee, which functions in cooperation with the school principal.

It has been the policy of the Office of Education to encourage the formation of advisory committees with a stable membership that would make a practice of calling on consultants for specialized information. Consultants are drawn, in the main, from such agencies as state and local employment services, the state Department of Labor, or the state office of vocational education.[27] The federal policy favors particularly the designation of a representative of the USES as a consultant for each committee, so that data on the labor market, current training needs, and specific job requirements may be made easily available. It also recommends the appointment of a representative of each craft or occupation to be added to the committees as alternating consultants when the introduction or abolition of courses is under consideration.[28]

The function of the local advisory committees that is closest to the work of education itself, as it proceeds day by day, is to determine the essential occupations and industries in a community

[26] U.S. Office of Education, *Digest of Annual Reports* . . . 1940 (Washington, 1941), p. 36.
[27] Ibid. p. 6.
[28] U.S. Office of Education, *Representative Advisory Committees* (cited above), pp. 4–7.

or in a state, the number of workers to be trained, the type of jobs, job specifications, possibilities of training for various jobs from the standpoint of instructors, equipment, and space, and also to select consultants. The state advisory committees have similar functions at a state level, but on the whole their work is of a more administrative nature.

In its conception and organization the policy on advisory committees is laudable. Vocational schools, like all other educational institutions, cannot develop effectively without the support of public opinion, and they can gain this only if they maintain the educational standards established for the nation, and, at the same time, render a substantial service to the national economy by filling the gap in the training needs of the country. There is no way to reach this goal other than through the cooperation, in advisory committees at all levels, between representatives of education and economic forces, for the purpose of attaining practical results as well as promoting the idea of vocational education.

The principles of employer-employee parity and the calling in of experts as consultants are also fundamentally sound. This system promotes consistency in vocational education practice and an understanding on a certain number of basic problems among the members of the advisory boards, without depriving them of the benefit of expert advice from craft, occupation, and labor market consultants. An expansion of in-school vocational education may witness a broadening of the scope of the advisory committees and a further specialization of the services of the consultants. Whereas, until recently, vocational courses centered on a few apprenticeable crafts, with the result that no more than a portion of the manufacturing industries and trades were represented in the advisory committees, a wider cooperation will be sought and found in the future as the vocational education program expands, and eventually advisors and consultants will be taken from the whole realm of the industrial economy. A great segment of the population which hitherto has had little knowledge of in-school vocational education will thus become familiar with a vigorous and promising branch of our secondary education.

VII

Technical Institutes

Development

TECHNICAL institutes, although they antedated technical high schools by many years, have never achieved uniformity of type or increased to a considerable number. Founded or sponsored by individuals with very definite and personal conceptions of what such schools should be, the technical institutes have so long been subjected to these varied influences that they are just now beginning to emerge from the experimental stage. Largely through the efforts of the Society for the Promotion of Engineering Education (SPEE), the term, 'technical institutes,' has recently become standardized and has come to mean a type of institution quite distinct from the technical or vocational high school or trade school.

It is, of course, the possession of certain common features that enables these institutions to be designated as technical institutes in the currently accepted sense of the term. With the exception of private trade schools, they are the only institutions of vocational education that are not secondary in character but whose activities involve work on a full-time day basis. But while they do not operate at the secondary level neither are they of college grade, because of the content of their curriculums and the average length of their programs. Inasmuch as they are not considered to prepare for 'trade and industrial pursuits' in the sense of the Smith-Hughes and George-Deen acts, they receive no federal aid. They are either privately or publicly operated, but even in the latter event they are outside the jurisdiction of the public school system. The programs are generally two or three years in length, but may be one or four. Minimum entrance age is from sixteen to eighteen. High school graduation is frequently required for entrance and is almost always preferred; previous industrial experience is generally not required although usually held desirable.

It is not a new idea that specialized training should be provided for the 'intermediate group' engaged in technical and supervisory occupations at the level between manual pursuits and the professions. It was inherent in the establishment of the mechanics' institutes early in the 1820's, and interest in this type of training increased with the rise in importance of technical occupations in the economy. Yet the number of institutes has remained small. A substantial report on technical institutes made by SPEE in 1928–29,[1] although it did not claim to be exhaustive, listed 34, of which only 9 were designed as 'predominantly technical institutes'; 15 were predominantly degree-granting colleges or universities which included technical courses in their programs; and 10 were 'industrial schools of mixed character.' Full-time day courses were offered by only 19 of the institutes, evening courses by 14, and cooperative half-time day courses by 2.

One of the chief deterrents to the development of the technical institute has been the persistent trend in this country toward engineering college education. As a result of the passage in 1862 of the Morrill Act, which gave a tremendous impetus to American technical education through the establishment of land grant colleges, the existing technical institutes gravitated toward the conventional form of engineering colleges and were gradually reorganized into degree-granting institutions. Once established, the schools of engineering enjoyed greater prestige than the technical institutes and had no interest in encouraging techical institute training since it would have meant a reduction of their own potential student body. Furthermore, parents and students preferred the wider professional opportunities, open to graduates of engineering colleges, to the more limited future for technical institute graduates, even

[1] Society for the Promotion of Engineering Education, *Report of the Investigation of Engineering Education*, 1923–29, vol. 2, Part 2 (Pittsburgh, 1930), pp. 1–271.

when withdrawal from college before completion of the course was a distinct probability.

Contributors to the SPEE report urged expansion of the technical institutes on the grounds that the needs of the economy could scarcely be met by less than 250 such schools. They shared with the National Industrial Conference Board the belief that, in an average year, industry, trade, and technical services could absorb from 40,000 to 50,000 men so trained. At the time the report was made, there were, annually, barely 9,000 graduates of engineering colleges, and probably less than 1,500 from technical institutes of post-secondary grade. If their number has increased meanwhile, so have the number of vocational-technical pursuits for trained workers; thus the need for more schools still exists.

Although technical institutes share the vocational-technical goals and a good part of the scientific and technical content of the training given by technical high schools, they differ considerably from them in many respects. The primary distinctions are that their curriculums are confined to narrower fields of industrial production than those of the technical high school, and that their teaching of applied and practical technical knowledge is concentrated on training rather than on education. The main emphasis is on vocational-technical subjects. The technical subjects take precedence over scientific subjects, and these, in turn, over mathematics. In general, mathematics and science together do not exceed 30 per cent of the entire instruction time; if they attain a higher proportion in the first year, they are accorded less time in the second or third. They are frequently given in the form of applied science, applied chemistry, physical elements of engineering, or the like. General education subjects are usually not included in the programs, or are reduced to a minimum that generally comprises only business English or business correspondence.

Among the more notable technical institutes are Pratt Institute in Brooklyn,[2] the Rochester (N.Y.) Athenaeum and Mechanics

[2] This has become an engineering college, but still offers three-year technical programs of noncollege grade.

Institute, the Ohio Mechanics Institute at Cincinnati, Chicago Technical College, Wentworth Institute in Boston, and Bliss Electrical School in Washington, D.C. The Newark (N.J.) Technical School, and the Lowell Institute School for Industrial Foremen conducted at the Massachusetts Institute of Technology, are evening schools of the same type. All these institutions have made important contributions to vocational-technical training in various fields. Bliss offers a one-year electrical engineering course; Chicago Technical College gives two-year courses in architecture, building construction, and civil, electrical, and mechanical engineering; Rochester Athenaeum has three-year cooperative electrical, mechanical, and chemical courses; Wentworth offers two-year courses in machine construction, electrical construction, power plant, architectural construction, and foundry.

In 1940–41, only three technical institutes with a total enrollment of 929 students offered cooperative courses—Rochester Athenaeum and Mechanics Institute, Ohio Mechanics Institute, and Wyomissing (Pa.) Polytechnic Institute. With three exceptions, all the cooperative curriculums were in engineering, the courses varying in length from two to three years of a relatively low number of weeks of instruction, compared with the number required by degree-granting institutions.[3] In contrast to cooperative programs in the colleges and universities, where the students remain in school full time during the first year,[4] cooperative programs in these technical institutes may be embarked on right at the start.

The nature of the work of technical institutes may be well illustrated by the program of the cooperative course in instrument making given by the Rochester Athenaeum.[5] In the first year the student devotes 4 hours a week to mathematics, 5 to mechanical

[3] Two-year courses at Ohio Mechanics, 38 weeks; 2½-year course at Wyomissing, 50 weeks; 3-year curriculum at Rochester Athenaeum, 57 weeks.

[4] Leo F. Smith, 'Cooperative Work Programs,' in *Journal of Higher Education*, vol. 15, no. 4 (April 1944), pp. 209 ff.

[5] U.S. Office of Education, *Vocational-Technical Training for Industrial Occupations*, Bulletin No. 228 (Washington, 1944), pp. 246–7.

drawing, 12 to machine shop and instrument making, 3 to psychology, 4 to mechanics and heat, and 2 to English and study techniques. The second year's program includes economics for 3 hours a week; drawing and mechanism, 6; electricity, 6; strength and properties of materials, 6; instrument making, 9. Subjects comprising the schedule for the third year are optics and sound for 3 hours a week; instrument and tool design, 9; materials laboratory, 3; instrument making, 9; industrial management, 3; and technical projects, 3.

Another typical program is the two-year course in steam and Diesel engineering given at the Wentworth Institute.[6] In the first year a total of 200 school work hours and 235 home study hours are spent on applied science (statics, kinetics, applied heat); 240 and 140, respectively, on steam and Diesel engines (construction and operation); 200 and 235 on electricity (direct current machinery); 190 and 0 on mechanical drawing; 120 and 150 on mathematics (application of arithmetic, algebra, and trigonometry); 90 and 0 on welding (oxyacetylene and arc welding); 30 and 40 on English (letter writing and technical reports). The distribution of total school work and home study hours for the second year is as follows: 360 and 250 for steam and Diesel engines (operation and testing of engines and auxiliaries; water, fuel, oil, and gas analysis); 180 and 175 for electricity (alternating current machinery); 75 and 95 for applied mechanics and testing of materials; 30 and 40 for English (letter writing, technical reports, public speaking); 180 and 50 for machine shop; 175 and 25 for mechanical drawing; 45 and 50 for mathematics (advanced work in algebra and trigonometry).

JUNIOR COLLEGE ROLE

In recent years, courses similar to those given in technical institutes have begun to appear in the curriculums of junior colleges. This is not an illogical result of junior college development, especially in the southern and western sections of the country, but

6 Ibid. pp. 246-7.

whether it is a trend to be encouraged remains to be demonstrated.

Junior colleges operate either as an undergraduate division of college or as a terminal institution, in both cases on a two-year basis. In the former capacity they are closely linked with collegiate institutions; in the latter they appear rather as an extension of high school contributing to the never-ending effort to prolong the school attendance of American youth. A few junior colleges give additional emphasis to this orientation by offering a four-year program extending from the 11th through the 14th grade, or, in other words, from the third year of high school through the second of college. In several junior colleges, the two-year course leads to the degree of Associate of Arts or some similarly named degree; this trend of conferring degrees on junior college graduates appears to be spreading.[7]

Even in their terminal courses junior colleges tended to adjust their work to that of the first two college years. No noticeable change occurred until, with the expansion of vocational education and training, two-year courses of a vocational character penetrated the junior college programs. In 1940–41, approximately 34 per cent of all junior college training in the United States was terminal in nature, and the 'vocationalization' of the program was well under way.[8] In California, for example, the Los Angeles Junior College has for several years been offering numerous semiprofessional courses of study; similar offerings are reported by Pasadena Junior College and Sacramento Junior College.

As the terminal education function gained more importance, junior colleges also entered the field of vocational-technical training or, to use a term frequently found in the junior college literature, 'technical institute training.' Most examples of this kind of training

[7] Raymond E. Davis, 'Function of the Junior College in Engineering Education,' in *Journal of Engineering Education* (February 1933), pp. 429–37; Arthur G. Gehrig, 'Technical Courses at Pasadena,' ibid. pp. 458–62.

[8] Howard A. Campion, 'Vocational Programs in Junior Colleges,' in National Society for the Study of Education, *Yearbook*, No. 42, Part 1: *Vocational Education* (Chicago, 1943), pp. 407 ff.; American Association of Junior Colleges, *Present Status of Junior College Terminal Education* (Washington, D.C., 1941), p. 24.

are found in the West, where it developed out of the special educational needs of the region. Inasmuch as the technical institute, on the other hand, is the result of training needs of the industrial areas east of the Mississippi and north of the Ohio and Potomac rivers, the work of the two types of institutions shows no regional overlapping.

Despite this extension of activity, it would be an error to overestimate junior college terminal technical training. Numerically, the findings are not impressive. A study based on the curriculums of 270 junior colleges in 1930–31 reported only 21 terminal technical courses.[9] And according to one of the recent studies of the Commission on Junior College Terminal Education, fewer than 3,500 students were enrolled in strictly vocational-technical courses in the 293 junior colleges investigated.[10]

Furthermore, for a long time, the curriculum of the technical courses in the junior colleges differed greatly from those of the traditional technical institutes.[11] Subjects that bore no direct relation to technical fields—for example, English, speech, social science, humanities, or physical education—were accorded from 12 to 15 per cent of instruction time by junior colleges, whereas in technical institutes they were omitted entirely or, at best, were given only slight attention. Moreover, in junior college terminal technical education, mathematics, physics, and chemistry occupied about 50 per cent of the instruction time, while in technical institutes, where the technical subjects are the center of instruction, they account for no more than about 30 per cent.

It is obvious, therefore, that for the most part the junior college approach to technical training has had a closer relationship to that of the technical high school, or to the first two years of engineering college, than to that of technical institutes. This is under-

[9] Arthur W. Leighton, 'Technical and Engineering Education,' in *Junior College Journal* (December 1934), pp. 113–20.

[10] U.S. Office of Education, *Vocational-Technical Training* . . . (cited above), p. 189.

[11] Ibid. p. 181; Campion, op. cit. p. 407; Clyde C. Colvert, *The Public Junior College Curriculum* (Baton Rouge, La., 1939), pp. 99–114.

standable in view of the fact that the technical institute grew out of economic, and the junior college out of educational, needs. Technical institute training, therefore, has been determined far more by immediate practical considerations than has that of the junior college.

This situation may explain the lack of enthusiasm for junior college terminal technical training on the part of representatives of the engineering professions, and on the part of the ardent proponents of the technical institutes. At the time of its extensive investigation (1928–29), SPEE was unable to find any basis in experience for expecting the junior college to do successfully the work of the technical institute. Weighing its origin and real goal, the report considered the junior college an extension of secondary education, and deemed this essentially secondary environment unfavorable to the task of the technical institute. It asserted further that 'even in the so-called technical junior colleges, the only courses offered are the precise duplicate of the first two years of the university courses.'

Developments in the junior college subsequent to the publication of the SPEE report have given rise to no reversal of such unfavorable opinion, though there have been no other equally harsh judgments of this kind. Competent observers continued to feel dissatisfied.[12] Robert Hoover Spahr, one of the authors of the SPEE report, although he did not maintain the earlier completely negative attitude of the report toward junior college participation in technical education, reserved final judgment with the statement that 'time will tell the results of their rather interesting and voluminous efforts in this area of education.'

Recently, however, bolder steps in the direction of genuine technical institute training have been taken by some of the junior colleges, especially those in California, the state that has shown most enterprise in the junior college movement. With the impetus of the war emergency, junior colleges that specialized in two-year

[12] F. Theodore Struck, *Vocational Education for a Changing World* (New York, 1945), p. 486.

engineering courses gave them a more definitely technical institute character; others, like the one in Bakersfield and that in Meridian, Mississippi, added courses of this kind to their programs. The California colleges were largely instrumental in providing vocational-technical training for the aircraft industry, 60 per cent of which was located in that state.[13]

Curriculums took a more practical turn. Thus, Pasadena Junior College offered 13th- and 14th-year students a course in aviation technology comprising the following subjects: aeronautical welding; aeronautical woodshop; aeronautical machine shop; aeronautical drafting; descriptive geometry; aeronautical laboratory; technical reports; technical mathematics; aircraft design, drafting and construction; material testing laboratory; strength of materials; industrial organization; metal aircraft construction; aeronautical mathematics, physical education or Reserve Officers Training Corps. This is a purely technical institute curriculum in which the college curriculum features have been almost wholly abandoned in favor of highly concentrated technical training, with additional emphasis on related subjects; cultural subjects are entirely eliminated. Such a curriculum presupposes a teaching staff that should not be lacking in scholastic background but that cannot fulfill its task without substantial occupational experience—a far cry from the usual faculty in the junior college. The problem of teachers and teacher training is by no means the least barrier to the kind of terminal technical training in junior colleges that would yield satisfactory returns in terms of well-prepared technicians.

New York State Projects

A third type of institution that would provide proper training for intermediate technical and supervisory positions is suggested by the recently outlined New York State project for such education. This follows a middle road between the older, established technical institutes and the so-called technical institute training of the junior colleges. New York's interest in vocational-technical

[13] Campion, op. cit. pp. 415–20.

training on a post-high school level was first reaffirmed in 1937, when two-year technical courses were added to several schools that had been established some forty years before in rural areas for training in agriculture and home economics. But by including general education subjects and stressing mathematics and science, the curriculums of these institutions more closely approached those of the junior colleges than those of the traditional technical institutes.

Six years later, comprehensive planning crystallized in what is popularly known as the Strayer report.[14] In this plan, for the first time, business, industrial, and technical institutes were expressly mentioned as a special group within the instructional services to be established by an organization for vocational education. Since business and industry need workers with more technical knowledge than that possessed by workers on trade levels, institutes of this kind, offering one- or two-year courses to supplement and extend the practical courses given in high school, were suggested as being of value to both employers and workers.

The New York plan was presented as applicable to other large cities as well. 'When the pressure from students who seek admission becomes great, as is likely when the present war emergency period ceases, such schools may find it advisable to eliminate the present tenth school year and offer four years of work beginning with what is now the junior year of the secondary school period. There is a place for business and technical institutes in large American cities as part of an extended secondary school program.' [15]

The report suggests courses varying in content and length according to special fields, and includes in its recommendations 'that the educational offerings of the technical and the central vocational high schools be extended to a thirteenth and a fourteenth

[14] State of New York, Legislative Document (1944) No. 60, *Report of the New York City Sub-Committee of the Joint Legislative Committee on the State Education System* (Albany, 1944), Appendix 1: Report of the Survey of the Schools under the Control of the Board of Education, City of New York, pp. 311, 315–6, 319, 325, 334.

[15] Ibid. pp. 315–6.

year to include business, industrial and technical institutes related to the fields in which these schools now function on the secondary level—administration to remain for the present in the districts where these schools are now located.' [16] This implies a coordination with the work of the vocational and technical high schools and, in line with the organization of these schools, close cooperation between the schools, management, and labor—an interesting feature of the new planning that will foster the success of the technical institutes. Students of these institutes would be recruited not from among persons with work experience in industry, but from high school students whose shop experience, if any, would be confined to that acquired in vocational high school workshops.

The State of New York plans the establishment of 21 technical institutes, eleven of which are slated for New York City, while the other five are to serve Syracuse, Utica, Buffalo, Rochester, Albany, and other towns. Courses are to be two years in length. No degrees are to be offered, but certificates will attest to the completion of the work by the students.

When this plan was published early in 1945, New York City had already established the Fashion Institute of Technology and Design, the first technical institute of its type in the state, incorporated under a charter granted by the Board of Regents, and designed to serve as a model for other institutes to be established later. The Fashion Institute is the joint creation of the Educational Foundation for the Apparel Industry, established by leaders of management and labor, and the Board of Education of the City of New York. The close cooperation between educational authorities, management, and labor, in the establishment of the Fashion Institute, is further emphasized by the fact that management and labor leaders proceeded under the guidance of the chairman of the Needlecraft Educational Commission. This Commission acts as an advisory board to the Central High School of Needle Trades with which the Institute is administratively connected.

The Board of Education supplies the facilities for instruction

[16] Ibid. p. 334.

and a nucleus of the teaching staff; the Foundation supplies special materials for instruction, visiting lecturers, and 100 scholarships a year valued at $400 each for talented high school graduates from any high school in the United States.[17] The first graduates of the Institute were transferred into industry in the spring of 1946.

The Fashion Institute offers two major courses—one in the field of fashion, the other in industrial scientific management—and gives the students in either course a limited amount of instruction in the other. Of the 25 class units required in each of the four terms, 13 refer to the central subjects proper: apparel construction and design in the fashion course; and in management, a general course and laboratory work in scientific management, plus some units in elementary accounting, industrial cost accounting, marketing and quality control. The remaining 12 units are divided among the related technical subjects, and the cultural and academic subjects.

The related technical subjects in the field of fashion, distributed over four terms, are textile design, millinery design, applied textiles, textile testing, elementary accounting, industrial cost accounting, industrial scientific management, marketing, and quality control. The cultural and academic subjects are history of costume, industrial psychology, labor relations, contemporary literature, personality development through effective speech (oral report technique), advertising copy, human relationships (sociology), and world civilization. Report techniques, typewriting, and workshop experience are included in the curriculum as tool subjects, and 4 units distributed over two terms are devoted to leadership training. In addition to the 25 class units, 34 units of outside preparation, covering the same subjects, are required each term. Save for minor differences, the cultural and academic subjects in the curriculum for industrial scientific management are the same as in the fashion course. Related technical subjects of the management curriculum include poster, applied textiles and textile testing (these

[17] Mortimer C. Ritter, 'Fashion Institute of Technology and Design,' in *Occupations* (May 1945), pp. 457-9; Fashion Institute of Technology and Design, *First Annual Report* 1944-1945 (New York, 1945), p. 5.

two identical with offerings in the other course), mathematics, and art.

The breadth of the academic subjects, which cover about the same amount of time as the related technical subjects in the fashion course but more time in the management course, is remarkable.[18] So, too, is the inclusion of labor relations, not found as a separate subject in the vocational high school curriculums. The multiplicity of the academic subjects, however, implies that most are taught in two weekly periods during only one or, at best, two terms, and that the instruction is more suggestive than informational.

Among similar institutions planned for other industries, the technical institute for printing deserves special mention. In New York City the Graphic Arts Educational Commission, consisting of the representatives of education, of organized labor, and of employers in the graphic arts, is busily engaged in studying the problem of education and training for the printing trades, and the chairman of the commission has drawn up the following plan: a three-year vocational high school course, after junior high school, giving pre-apprentice training; a two-year technical institute for advanced training for junior positions in management, in production, and in shop; a four- to six-year school for apprenticeship training; a school for journeyman training; a professional and college technical institute for training potential teachers on a college level; a post-graduate school for management and upgrading training.[19] The two-year technical institute will be organized as a separate unit of the New York School of Printing and is designed to train for junior executive positions, such as assistant production manager, assistant estimator, job and billing clerk, assistant purchasing agent, and inventory clerk. The plan, as a whole, is outstanding, in that it covers all phases and aspects of vocational education and training, combines in-school and in-employment training, and integrates vocational high school and technical institute training with apprenticeship and journeyman training.

[18] Fashion Institute of Technology and Design, *Second Annual Report*, 4 June 1946 (New York, 1946), p. 10.
[19] William H. Friedman, *Post-war Education for the Printing Industry* (New York, 1945).

VIII

Statistical Survey of Vocational Education and Training

ENROLLMENTS

AS may be seen in Table 6, enrollments in vocational schools and classes showed a steady rise from a total of 164,186 in 1918 to a peak of 2,624,786 in 1942. The first important setback came in the following year when total enrollments fell off by 326,698, a decline directly attributable to wartime conditions. The early years of the war made no perceptible difference, but by 1943 many vocational teachers and members of the student body had been drafted into the armed services, others had entered war industries, and still others were finding it impossible to attend part-time and evening classes because of overtime work.

An enrollment of more than 2 million in vocational schools is admittedly impressive. Analysis of the composition of this vast group, however, reveals that, contrary to popular opinion, it is not the all-day classes but rather the part-time courses that attract most of the students and for which the major part of federal support is used. In 1942 the combined enrollments in the part-time and evening classes were 1,427,573 or 54.4 per cent of all enrollments in vocational classes. Enrollments in trade and industrial part-time and evening classes (including continuation classes) were 553,146, almost double the number in all-day trade and industrial classes. These figures indicate plainly how many persons beyond high school age feel the need for additional occupational training.

All-day vocational high school enrollments, with which this study is mainly concerned, numbered 1,197,213 in 1942, or 45.6

per cent of the total. But this figure in no way suggests how small an amount of vocational education and training was offered at the secondary level in agriculture, the trades, and industry, since about 50 per cent of the all-day enrollments were in home economics classes. In 1942, the peak year, enrollments in trade and industrial all-day classes were 297,451, or only 4.1 per cent of the total high school population, a proportion that in no way reflects the great

TABLE 6. ENROLLMENTS IN FEDERALLY AIDED ALL-DAY
VOCATIONAL HIGH SCHOOLS AND PART-TIME
AND EVENING CLASSES, 1918–43 [a]
(in thousands)

Type of Class	1918	1924	1930	1934	1938	1942	1943
All-day Vocational High Schools							
Trade & industrial	18.6	33.3	71.4	123.5	184.2	297.4	196.4
Agriculture	15.5	65.4	113.7	164.9	246.2	332.9	286.2
Home economics	8.4	36.3	56.4	142.5	358.0	566.8	542.9
Total	42.5	135.0	241.5	430.9	788.4	1,197.1	1,025.5
Part-time and Evening Classes							
Trade & industrial	99.3	120.4	210.9	168.9	346.9	447.4	312.1
Agriculture [b]	—	20.7	74.7	121.2	214.7	272.2	205.7
Home economics	22.4	120.5	118.6	155.4	269.4	387.2	330.8
Distributive	—	—	—	—	36.0 [c]	215.0	313.9
Continuation	[d]	256.1	336.3	174.6	154.7	105.8	109.9
Total	121.7	517.7	740.5	620.1	1,021.7	1,427.6	1,272.4
GRAND TOTAL	164.2	652.6	981.9	1,051.0	1,810.1	2,624.8	2,298.1

[a] Computed from U.S. Office of Education, *Digest of Annual Reports of State Boards for Vocational Education* . . . 1943 (Washington, 1944), Table 5, p. 80.
[b] Including day-unit classes.
[c] Organized in 1937 on the basis of the George-Deen Act.
[d] Included by official statistics in part-time classes; first separate listing, which appeared in 1920, put enrollment at 98,082.

importance of manufacturing, construction, mining, and transportation in the national economy. But the rapid increase in enrollments in these courses between 1930 and 1942, when compared with the increase in general high school enrollments,[1] is decidedly impressive. In 1930, only 1.5 per cent of all high school enrollments were in trade and industrial classes; since then the percentage has almost tripled.

The distribution of enrollments in trade and industrial classes among evening, part-time trade extension, and all-day courses for the 1926–42 period is shown by the following figures (expressed in thousands).[2] Enrollments in all-day classes have shown a steady

	Evening	Part-time trade ext.	All-day
1926	89.7	41.8	44.8
1928	114.6	42.5	57.4
1930	165.3	45.6	71.4
1932	151.0	44.5	93.4
1934	130.9	38.0	123.5
1936	120.2	125.9	145.6
1938	163.3	183.6	184.2
1940	167.9	241.1	206.9
1942	85.2	349.0	297.5
1945	70.2	151.5	174.5

growth. In the main, they have paralleled educational and economic trends, increasing in proportion to the growth of the entire high school population and faster than that of the general high school. The greatest proportional increases occurred between 1930 and 1934, the worst years of the depression. Obviously, unfavorable labor conditions affect high school attendance favorably.

The other types of classes, in contrast, follow exclusively economic lines and in quite a different way. The economic depression of the thirties disrupted the development of evening and part-time class enrollments as the decline in employment decreased the de-

[1] See Ch. III, p. 56.
[2] Computed from U.S. Office of Education, *Digest of Annual Reports of State Boards for Vocational Education* . . . 1943 (Washington, 1944), Table 5, p. 80, and *Statistical Abstract of the United States*, 1946, p. 141. The 1942 figure for part-time trade extension classes excludes part-time cooperative classes.

mand for adult vocational training. The sharp decrease in evening class enrollments in 1942, which preceded the general decline of 1943, may be accounted for by the lengthening of the working day for the group which this kind of training chiefly served.

REGIONAL DISTRIBUTION

A survey of 1942 enrollments in federally aided trade and industrial classes by regions, as shown in the following figures,[3] reveals their predominance in the industrial North Atlantic area with a total of 44 per cent in this section and the other 56 per cent more or

	All classes	All-day classes
North Atlantic	378,354	211,379
Southern	165,875	26,669
Central	163,645	34,455
Pacific	139,169	23,357
Hawaii	2,177	857
Puerto Rico	1,377	734
TOTAL	850,597	297,451

less equally distributed over the South, Central, and Pacific areas. In all-day classes alone, enrollments in the North Atlantic region accounted for 71 per cent, with percentages in other regions ranging from 12 to 8. In part-time and evening classes the regional variation was less pronounced. There were 115,997 enrollments in part-time trade extension or trade preparatory classes in the Atlantic region, and 83,942 in the South, the next highest on the list; 29,291 enrollments in evening classes in the Atlantic region were followed fairly closely by 25,623 in the Central area.[4]

The ten states with the highest enrollments in all-day trade and industrial classes in 1943 were New York with 60,113, Pennsylvania with 19,579, Massachusetts with 14,524, California with 12,-120, Illinois with 8,407, Texas with 8,181, New Jersey with 6,078, Ohio with 5,842, Michigan with 5,751, and Connecticut with

[3] U.S. Office of Education, *Digest of Annual Reports* . . . 1942 (Washington, 1943), p. 22.
[4] Ibid. p. 22.

4,457.[5] It is not surprising that these are almost all highly industrialized states; five are in the North Atlantic region, three in the Middle West, one each in the Far West and the Southwest. With the exception of Texas, which only recently has gained a ranking position in trade and industrial education, more than 65 per cent of the population of each of these states is concentrated in urban centers.

In the following figures a relationship is established between population, urban concentration, and trade and industrial high school attendance, with a view to measuring the extent of trade and industrial education in the ten states cited above.[6] New York

	Population in millions	% Concentration in urban areas	Enrollments in all-day trade & indus. classes	Enrollments per 1,000 population
New York	13.5	82.8%	60,113	4.5
Pennsylvania	9.9	66.5	19,579	2.0
Massachusetts	4.3	89.4	14,524	3.4
California	6.9	71.0	12,120	1.8
Illinois	7.9	73.6	8,407	1.1
Texas	6.4	45.4	8,181	1.3
New Jersey	4.2	81.6	6,078	1.4
Ohio	6.9	66.8	5,842	0.8
Michigan	5.3	65.7	5,751	1.1
Connecticut	1.7	67.8	4,457	2.6

ranks first as a result of the progressive policy pursued by both the state and New York City with regard to vocational education. Two New England states, Massachusetts and Connecticut, come next with regard to the ratio of enrollments to population. Of the other ten states only Pennsylvania has a ratio as high as 2 per 1,000.

Conversely, it is the South and West that have taken the lead in agricultural all-day classes. Of the ten states showing the highest enrollments, four are in the South, four in the Middle West, one in the Southwest, and one in the Atlantic area. The figures are as

[5] Figures for individual states were not published for 1942.
[6] U.S. Office of Education, *Digest of Annual Reports* . . . 1943 (cited above), Table 5, p. 80; *Statistical Abstract* . . . 1946 (cited above), p. 15.

follows: Texas, 28,907; North Carolina, 18,523; Georgia, 14,761; Illinois, 12,299; Wisconsin, 11,589; Tennessee, 11,354; Ohio, 11,190; Indiana, 11,131; Pennsylvania, 11,103; Louisiana, 10,130.[7]

Enrollments in home economics all-day classes (97 per cent of enrollees are girls) generally paralleled those in agricultural education. Texas, Georgia, North Carolina, and Illinois, which had the highest enrollments in agricultural all-day classes, also had the highest enrollments in home economics classes with 54,030, 31,207, 29,-173, and 22,893 respectively. On the other hand, home economics classes were poorly organized and attended in such states as New Jersey (2,030) and Connecticut (2,200), which explains why few industrial states rank among those with high total enrollments in all-day vocational classes.

As shown by the following figures on population, total enrollments in vocational all-day classes, and enrollments in agricultural, trade, and industrial, and home economics classes, in the ten states with the highest total enrollments in 1943,[8] Pennsylvania, Illinois, Texas, and Ohio rank high in all groups, indicating thereby a pronounced policy in favor of all branches of vocational education.

	Population in millions	Total enrollments	Agricultural enrollments	Trade & indus. enrollments	Home econ. enrollments
Texas	6.4	91,118	28,907	8,181	54,030
New York	13.5	81,864	9,164	60,113	12,587
Pennsylvania	9.9	49,196	10,328	19,579	19,289
Georgia	3.1	45,468	13,100	1,161	31,207
N. Carolina	3.6	44,051	12,775	2,103	29,173
Illinois	7.9	43,599	12,299	8,407	22,893
Ohio	6.9	35,976	10,523	5,842	19,611
Indiana	3.4	35,145	10,675	2,558	21,912
Virginia	2.7	33,151	7,948	2,437	22,766
Louisiana	2.4	33,842	9,700	3,603	20,539

[7] U.S. Office of Education, *Digest of Annual Reports . . .* 1943 (cited above), Table 5, p. 80.

[8] Ibid. Table 5, p. 80; *Statistical Abstract . . .* 1946 (cited above), p. 15.

The figures for New York, Massachusetts, and Connecticut reflect marked interest in trade and industrial all-day classes.

TRADES AND COURSES

In the 3,202 trade and industrial courses listed by the Vocational Division of the United States Office of Education in 1940, 109 trades were being taught.[9] Inasmuch as no new breakdown has since been published, the figures for that year will have to serve as a basis for discussion.

The number of trades, courses, and enrollments in each of seven large trade groups may be seen in the following tabulation. The largest number of courses were in the machine and metal trades and the closely allied auto mechanics, aviation, and electrical group, these together accounting for almost half of all the courses. Construction and woodworking trades are also represented by a large number of courses. Some of the large groups, however, included components of other groups, which makes it advisable to interpret the figures with caution.[10]

	Trades	Courses	Enrollments
Machine, metal & related trades	20	833	56,883
Auto mech., aviation, elec.	19	740	64,928
Constr. & woodworking	17	823	29,500
Food trades & serv. occupations	20	260	18,000
Textiles & clothing	13	218	30,000
Printing & related artistic trades	12	307	16,200
Chem., tech., misc.	8	21	2,500

[9] U.S. Office of Education, *Directory of Federally Aided All-Day Trade and Industrial Education Programs* (Washington, 1940), pp. I–III. The number of courses shows the frequency of the different trades in the vocational high school programs throughout the country. If two or more classes in the same trade are enumerated within a single school, they are counted as one course.

[10] For example, all drafting is lumped together with the machine and metal trades, although some of the courses or part of them may be given in connection with architecture, construction, and woodworking; the same is true of the general vocational courses, industrial design, and others. Furthermore, some of the maintenance and repair courses, which are usually identified with the service occupations, are counted among the machine and metal trades because a knowledge of these trades is considered prerequisite to maintenance and repair.

Within the seven large trade groups, the separate trades appearing most frequently in vocational high school curriculums are auto mechanics (359 courses), machine shop (301), electricity (252), carpentry (227), and printing (214). All these courses are in recognized apprenticeable trades and offer all-round basic training along trade unit lines. The predominance of apprenticeable trades is due to tradition and also to the fact that their broad scope affords a solid basis for technical and operational knowledge, which can later be effectively integrated with any specialized job or occupation.

The problem of expanding trade education has recently been approached by the introduction of courses either in more specialized, artistic, or technical trades, or in the service occupations. Among the former, for example, are special courses in machine design, ornamental design, showcard writing and design, oil production and refining, and industrial chemistry. Exploration and penetration into new fields is an important development, in view of the need to extend the vocational courses according to the diversified demands of the labor market.

Statistically, enrollments and courses have not traced the same pattern. The highest enrollments were in auto mechanics, aviation, and electricity courses, trades that ranked third in the tabulation of number of courses. Machine, metal, and related trades, which had the largest number of courses, had the second highest enrollments, while textile and clothing groups, which were sixth in regard to number of courses, held third place in enrollments. The explanation lies in the fact that the textile and clothing vocational high schools are large trade unit schools concentrated in a few big cities, while metal trade and mechanics schools and classes are widely distributed over the country and many of them have relatively few students. This is even more true of the 823 construction and woodworking courses in which only 29,500 students were enrolled.

The distribution of students among the separate trades in each of six large groups, the number of courses given, and the number of states in which they were found are shown in the figures that follow.[11]

Auto mechanics ranked first, with women's garment work and electricity next in order; these three trades were the only ones in

	Total enrollments	No. of courses	No. of states
Machine, metal & related trades			
Drafting	5,929	139	26
General industrial—metal	8,820	58	26
General vocational	16,126	99	14
Machine shop	16,748	301	40
Sheet metal	3,240	84	26
Welding	2,379	51	21
Auto mechanic, aviation, electricity			
Auto mechanics	26,929	359	45
Aviation	8,520	40	20
Electricity	20,487	252	40
Radio	2,442	32	18
Construction & woodworking			
Cabinetmaking	4,496	157	27
Carpentry	5,212	227	38
General industrial—building	6,537	166	30
Plumbing	1,983	47	16
Woodworking	7,268	81	21
Food trades & service occupations			
Food trades	6,581	82	25
Cosmetology	6,266	83	25
Household service	1,076	24	10
Textiles & clothing			
Garment & needlework trades, women's	23,471	100	32
Millinery	2,541	21	11
Printing & related trades			
Commercial art	3,450	54	21
Printing	12,634	214	40

[11] Enrollments computed from U.S. Office of Education, *Digest of Annual Reports* . . . 1940 (Washington, 1941), Table 9, p. 30; data on courses computed from U.S. Office of Education, *Directory* . . . (cited above), pp. I–III.

which more than 20,000 students were enrolled. In machine shop trades only 16,748 students were enumerated; to these must be added, however, many who were listed as enrolled in general industrial vocational classes. Moreover, sheet metal work and welding, and also auto mechanics, are closely allied to machine shop work; total training in this field therefore was undoubtedly greater than indicated by the number of machine shop enrollments. The only other trades with enrollments of more than 1,000 each were patternmaking, marine engine mechanics (given only in one school), painting, paperhanging and woodworking, shoemaking and shoe repairing, men's garment trades, and janitor service.

Of the 218,000 enrollments in trade and industrial classes about 46,000 were female; half of these were in the ladies' garment trades, the other half distributed among cosmetology (6,164), household arts (944), food trades (4,810), general vocational (4,487), millinery (2,541), and such fields as nursing, costume design, interior decorating, and laundering. Even before 1940, the infiltration of women into the occupations traditionally held by men was felt, although only to a very slight degree.

The 3,202 courses were given in 1,089 schools located in 827 cities. The distribution of these courses among the trades, total enrollments in each group of courses, the number of states in which they were offered and the states giving the highest number of courses in each group may be seen in the following figures.[12] Sixteen trades dominated secondary trade and industrial education, accounting for 75 per cent of the courses and 80 per cent of the enrollments, while the remaining 25 and 20 per cent respectively were distributed among the other 93 trades. General vocational education for work in several trades was most frequent in Massachusetts.

That the number of courses and enrollments often followed divergent lines is proved again by the following figures. For instance, two woodworking trades—cabinetmaking and carpentry—were reported as being offered in 384 courses with only 9,708 enroll-

[12] Computed from U.S. Office of Education, *Directory* . . . (cited above), pp. I–III.

	No. of courses	Total enrollments	No. of states	State giving most courses
Auto mechanics	359	26,929	45	Calif. (50)
Machine shop	301	16,748	40	Pa. (46)
Electricity	252	20,487	40	Pa. (42)
Printing	214	12,634	40	Calif. (27)
Carpentry	227	5,212	38	La. (24)
Garment & needlework (women's)	100	23,471	32	N.Y. (16)
Gen. indus.—bldg.	166	6,537	30	Ill. (26)
Cabinetmaking	157	4,496	27	Pa. (24)
Drafting	139	5,929	26	Pa. (25)
Gen. indus.—metal	58	8,820	26	Okla. (8)
Sheet metal	84	3,240	26	N.Y. (15)
Food trades	82	6,581	25	N.Y. (12)
Welding	51	2,379	21	Calif. (10)
Woodworking	81	7,268	21	N.Y. (14)
Commercial art	54	3,450	21	Ill. (10)
Aviation	40	8,520	20	Calif. (11)
TOTAL	2,365	165,701		

ments. Both trades are typical of the one-school small community. Aviation, on the other hand, with a not much smaller number of enrollments (8,520), was offered in only 40 courses, or hardly more than one-tenth of the number of courses given in cabinet-making and carpentry.

Specific industries often determine the trades taught in local vocational schools. Thus, the only school for glovemaking is in Gloversville, N.Y., the center of the glove industry; six of the fourteen textile vocational high schools are in the weaving centers of South Carolina; and the largest needle trades school is in New York City.

RELATION OF TRAINING TO INDUSTRIAL NEEDS

To date, the role of the vocational high schools in supplying the labor force with trained workers has been much smaller than commonly supposed. While this qualification applies to all the major fields in the province of vocational high schools, it is particularly true of the trade and industrial classes. In 1940, the high school population was approximately 7.1 million—6.1 million in general high schools, and 1 million, or 14.1 per cent, in vocational high schools. But the proportion of the labor force engaged in the craft trades and as farmers, operatives, or other manual workers was no less than 68.2 per cent of the gainfully occupied population (70 per cent, if the 500,000 listed as foremen in the technical trades are included). This disparity is even more striking if the figures for only the male students and male gainfully occupied are compared. About 73 per cent of the gainfully employed male population were in the categories under discussion, while less than 14 per cent of the male high school population were enrolled in vocational high schools with a view to preparing for work in these specific fields.

If one compares the enrollments in all-day trade and industrial classes with the number of persons employed in craft trades only, the percentage of enrollments (less than 3) is still far below the percentage of craftsmen in relation to all gainfully occupied persons (11.8, to which may be added 1 per cent for foremen). And if one considers that many of the courses in which these students are enrolled also prepare for occupations in which operatives play a large role, such as those in the garment trades, the inadequacy of the number of trainees for craft trades becomes even more obvious.

The disparity shows up even more clearly in the following figures (expressed in thousands) on enrollments in some of the most frequently taught trades in the vocational high schools and on the number of gainfully occupied in these trades.[13]

Assuming an average tenure of 28 years in an occupation, the annual replacement rate would have to be 3.6 per cent. Assuming also three and a half years as the average term for students preparing for a trade in vocational high school (some entering in the 9th grade, others in the 10th), the number of enrollments should repre-

[13] Enrollments computed from U.S. Office of Education, *Digest of Annual Reports* . . . 1940 (cited above), Table 9, p. 30; figures on gainfully occupied computed from Sixteenth Census of the United States, 1940, Population, vol. 3, *The Labor Force*, Part I, U.S. Summary (Washington, 1943), Table 58.

sent about 12.6 per cent of the gainfully occupied in the respective trades. From the figures below it can be seen that the actual percentages were far below this level even in those trades that were most popular in vocational high schools.

	Vocational h.s. enrollments	Gainfully occupied	Enrollments in % of gainfully occupied
Electricity	20.5	252.9	8.1%
Sheet metal	4.0	91.6	4.4
Machinists	16.7	521.1	3.2
Mechanics	27.1	949.7	2.9
Plumbing	2.0	216.1	1.0
Foundry	.5	87.6	0.6
Tool & diemakers	.2	96.9	0.2
Forging	.1	87.2	0.1

In the machine and metal industry, all craftsmen, operatives, and persons in occupations such as those of locomotive engineers (excluding foremen and managers of small plants as well as laborers) totaled 4.2 million. The total enrollment, however, in all courses aiming at preparation for these occupations was approximately 121,000 or only 2.9 per cent of those employed.

Figures on some of the building and woodworking trades, as given below (in thousands), reveal an even greater difference.[14]

	Vocational h.s. enrollments	Gainfully occupied	Enrollments in % of gainfully occupied
Carpentry	5.2	773.6	0.7%
Cabinetmaking	4.5	58.8	7.7
Bricklaying	.9 ⎱	141.7	0.9
Masonry	.4 ⎰		
Plastering	.2	52.9	0.4
Painting	1.4	350.3	0.3

In most cases the ratios do not reach even 1 per cent. They are so low that with the exception of cabinetmaking it can hardly be said that the vocational high schools have played any measurable part in the preparation for these trades.

In the printing trades, where the number of craftsmen was 241,-

[14] Data computed from sources cited in note 13.

000, only 12,634 or 5.2 per cent were enrolled in vocational courses. This figure represents a better proportion than exists in the trades mentioned above, but is still far below the desirable minimum of 12.6 per cent.

On the whole, therefore, the results confirm the extent to which vocational education will have to be expanded even if only to prepare for the predominant craft trades, and for foremanship and small shop management, not to speak of the great number of semiskilled occupations.

IX

Informal In-Employment Training

IN-EMPLOYMENT training, varied as it is, has the single common feature that it is training given within the framework of employment. It may well be divided into two main groups—apprentice training, and the far more prevalent informal training on the job. The essential difference between the two systems lies in the fact that the apprentice holds his job for the purpose of obtaining systematic training over an unbroken period of years, while the other trainee holds his job for the job's sake, to which learning is only incidental.

PREVAILING TYPES

In contrast to the more or less standardized working schedules for apprentices, to be discussed in subsequent chapters, the usual training on the job includes a great many different procedures through which the trainee may progress in almost any imaginable fashion. To date, the most purposive and systematic training of this kind is that which is given a new operative in the large mass production industries. The worker is assumed not to know the job that lies ahead of him and is therefore taught the few operations he is to perform. In plants where the work is broken down into extremely narrow operations, the actual teaching may take only a few minutes, but the new worker will usually require a certain extended period of time before he is capable of performing his particular job continuously, evenly, and with sufficient speed and accuracy. If the work cannot be taught so quickly, or if it requires the handling of more expensive machinery, tools, or materials, the future operative may even receive pre-assignment instruction in a special section of the factory—that is, training given in so-called vestibule schools after the worker has been hired but before he is given actual productive work. The time spent by a new worker on pre-assignment training is usually brief, ranging from one to fourteen days, and in most cases it has to be supplemented by some additional instruction directly on the job.

Such off-the-job training assumed considerable proportions at the beginning of the war when all industry became acutely aware of training problems. Large firms even added training directors and special trainers to their staffs to handle this particular problem. A similar form of vestibule school training had been utilized during World War I but was abandoned soon after. In 1937 when the National Industrial Conference Board made its survey of industrial training, only 8.5 per cent of the firms replying to the questionnaire reported that they had vestibule schools, though 80 per cent claimed to give some sort of systematic training.

Another exceptional form of in-employment training was that developed during the last war through the cooperation of the vocational high schools, war industries, and the federal government, whereby the high schools employed their facilities for short-term training on a large scale, in accordance with the immediate needs of local plants. In many cases, workers were hired and put on the payroll while they were still receiving training in the vocational high school. Thus the training was technically within the framework of employment but was neither on-the-job training nor plant pre-assignment instruction.

One should not, however, infer from the description of these special training arrangements that the usual in-employment training offers any such systematic program. For the most part it consists of having the foreman or one of the regular production workers show the new worker the job that has to be done. The rest is then up to the worker, and thus 90 per cent of all informal in-employment training should probably be called on-the-job *learning* rather than on-the-job *training*.

Informal training or learning on the job applies not only to the preparation of the operative in mass production, for whom it is not wholly inadequate, but also, to a large extent, to the training for more diversified and skilled work. That this situation exists is obvious from the small number of apprentices in industry. In the National Industrial Conference Board survey, 57.7 per cent of the 473 companies covered reported apprentice training, but the actual number of apprentices was only 7,322 or 1.1 per cent of the persons employed. On the other hand, on-the-job training was reported by practically every company that professed to give any training at all. Thus it appears that even for craftsmen, training on the job is virtually the only training available. This is the salient and, at the same time, the weakest point in in-employment training.

If such training is at all systematic, the new employee starts at the lowest level, which may mean transporting supplies, cleaning equipment, or doing other odd jobs of this nature. Under favorable conditions and if the worker is eager for advancement, he may then become a helper for an experienced employee, and, on the basis of what he can observe and with some opportunity to perform the various operations, he may later try his hand as a skilled worker in the same or in some other plant.

In other instances the worker's way will be less smooth and direct. Even without having had the opportunity to acquire skills, he may nevertheless find employment by claiming to be a skilled worker, and then lose his first few jobs in rapid succession because he does not possess the skills he claimed. Finally, by trial and error, he may learn enough to enable him to hold a job, although possibly not in the trade he originally selected. Correspondence courses or brief attendance at private trade schools has in the past often helped workers to cope successfully with the problems of entering and learning a trade in such a way. The amount of skill acquired by this rather slipshod method of 'stealing a trade' depends largely on the interest and aptitudes of the individual worker and on his luck in obtaining jobs and work that give him an opportunity to improve his occupational techniques and knowledge.

In the many business enterprises investigated for the purposes of this study, the methods of on-the-job training described above were used almost to the exclusion of any other, and despite their shortcomings they were not considered by management in general as inadequate as a preliminary analysis of the situation would suggest. Even small shops have adopted these methods, making the best of what is obviously the simplest and most direct way of enabling the worker to perform the necessary operations.

Closer analysis, however, reveals that such training can be used successfully only because many key positions in the work process are held by older, experienced, and well-trained workers. If the percentage of these key men is high enough, apparently all production requirements, including even diversified and custom work, can be met. During the war, it is true, the proportion of skilled labor in war production industries was extremely low, and the problem of utilizing the limited supply to the best advantage had to be solved by re-engineering, further breakdown of jobs, and the extensive use of lead men and setup men to prepare and supervise the jobs of newcomers to the labor force. Such a readjustment was possible only because war industries were largely a matter of mass production, but it has never been accepted that these measures could cope successfully with the peacetime needs of the economy as a whole.

Definition of Training Time

It is manifestly impossible to make generalizations in terms of the nature of in-employment training in various manufacturing industries, because the countless operations taught vary too widely for comparison. The only common denominator is the length of training given. It is, therefore, on the basis of findings with reference to the time spent on training that certain conclusions have been drawn regarding the distribution and degree of skills indispensable to the proper functioning of a large sector of our national economy.

Length of training, or the amount of time that is necessary for learning each of the many manipulative skills required for modern production, is one of the most controversial issues in any discussion of occupational training. Opinions vary widely, some holding that in modern technology nearly all jobs can be learned in a few hours or days, while others maintain that training for nearly all trades requires several years. Even when the discussion is narrowed to a single trade—that of tool and diemakers, for instance—there is strong disagreement. According to some authorities it takes ten years to become a skilled toolmaker; on the other hand, many large plant owners will vouch for the fact that tools and dies for war production were turned out by men who, with few exceptions, had had no more than a few months of training.

The root of such a contradiction is confusion over the terminology involved rather than a basic difference of opinion on the point at issue. The first matter to be clarified is the distinction between training for a job and training for an occupation. In small shops, in repair work, and in diversified production, the terms 'job' and 'occupation' may be interchangeable; in mass production, this is by no means the case. An operative in mass production may work at a special machine equipped with single-purpose jigs and with tools already ground and set to cut one work piece to a given size for which the machine has been adjusted in advance. In these circumstances the skill needed for the actual operation is indeed very limited and the required training time is therefore correspondingly short. But such an operation or job involves only one simple skill within a traditional occupation or craft, the mastery of which requires much longer training.

Once this distinction has been established, the next major question is what constitutes required training. As a rule, it is assumed to include all the essentials for converting a 'green' worker—that is, a completely inexperienced worker—into an efficient performer of the required operations. But a 'green' hand is chiefly a theoretical concept, for virtually all workers entering industry have had elementary and some high school education and are thus familiar with the discipline of learning. Furthermore, most workers have had a certain amount of shopwork or manual training in school, and have handled tools or even machinery. It is also important to point out that only a small proportion of the new employees in any plant have just left school. Most so-called 'green' workers have been employed before, either in the same or in a related industry, and have thus acquired work habits and improved their manual dexterity. Statistically determined training periods should therefore be understood as the period of training over and above the acquisition of such educational and occupational background.

Statistical results on the length of training also vary according to the degree of efficiency that a worker is expected to achieve in the stated period. A beginner in the clothing industry, for example, may learn in a few minutes how to start and stop a power-driven sewing machine, in a few hours how to sew a straight seam, and in a few days how to work on clothing that is to be placed on the market. It may, however, take four weeks before the worker earns his wage rate, three months before he reaches the average piece rate, and from six to nine months before complete independence and top efficiency are attained. Statements concerning the length of training are therefore misleading unless it is clearly understood that professional speed is to be acquired during the designated period of training.

The length of training required to achieve satisfactory performance has been the subject of many investigations, but they are all concerned with the training of the employed; pre-employment training, especially vocational training in school, and its bearing on the length of in-employment training are not considered.[1] The investigations, moreover, are usually confined to length of training for a job and do not take into account systematic apprentice training for a trade. Nor do they include the length of training in very small shops or repair work; they are mainly concerned with manufacturing industries. It should also be kept in mind that the training period required to prepare a worker to perform a single job

[1] In the literature on vocational training, the term 'post-employment training' as contrasted with 'pre-employment' training is frequently used. This study prefers 'in-employment training' since 'employment' implies not only the act of hiring a worker but the entire period of the worker's service.

or operation acceptably seldom corresponds to his complete in-employment training. The average worker changes jobs frequently and each time receives some new training, however little; as a result he may be trained one, five, or twenty times in the same, related, or unrelated industries. A basic distinction has therefore to be made between the length of training for a single job and the accumulated training received by a worker during his occupational life.

LENGTH OF TRAINING IN VARIOUS INDUSTRIES

The 1937 National Industrial Conference Board survey investigated not only types of in-employment instruction but also maximum length of training in a representative group of 473 companies with an aggregate of 626,668 employees.[2] Replies from 375 companies to a questionnaire on the subject of training time required for the ordinary occupations supply the basis for the following figures.

	No. of companies	% of total		No. of companies	% of total
1 week	17	4.5	1 year	31	8.3
2 weeks	12	3.2	2 years	35	9.4
3 weeks	17	4.5	3 years	19	5.1
4 weeks	32	8.5	4 years	24	6.4
2 months	50	13.3	5 years	9	2.4
3 months	44	11.7	More than		
4 months	6	1.6	5 years	2	0.5
5 months	2	0.5	Varying		
6 months	52	13.9	periods	23	6.2

Combined in larger units the results appear as follows:

	No. of companies	% of total
2 months	128	34.0
3 to 6 months	104	27.7
6 months to 2 years	66	17.7
More than 2 years	54	14.4
Varying periods	23	6.2

[2] National Industrial Conference Board, *Training for Industry*, Studies of the National Industrial Conference Board, No. 237 (New York, 1937).

Of the 375 companies involved, 34 per cent reported a maximum training period of 2 months or less, and 27.7 per cent a period of 3 to 6 months; in other words, 61.7 per cent, or more than three-fifths, of the companies trained their workers for production in 6 months or less. The results are expressed not in numbers and proportions of employees or operations but according to companies only, thus obscuring important data; no further breakdown of the figures has been attempted.

An earlier and more intensive study of training time was conducted in 1931 by Charles A. Koepke and his associates at the University of Minnesota, and was repeated in 1936 for purposes of comparison.[3] These investigators attempted to determine the most effective training periods for a variety of operations, but their findings were not so representative as those of the National Industrial Conference Board, since coverage was restricted to 88 firms in 33 industries involving only 4,133 operatives or jobs. In so far as it was possible, the selection of plants in any one industry was made on the basis of representativeness, but it is obvious that the results could have only a relative and regional value.

The 1931 results yielded the following schedule of training time for satisfactory performance of all operations. Without publishing figures for earlier periods, Koepke asserted that these

	% of jobs
Less than 2 weeks	22
2 weeks to 2 months	33
3 to 9 months	17
10 months to 2 years	16
2 to 4 years	8
More than 4 years	4

percentages revealed a drastic shortening in training time, a development which he attributed to the breakdown of a great many industrial operations into small units. Although the methodological

[3] Charles A. Koepke, *A Job Analysis of Manufacturing Plants in Minnesota* (Minneapolis, 1934) and *Changes in Machinery and Job Requirements in Minnesota Manufacturing* 1931–1936 . . . (Philadelphia, 1939).

approach of the Koepke survey differed greatly from that of the National Industrial Conference Board investigation, the figures of both confirm the fact that a training period of less than 3 months is all that is necessary for half the jobs, and that high skills, acquired in a minimum of 2 years, are required for about 12 per cent.

On the basis of his 1936 survey Koepke contended that advances in production techniques were continuing to cut down training time. Comparison with the 1931 study reveals that increases in training periods below 2 months considerably surpassed decreases, and that decreases in periods above 2 years exceeded increases. The number of production workers whose training periods were below 9 months increased 17 per cent—from 487 in 1931 to 572 in 1936. While these findings were confined to regional or local conditions, they nevertheless corroborated a nationwide trend. Koepke concluded that 'the process of increasing division of labor through increased mechanization is still running its course although that course may not now be so rapid or so revolutionary as before.' [4]

In order to be able to form an independent judgment on the subject of training time, this study made its own investigation of a representative group of companies in various industries—shipbuilding, radio, metal, electrical, textile, paper, glass, and others—with a total of 80,004 workers. The situation in 1941 and 1942 is indicated by the following figures. The deviations from Koepke's

	% of jobs
Less than 4 weeks	29
1 to 3 months	14
4 to 9 months	32
9 months to 2 years	14
More than 2 years	11

results, such as a higher proportion in the 4 to 9-months group and a smaller proportion in the 1 to 3-months group, are minor, indicating perhaps a difference of only several weeks of training. The lack of data on the numerical and representative strength of

[4] Koepke, *Changes in Machinery* . . . (cited above), p. 36.

the firms investigated in both studies may also have some bearing on these differences.

Expressed in larger units of time, however, a comparison of the surveys made by the National Industrial Conference Board, Koepke, and the authors of this study reveals a remarkable similarity in the findings, which may be seen in the following figures. The percentages given for the National Industrial Conference Board refer, of course, to the total number of companies investigated, while those of the other two pertain to the total number of operations or jobs. All three surveys suggest that a considerable

	Less than 9 mos.	9 mos. to 2 yrs.	More than 2 yrs.
Natl. Indus. Conf. Bd.	70.4%	14.4%	15.2%
Koepke	72.0	16.0	12.0
Authors	75.0	14.0	11.0

portion of the jobs require a training period of only a few months and that about 20 to 30 per cent require not more than a few weeks of training for satisfactory performance.

But another and equally important fact is revealed by the tabulations: namely, that a sizable share of jobs even in large manufacturing plants—some 12 per cent or more—call for highly skilled workers. These jobs cannot be satisfactorily filled without substantial training over a period of years. Koepke emphasized that the highest skills continually lost ground but he admitted that the change was gradual and had ceased to be spectacular.[5] Still more explicitly, the National Industrial Conference Board study contended that 'the opinion advanced at one time that intensive and progressive mechanization was reducing the need for highly skilled labor had not been borne out by events. While a less comprehensive mechanical training than formerly may give adequate preparation for many occupations, a high degree of special skill is necessary to secure best results from elaborate and intricate machines, and such skills can be built satisfactorily only on a sound foundation of the fundamentals of machine operation.'[6]

[5] Ibid. p. 43.
[6] National Industrial Conference Board, op. cit. p. 28.

Thus the counterpart of the continuous shortening of the training time for the majority of jobs is the stability of the proportion
of jobs for which highly skilled workers are needed in industry.
While the latter constitute a minority, they are indispensable to
the work of the vast remainder of production workers.

LENGTH OF TRAINING IN SPECIFIC INDUSTRIES

Approaching the subject of length of training from another
angle, an examination of training policies and characteristics in certain individual industries was made. A series of industry manning
tables published in 1943 and 1944 by the War Manpower Commission served as a basis for the accompanying figures showing, for
fifteen different industrial groups, the percentage distribution of
workers by the length of their training periods.[7]

	A (over 24 mos.)	B (13–24 mos.)	C (6–12 mos.)	D (3–6 mos.)	E (2 mos. or less)
Bitum. coal mines (udrgrd.)	22.1%	19.3%	20.4%	26.4%	11.8%
Bitum. coal mines (strip)	24.3	11.6	18.7	17.1	28.3
Gray iron jobbing foundries (less than 100 workers)	25.8	14.3	13.4	34.6	11.9
Gray iron jobbing foundries (more than 100 workers)	16.1	5.6	14.0	29.4	34.9
Forgings	20.1	7.1	13.3	31.6	27.9
Ball & roller bearings	13.4	6.7	14.3	45.1	20.5
Machine tool accessories (re-engineered)	30.5	16.3	16.3	27.6	9.3
(slightly or not at all re-engineered)	66.8	12.5	5.0	10.3	7.5
Nonferrous metal foundries	27.5	11.8	10.5	36.9	13.3
Metal aircraft parts	13.2	9.6	17.8	42.2	17.2
Fabricated plastic products	8.4	4.7	8.9	36.2	41.8
Commun. equipment (radio, radar, etc.)	5.6	4.1	5.6	36.3	48.4
Southern sawmills	8.0	5.6	13.1	40.2	33.1
Pulp, paper, paper products	14.0	10.4	11.0	26.2	38.4
Motor truck transport.	7.6	6.9	39.0	39.5	7.0

[7] The tables have been computed on the basis of two or three dozen
samples per industry, taken from various states and regions, and analyzed

The percentage of workers in training grades *A* and *B* (13 months or more of training) is remarkably high, especially in the iron industry and the metal trades. Omitting all reference to the machine tool accessories industry, which has a particularly great need for highly skilled labor, from 20 to 40 per cent of the workers are found in these two training groups, amounting to an industrial average of 28.5 per cent.[8] The percentage of skilled labor is also exceptionally high in the bituminous coal mines; it reaches 25 per cent in the pulp, paper, and paper products industries, and does not fall below 13 per cent in any of the others with the exception of communications equipment where it is 9.7 per cent.

On the whole, the figures of this tabulation indicate a higher percentage of long training periods than do those of Koepke and our own investigation, but too much importance must not be attached to this variation. In the first place, the particular industries selected for the manning tables would inevitably show a high percentage of skilled workers. And in the second, because of the abnormal manpower situation in wartime the accuracy of the manning tables may be questioned. It is even suggested in the text of the tables that estimates of training time may have been inflated by the industries in question in order to emphasize the 'essential' aspect of workers and jobs and thus gain military draft deferment for their employees. But the allowance of even a liberal margin for error and inconsistency does not decisively alter the fact that skilled occupations, although constantly disappearing and reappearing in new categories as a result of technological changes, continue to exist as such, and to resist any substantial reduction in the length of training required for their adequate performance.

The automobile industry, as is well known, is outstanding for its exceptionally short training periods, which were made possible by a drastic transformation of production techniques in the two

---

and computed by the Division of Occupational Analysis and Training Tables (Bureau of Manpower Utilization) of the War Manpower Commission.

[8] This percentage represents an unweighted average, giving equal weight to each industry irrespective of the number of persons employed or the number of plants covered by the investigation.

decades preceding the outbreak of World War II. Between 1919 and 1929, productivity in the automobile industry alone rose 134 per cent compared with an increase of only 43.2 per cent in industry as a whole. Most operations have been simplified and specialized to such a degree that they require a minimum of skill for satisfactory performance. R. J. Thomas, former president of the United Automobile Workers, reporting to the Temporary National Economic Committee of the Congress in 1940 [9] on the development of this industry, asserted, on the basis of data furnished by workers, that in the plants of the Ford Motor Company the following conditions obtained: 43 per cent of the workers required 1 day to learn their jobs; 36 per cent, up to 8 days; 14 per cent, 1 week to 1 month; 6 per cent, 1 month to 1 year; and 1 per cent, more than 1 year.

These figures are substantiated by the superintendent of the Ford Industrial Schools [10] who reported that practically all employees with the exception of apprentices were trained on the job in a period not exceeding 4 weeks.[11] As Mr. Thomas pointed out, however, during the first decade of rapid expansion in the automobile industry, highly skilled workers—carpenters, blacksmiths, cabinetmakers, sheetmetal workers, and the like—were attracted into the industry by high wages, thereby creating a reserve of skills that could be drawn on for a considerable time.

The training schedule of a dry dock and shipbuilding company employing 26,000 workers indicates conditions in that industry before the war. The following figures show what percentages of the workers were in each training bracket. The group receiving the longest training included the apprentices who constituted 2 per cent of the total labor force. Of the workers who were trained from 1 to 3 months, 20 per cent were trained on the job and 5 per cent in vocational schools; for all other groups, training on the

[9] U.S. Temporary National Economic Committee, *Investigation of Concentration of Economic Power*, Hearings before the T.N.E.C., Congress of the United States (76th Congress), Part 30: Technology and Concentration of Economic Power (Washington, 1940), pp. 16361–2.

[10] Letter to the authors from F. E. Searle, Ford Motor Company, Dearborn, Michigan, 29 June 1943.

[11] This statement refers to factory employment only.

job was the only method employed and was considered by the director of training to be most desirable.[12] The length of training in this industry, with about 75 per cent of the labor force receiving less than 9 months and 15 per cent getting more than 2 years, corresponds to the proportions in other industries; the percentage trained for 4 to 9 months is higher than the average in manufacturing industries.

Less than 4 weeks	10%
1 to 3 months	25
4 to 9 months	40
9 months to 2 years	10
More than 2 years	15

The hat and millinery industry offers a good example of one in which technological changes have been hardly noticeable in recent years.[13] The percentage distribution of the 60,900 members of this industry by the length of their training periods is shown by the following figures. A training period of up to 6 months for 73

1 to 5 weeks	3%
6 to 13 weeks	13
3 to 6 months	57
1 to 2 years	5
2 to 3 years	12
More than 3 years	10

per cent of the labor force in this industry corresponds to the industrial average. But the percentage trained in only a few weeks is lower than the average in manufacturing industries, while a larger proportion than is usual falls within the 3 to 6 months bracket. The 22 per cent trained for more than 2 years is above the average standard. Within the industry itself there was considerable variation in training periods. In the fur felt hat industry 40 per cent were trained for more than 3 years, and the remaining

[12] Letter to the authors from James I. Teat, Alabama Dry Dock and Shipbuilding Company, Mobile, Alabama, 24 April 1943.

[13] Data provided by Alfred Braunthal, research director, United Hatters, Cap and Millinery Workers (AFL).

60 per cent in less than 6 months, while in the men's cap and cloth hat industry only 15 per cent are trained for 1 to 2 years and the remaining 85 per cent in less than 6 months.

Despite certain marked deviations, individual industries tend to follow the training pattern of industry as a whole. Technological progress, especially widespread mechanization and advancing division of labor, has been instrumental in reducing training time for a considerable portion of the labor force. Nevertheless, the need for highly skilled labor remains more or less constant.

Length of Training in War Industries

With the huge defense program of 1940 and 1941 and the war production needs of the years immediately following, American industry was faced with a formidable manpower problem. Millions of workers, many of them women, entered the labor market for the first time and had to be given initial training; others who shifted from civilian to war production had to be retrained.

Under these conditions it was imperative to cut training time in war industries to a minimum and to concentrate the instruction on bare essentials. The War Manpower Commission industry manning tables show remarkably little, if any, influence of wartime conditions on length of training, but these tables must be interpreted with caution, as has already been pointed out. Figures gathered especially for this study furnish evidence of marked effects, and permit interesting comparisons with training periods under prewar conditions (Table 7).

Without exception, although to varying degrees, these examples show a significant increase of short training periods and a sharp decline of longer training time. The continuance of apprenticeship, even on the limited prewar scale, was rendered almost impossible by the urgency of the situation. On the other hand, there were no signs of the disappearance of skilled jobs despite wartime pressures. To a smaller or greater extent they survived.

In judging the shortening of training periods in various industries, it must be remembered that the degree to which job re-

TABLE 7. PERCENTAGE DISTRIBUTION OF WORKERS IN SELECTED
REPRESENTATIVE INDUSTRIES, BEFORE AND DURING WORLD WAR II,
BY LENGTH OF TRAINING PERIOD

Industry	Under 4 wks.		1–3 mos.		4–9 mos.		9 mos.–2 yrs.		Over 2 yrs.	
	Prewar	War	Prewar	War	Prewar	War	Prewar	War	Prewar	War
Elec. products [a]	20%	30%	25%	30%	25%	20%	15%	12%	10%	8%
Plastics div., elec. co. [b]	—	10	—	20	50	50	10	10	40	9
Dry dock & shipping [c]	10	29	25	40	40	20	10	10	15	1
Metal [d]	30	80	35	8	25	4	10	6	—	—
Paper [e]	—	—	10	20	10	30	80	50	—	—
Glass [f]	38	57	19	28	28	5	10	5	5	5

[a] Employing 2,000 men, 10,000 women.
[b] Employing 6,000 men, 650 women.
[c] Employing 22,000 men, 4,000 women.
[d] Employing 1,069 persons.
[e] Employing 2,903 men, 479 women.
[f] Employing 4,369 men, 1,874 women.

engineering was possible exerted a strong influence on training practices. The magnitude and nature of the work prevented some plants from re-engineering their jobs, while others, because of their occupational structure, were able to do so with little or no disturbance. The importance of re-engineering for length of training is reflected even in the manning table data for the machine tool accessories, which reveal the following contrast between the two types of plants (the figures refer to the percentage of employees in each training period category).[14]

	Type I *(Re-engineered)*	*Type II* *(Not re-engineered)*
A (over 24 mos.)	30.6%	66.8%
B (13 to 24 mos.)	16.2	12.5
C (7 to 12 mos.)	16.3	5.0
D (3 to 6 mos.)	27.6	10.3
E (2 mos. or less)	9.3	7.5

Through production planning and job re-engineering, Type I plants were able to operate with extended training for only 30.6 per cent of the employed, while Type II plants required the training for 66.8 per cent. Type I plants could make wide use of unit-skilled machine operators; Type II plants, on the contrary, operated with a production staff composed almost entirely of multiskilled men. In Type I plants, toolmakers, diesinkers and setters—the most highly skilled craftsmen—comprised only 11.5 per cent of the entire labor force; in Type II plants they accounted for 45 per cent or four times as many. But in the machine shop and related occupations the ratio is reversed: they constituted 44 per cent of the labor force in Type I plants and only 8 per cent in Type II plants.

The most decisive factor in re-engineering is the size of the plant. In small factories employing only a few dozen workers, job breakdown is almost out of the question, and in plants employing 50 to 100 workers its possibilities are definitely limited. The following

[14] Allowance must be made for errors and inconsistencies in the manning tables, already referred to in the text.

figures on the distribution in 1939 of wage earners in manufacturing industry, according to the size of the plant (number of workers employed), indicate the limits of re-engineering.[15]

1 to 5 workers	2.6%
6 to 20	6.9
21 to 50	9.7
51 to 100	10.8
101 to 250	18.7
251 to 500	16.1
501 to 1,000	13.0
1,001 to 2,500	11.9
2,501 or more	10.5

Of the total labor force, 19.2 per cent worked in plants employing fewer than 50 workers, and an additional 10.8 per cent in plants employing 50 to 100 workers. Thus it appears that a sizable portion of the labor force, even in the manufacturing industries, is absorbed by small plants in which no rapid or extensive job breakdown can be expected. The skills needed in these small shops continue to cover a much wider range than those required for a particular job or operation in larger plants.

In reviewing the effect of drastically shortened training periods, several large companies who were called upon to evaluate this development pointed out that 'their estimates represented as much as 50 per cent reductions from their normal training time and that they could not maintain an efficient organization in normal times by adhering to these standards.' [16] Some of the methods devised for this accelerated training may, of course, have some bearing on peacetime production, but their applicability to the economy as a whole should not be overestimated.

TRAINING FOR VERSATILITY

Industrial training policies have in recent years been strongly influenced by the potential occupational mobility to be derived

[15] Sixteenth Census of the United States, 1940, *Manufactures*, 1939, vol. 1, p. 120.

[16] National Industrial Conference Board, 'Time Schedules in Job Training,' in *Studies in Personnel Policy*, No. 55 (New York, 1943), p. 2.

from short training periods. In a sense, this amounts to making the best of an existing situation. The growth of new industries and new production methods, and the vigorous expansion of production, as a whole, encouraged workers to shift from job to job and from industry and industry. For example, in 1931, among 26 industries in Minnesota there were 8 in which more than 85 per cent, and 17 in which more than 50 per cent, of the operations were being performed by workers who had transferred from unrelated industries. And in 1936, 40 to 50 per cent of the workers in the same state were found in jobs to which they had shifted from unrelated industries during the previous five years.[17]

Faced with the fact that workers were insistent on mobility, a number of plants apparently decided to train their new employees for versatility, in an effort to build up a body of reserve skills on which the plant could draw as needed and to give the worker a chance to change jobs within the plant—a system with obvious advantages to both worker and employer. The actual extent of such multioperational training can be ascertained only with difficulty. The Essex County vocational schools, after investigating the requirements for semiskilled workers with a view to developing multioccupations courses, stated that 'only in a very few instances is anything being done in industry to develop in semiskilled workers the ability to do more than one highly specialized job or process.'[18] The National Industrial Conference Board, on the other hand, reported that of 473 companies queried, 222 or 47 per cent claimed to have an established policy of training employees for versatility, while 34 others or 7 per cent noted the occasional adoption of such a policy. Most of these programs were scattered throughout the electrical, machine and machine tool, automobile and automobile parts industries. A variety of goals were set for the training: in addition to the plantwide systems reported by 15.2 per cent of the companies, there were special types for interdepartmental transfers (27 per cent), rotation within a department (21.9 per cent), training for promotion or upgrading (12.5 per

[17] Koepke, *A Job Analysis* . . . (cited above).
[18] Thomas L. Norton, *Education for Work* (New York, 1938), p. 192.

cent), and for the development of selected employees only (7 per cent).[19] Koepke also stated that most of the companies investigated pursued a definite policy of moving workers from one type of job to another in order to relieve the monotony of routine work.

Actual training practices may well lie between these two extremes. The holding of many jobs in the same or consecutive employment by the same worker is the rule and not the exception. All companies endeavor to have more than one worker who can perform certain crucial operations on their production lines. And if a particular operation ceases to be needed because of changes in production, the usual practice is to give the worker an opportunity to fill another job in the same plant. Also, if one of the more difficult jobs is open, it is generally assigned to an old worker who has performed similar operations rather than to a new employee. Other transfers are made because more pleasant jobs become available or simply because a worker is eager to change. All these shifts within a plant lead to retraining in the same way that a complete change of employment would. Since such mobility and retraining are not restricted to young workers—according to the National Industrial Conference Board survey, 83 per cent of the companies that trained young workers also trained workers between thirty and forty years of age [20]—the total amount of multijob training is indeed considerable. Nevertheless, systematic rotation of a substantial portion of the operatives in industry for the express purpose of promoting versatility remains relatively rare.

Within the last decade, it is true, a more determined effort has been made to increase the reservoir of skilled labor. With the expansion of economic activity in 1936–37, the shortage of skilled labor became acute in many industries. It was clear that revitalization of the necessarily slow apprenticeship system could not solve the immediate problem, and that a time-saving system would have

[19] The objectives of their versatility training programs were not specified by 16.4 per cent of the companies.

[20] National Industrial Conference Board, *Training for Industry* (cited above), p. 20.

to be applied. Many of the difficulties were overcome by upgrading routine workers and thereby giving them an opportunity to acquire a wider range of skills. In other cases the new trainee assumed the more formal position of a learner who received systematic instruction designed to make him a partial trade specialist. In general, 3 to 5 months were allotted to training, depending on the number of machines whose operation was to be mastered. Despite strong labor union opposition to this 'dilution of skills,' [21] production for war made learnership at least temporarily unavoidable.

The program for learners at Thompson Products, Inc., of Cleveland, is a successful example of this method of training. It was introduced in 1939 as a substitute for the company's regular four-year apprentice training course, which could not supply the demand for skilled workers as fast as they were needed. Most of the operators were trained in 15 weeks; the training for automatic screw and internal grinding machine operation required 17 to 22 weeks, in each of which 38 hours were devoted to actual shop practice and 4 to classroom work.[22] Although the learners' program reduced by 72 per cent the usual 18 months estimated by these manufacturers as sufficient for the acquisition of the necessary skills, the foremen reported that it produced 95 per cent efficiency, as compared with 50 per cent efficiency on the part of workers hired from the outside and not put through the course. The company attributed this result to the fact that a combination of theoretical training and shop practice imparted a clearer understanding and more intimate knowledge of the principles involved in the machines and, as a consequence, more intelligent performance of the work. It should not be overlooked, however, that the prerequisites for learnership at the Thompson company were graduation from technical high school and a minimum age of about twenty-five. Also, many of the learners were chosen from

[21] United Steel Workers of America, *Industrial Training*, Publication No. 4 (Pittsburgh, 1940[?]), p. 1; UAW–CIO International Education Department, *Apprenticeship and the UAW–CIO* (Detroit, 1941), pp. 5–6.

[22] Ray Livingstone, 'From Learner to Skilled Operator in Five Months' Time,' in *Factory Management* (May 1940).

workers already employed by the plant and whose capacities for further development had been demonstrated.

During the war, when systematic upgrading and learnership programs reached their peak, many other claims of successfully shortened training periods were put forth. The details of the programs vary according to the needs of individual plants. The achievements of this kind of training on a basis less rigid than that of apprenticeship, but more organized than mere on-the-job training, make it probable that similar procedures will be retained by American manufacturing industry.

X

Apprenticeship: Its Organization and Status

FOR various reasons already outlined in the opening chapter of this study, apprenticeship in the United States never gained either the scope or prestige that it has always enjoyed in European countries. Neither the economic nor the social development of this country favored the expansion of any form of indentured labor. Indeed the whole problem remained so far in the background that not until twenty years after the importance of in-school vocational education had been acknowledged by federal legislation did apprenticeship become a matter of national concern.

It is true that a number of state and private ventures in the field preceded the passage of the Fitzgerald Act in 1937. The demand for skilled labor imposed by our role in World War I prompted several attempts to promote apprenticeship. For example, in 1915 the apprenticeship law of Wisconsin was revived, amended, and put in working order. This contained provisions for indenture, instruction time, regulation of wages and hours, working schedules, and supervision by the State Industrial Commission—all of them items that were later incorporated in the Fitzgerald Act. A board created to administer the law was composed of employers, unions, and continuation school representatives; its secretary was the full-time supervisor of the apprentices. But for a long time the Wisconsin law remained an isolated attempt to regulate apprenticeship on a statewide basis.

In 1921 the building trades launched a national apprenticeship program, in an effort to relieve an acute shortage of skilled labor in this field. An apprenticeship commission, composed of representatives of workers, employers, and members of the Building

Congress, was set up to act in an advisory and supervisory capacity. For each of the separate trades there were state and local commissions, the latter of which fixed the terms of the apprentice agreements.

Some years later the National Metal Trades Association promoted a campaign for a national apprenticeship program. This called for the organization of industrial America into apprenticeship districts and the appointment of directors for each district as well as one for the national organization.

None of these efforts met with any substantial success but they served as a useful basis for the subsequent federal legislation.

THE FITZGERALD ACT AND ITS APPLICATION

The purpose of the Fitzgerald Act is to establish labor standards for apprenticeship; to extend their application to apprenticeship contracts; to bring employers and employees together for the formulation of apprenticeship programs; to cooperate with state agencies engaged in the formulation and promotion of standards, and with other federal agencies. Under the terms of the Act, two national agencies were created for its implementation: the Federal Committee on Apprenticeship and the National Apprentice-Training Service. The first of these is composed of two representatives of management and two of labor, and one each from the Department of Labor and Office of Education; and its main function is to develop standards and to shape policy. The second is the administrative branch, which advises the Committee on the setting up of standards, publishes the standards finally agreed upon, and registers all agreements between management and labor. Originally organized as a division of the Department of Labor, the Service was transferred during the war, first to the Office of the Administrator of the Federal Security Agency and, in 1942, to the War Manpower Commission. In September 1945 it was returned to the Department of Labor.

The success of the agencies depended entirely, of course, upon effective decentralization. The state labor departments were therefore requested to create state apprenticeship councils of which there are now twenty-four.[1] These are patterned after the federal Committee with equal representation of employers and labor, and of state departments of labor and state boards of vocational education. The state councils formulate their own standards and procedures, basing them on those of the federal Committee.

Following a somewhat different plan of decentralization from that of the Committee, the National Apprentice-Training Service established regional offices, of which there are now twelve, each with a small staff headed by a supervisor representing the national unit in Washington. The regional officers cooperate with and advise the state councils, or deal directly with management and labor in states where no councils exist.

Although the actual development of these agencies resulted from the initiative of public authorities, management and labor alone were responsible for the creation of proper bodies to administer the apprenticeship law at national, local, and plant levels. Employers' associations and trade unions therefore appointed joint apprenticeship committees to function at the national level in developing standards and encouraging local employers and labor unions to set up apprentice-training programs to conform with the standards set by the federal Committee. These national joint trade committees work in close cooperation with the Apprentice-Training Service, obtaining from it statistical reports or analyses of trade training problems, copies of new local training programs, and data on appointments to local joint committees, and furnishing, in their turn, advice to the Service on the handling of special training problems in the respective industries.

At the local level, joint apprenticeship committees for particular trades were newly created, or built up from existing employer-employee organizations. These committees are responsible for developing local standards for the employment and training of all

[1] Arkansas, California, Connecticut, Florida, Iowa, Kansas, Kentucky, Louisiana, Massachusetts, Minnesota, Montana, Nevada, New Hampshire, New Mexico, New York, North Carolina, Ohio, Oregon, Pennsylvania, Rhode Island, Vermont, Virginia, Washington, Wisconsin.

apprentices in the trade either by organizations of employers or others who subscribe independently to the written apprentice agreement.

Individual plant apprenticeship committees have also been established on a labor-management basis. These committees set up standards, provide a full- or part-time supervisor of apprentices, and outline his functions in relation to those of the committee. It is also possible for employers who are not members of an organization, and whose employee organizations are not particularly concerned with the training of skilled workers, to establish their own apprenticeship systems and register with the state council or the regional office.

To sum up—the system includes national agencies, state councils, and regional offices, composed of representatives of management, labor, and government labor and education offices; and management-labor committees operating at national, local, and plant levels. In all its connections with apprentice training the government acts only in an advisory capacity, exerting no compulsion whatever. While the Apprentice-Training Service develops the programs of employment and training according to the standards set by the federal Committee, the working out of details is left entirely to labor and management, who devise the standards for individual trades on a national level, but assign to local and plant representatives the task of implementing the rules and regulations according to specific local conditions. In general, the local joint committees function for the smaller enterprises, while plant committees operate in large establishments. Thus the local and plant committees do the final practical job. Their powers range from the enforcement of standards and the supervision of training to selecting apprentices and determining their number. The effectiveness of their work depends upon how well they succeed in promoting good training and protecting labor standards.

The Joint Apprenticeship Committee of the New York Electrical Contractors' Association and Local 3 of the International

Brotherhood of Electrical Workers (AFL) is a good example of a local joint committee formed by an established employers' association and a strong union. The duties of this committee include: determining the need for apprentices in the locality, and the shop facilities available for the necessary experience on the job; establishing minimum standards of education and experience; determining the employer's competence to give training; making certain that apprentices are under agreement, that they are continuously employed, adequately instructed, or transferred to another employer if necessary; determining the quality and quantity of experience and making sure that the apprentice obtains it; arranging for tests on progress in manipulative skills and technical knowledge; hearing and adjusting all complaints of violation of apprentice agreements; assuming responsibility, in general, for the successful operation of the apprenticeship standards; keeping in constant touch with apprentices, employers, and journeymen; cooperating with public and private agencies and with the director of apprentice training and the instructor of related training; developing public interest in apprentice standards. Other duties involve notifications, registrations, recommendations for examination, and maintenance of careful records of apprentices.

The duties of plant apprenticeship committees are somewhat less extensive since only one employer is involved in an agreement, but in individual cases they are more important. In addition to supervisory and claim-adjusting functions, which *mutatis mutandis* are similar to those of the local committees, the plant committees frequently pass on apprentices after preliminary examination and approval by the personnel director of the company. And in some instances, they may adjust the ratio of apprentices to journeymen and decide on the number of apprentices to be employed in a plant.

Adjustment practices are especially necessary in large plants that have a number of divisions at work on a variety of products in diversified apprenticeable trades. What is involved in this kind of planning is demonstrated by the experience of the Tennessee

Valley Authority which employed 271 apprentices among 5,000 skilled craftsmen in 1941 and had to make agreements with fifteen different trade unions. TVA reviewed this work as follows:

'The determination as to how many apprentices shall be employed and what shall be the ratio between apprentices and journeymen in each of the crafts is made by the Central Joint Council. When, as in earlier days, it was the custom to assign ratios for each local project separately, it was found that fluctuations in project activity, and consequently in employment, adversely affected the continuity of employment of apprentices. . . . It was, therefore, recently decided by the Central Joint Council to stabilize the employment of apprentices by establishing craft ratios applicable to the Authority as a whole. In this step, both management and labor were in complete accord. Thus, in accordance with present practice, it is now possible for the number of apprentices relative to the number of journeymen in the same craft to be greater or less than the accepted ratio at a given project without upsetting the programs as a whole . . . The rate of hiring apprentices within the limits of this stabilization understanding is determined by the total construction schedule, which is planned well ahead of time. As a result, fluctuations in the employment of apprentices are negligible, and it is possible for the Authority, through the council, to determine in advance how many additional apprentices it will need.' [2]

While the apprenticeship committees set, supervise, and enforce rules, the training supervisors are the executives proper. They work at a local or plant level, and their relationship to the apprenticeship committees varies; sometimes they are members of these committees, sometimes not, but in any event they are responsible to them. There are instances in which the salaries of the training supervisors and of their staffs are paid by the union, an arrangement that strengthens union influence. In other cases, the training supervisors are members of the plant personnel.

[2] U.S. Apprentice-Training Service, *Report on the Apprentice-Training Program of the Tennessee Valley Authority* (Washington, 1942), p. 5.

STATISTICAL ANALYSIS

When the census of 1940 was taken, the Fitzgerald Act had been in existence barely three years. It would therefore be unjustifiable to use the census figures as a measure of the effect of the Act on apprentice training. The number of apprentices given was some 84,000—only 6,600 higher than the 1930 figure.[3]

Although the Apprentice-Training Service felt unable to estimate with assurance the number of apprentices at the end of 1942, it settled on 200,000 as a best guess. This figure, which is so much higher than the 1940 census report, is explained by the Service by the fact that many more young people, especially those of 16 and 17 years of age, entered war industries as 'apprentices.' [4] There is no evidence, however, that the need for quick training during the war emergency had resulted in an expansion of regular apprenticeship. An increase from 84,000 to 200,000 within two years is so unlikely that the Apprentice-Training Service estimate must have included many wartime learnerships. Significantly enough, in 1942 only 45,000 apprentices, employed in about 5,000 firms and covered by 2,304 agreements, were actually registered with the Service as conforming to the standards recommended by the Federal Committee on Apprenticeship. As the war progressed, the number of bona fide apprentices showed a drastic decline, reflected in the appallingly low figure of only 16,000 registered apprentices at the end of hostilities.

It is true that many small firms that employ apprentices may not have registered with the apprenticeship authorities. The development of apprenticeship systems independent of federal administration is noted in an American Iron and Steel Institute survey of 28 firms employing 500,000 workers. The information gathered in connection with this survey seems to indicate that the apprentice training programs generally employed in the iron and steel industry involves much more than the minimum of 4,000 hours of em-

[3] This figure does not include some 8,000 unemployed apprentices.
[4] U.S. Apprentice-Training Service, *Apprentice Training for America's Youth* (Washington, 1943), p. 1.

ployment, but that only 50 per cent of the programs include sup-plemental educational courses. Where such educational courses are included, they involve 144 to 200 hours of classroom instruction per year. Only about 40 per cent of the companies require formal contracts with all of their apprentices, and an additional 10 per cent provide contracts only for special trade groups. The written agreements, however, usually do not embody definite schedules of work assignments. The progressively increasing scale of wages, at levels generally well above the federal standards, appears to be typical of the steel company programs. It does not appear to have been general practice among steel companies to seek approval of their training programs by their respective employees' bargaining agencies; and only 1 in 28 has had the approval of the Federal Committee on Apprenticeship.[5]

An analysis of the 45,000 apprentices registered in 1942 shows that they were concentrated mainly in California (7,088), Illinois (2,925), Michigan (6,845), New York (2,069), Ohio (3,600), Washington (1,952), and Wisconsin (3,593). As for the industrial distribution, 33,000 of the 45,000 were in the machine and metal in-dustries—three times as many as in all other industries combined. This was, of course, a reflection of the enormous expansion of armament manufacture.

The insignificant number of apprentices in the labor force as a whole is emphasized in the following trade-by-trade analysis show-ing the development over two decades.[6] The number of apprentices

	1920	1930	1940
Carpenters	4,805	4,138	7,428
Electricians	9,562	4,611	3,430
Machinists	39,463	13,606	14,198
Plumbers	7,386	5,937	5,311
Other bldg. & hand trades	12,737	11,841	14,161
Printing	11,603	10,928	10,020

[5] American Iron and Steel Institute, *Practices Relating to Apprentice-Training Programs in the Iron and Steel Industry,* ed. by Grover C. Brown (New York, 1941).

[6] For the development of apprenticeship as a whole, *see* figures in Ch.

in carpentry has remained fairly stable. The high number of electrician and machinist apprentices in 1920 was probably a result of the immediately preceding war years, while the low figure for electricians and plumber apprentices in 1940 reflected the depression in the building trades. The printing industry, despite its comparatively extensive apprenticeship system, also showed a smaller number in 1940 than in either 1930 or 1920.

The apprentice-journeyman ratio is correspondingly low, as shown by the following figures on several major trades in 1940.[7]

	Apprentices	Journeymen	Ratio
Carpenters	7,428	766,213	1:103
Electricians	3,430	227,102	1:66
Machinists	14,198	521,093	1:37
Plumbers	5,311	210,815	1:140
Printers	10,020	240,881	1:24

Assuming that twenty-eight years is the average tenure for a worker in a trade (allowing for dropouts due to change in trade, advancements, or natural causes) and that four years is the average for apprenticeship, the ratio of apprentices to journeymen should be 1:7. In each of the trades cited above it is considerably lower, carpenters and plumbers showing the greatest discrepancy. Even the printing industry, which has the most satisfactory ratio, could absorb three times as many apprentices without causing an oversupply of skilled labor. The ratio given for machinists may be misleading, since apprentices in this trade have to replace not only journeymen machinists but also most of the mechanics, who numbered nearly a million in the 1940 census. It is clearly apparent that apprenticeship does not yet play a measurable role in any trade with the possible exception of printing.

The concentration of apprenticeship programs in large enterprises is typified by conditions in the machine and metal industry

I. Figures for 1920 and 1930 taken from Fifteenth Census of the United States, 1930, *Population*, vol. 5 (Washington, 1933), p. 40; figures for 1940 were taken from *Statistical Abstract of the United States*, 1946, p. 183, and refer to both employed and unemployed apprentices.

[7] *Statistical Abstract . . .* 1946, p. 183.

in 1943, summarized in the following figures.[8] Just two large businesses employ, between them, 5,600 or 20 per cent of all apprentices listed in this table. On the basis of the ratios of apprentices to journeymen, it can be presumed that enterprises with more than 10 apprentices are those employing at least several hundred workers each. This would imply that more than two-thirds of the apprentices in the machine and metal industry are employed by such large companies. In this country, therefore, small shops do not play nearly so important a role in the training of apprentices as they do in most European countries, although it must be kept in mind that the figures refer only to registered apprentices, and that apprentices in small shops are registered less often than those in the large enterprises.

No. of apprentices per enterprise	No. of enterprises	Total apprentices in group
1 to 3	3,506	4,069
4 to 10	773	4,959
11 to 25	240	2,422
26 to 100	109	5,615
101 to 500	27	4,717
501 to 1,000	1	631
Over 1,000	2	5,600
TOTAL	4,658	28,719

From the foregoing account it may be concluded that the Fitzgerald Act has not yet had full effect. It has contributed to the standardization of apprenticeship regulations and to the further organization of apprenticeship without, however, having extended its scope beyond more than approximately half of all apprentices. It has not markedly affected the number of apprentices. In the prewar and war years it was applied under conditions that cannot be considered normal, and it would be premature, therefore, to pronounce the legislation ineffectual.

[8] Compiled from U.S. War Manpower Commission, *Apprenticeship Systems in the United States* . . . May 1943 (FCA-192:042443).

Postwar Developments

As a result of the rather special postwar conditions, systematic in-employment training is experiencing an expansion that may well alter the face of American industrial training. The prevailing high level of production and employment has made employers eager to secure a well-trained labor force. At the same time, millions of young men, recently discharged from the armed services and intent on planning their business careers, recognize the advisability of acquiring further education or training along lines that will insure their orderly advancement. These two factors alone would have resulted in increased attendance in schools and colleges and in an expansion of apprenticeship and other forms of occupational training. But veterans are further encouraged to return to school or to enter into some industrial training arrangement by the provisions of the GI Bill of Rights, which grants them federal subsidies of $65 to $90 a month for varying periods of time while they are so engaged.

In order that a veteran trainee may receive these federal benefits in addition to regular payments from his employer, it is necessary that he be certified as eligible by the Veterans Administration and that his employer offer a training program acceptable to the state authorities. In the case of an apprenticeship this usually means that the employer agrees to conduct a program of training corresponding to the general standards formulated by the various joint apprentice committees.

The marked effect of this legislation is indicated by the rapid increase in the number of apprenticeship trade programs registered with the Apprentice-Training Service. By the end of May 1947, in the building trades alone these programs covered 51,513 establishments.[9] Apprenticeship programs are, of course, not the separate formal agreements between employer and apprentice, but only sets of rules under which either an individual employer or an

[9] U.S. Apprentice-Training Service, *Monthly Report on Apprenticeship Programs in the Building Trades* (FCA-1511:050847).

entire trade or industry may hire apprentices. The actual number of apprentices at any given time can only be estimated, since statistics are available only for certain groups.

For the building trades, the Apprentice-Training Service reported 98,126 employed apprentices, as of 30 April 1947. This figure included registered as well as nonregistered apprentices and was broken down for the separate trades as shown by the figures below.[10]

Trowel trades	12,611
Woodworking trades	36,241
Painting & related trades	7,741
Pipe trades	14,980
Electrical trades	15,397
Sheet metal trades	7,312
Other building trades	3,844

The number of apprentices in all trades registered with the Apprentice-Training Service at the end of April 1947 was reported to be 133,369.[11] The total at this time, therefore, was probably not much below 200,000.

The large proportion of veterans among apprentices may be seen in selected New York State figures. Of 5,480 apprentices in the building trades at the end of June 1946, 4,737 were veterans, and of 2,153 in the printing trades, 1,612 were veterans. The total reported for other trades was 3,507, of whom 2,957 were veterans. For the country as a whole the Washington office of the Apprentice-Training Service reported that 90 per cent of the new apprentices were veterans. In view of the fact that a large proportion of the particular age group involved would necessarily have been members of the armed forces this percentage is not too startling.

Federal subsidies, however, are not restricted to veterans serving regular apprenticeships. They are also granted for other forms

[10] U.S. Apprentice-Training Service, *Building Trade Apprentices in Employment* (FCA-1533).

[11] U.S. Apprentice-Training Service, *Apprentice Registration Actions Reported by Type of Action and State* (FCA-1252).

of approved training on the job. The jobs to be learned in such programs are not in the apprenticeable trades but 'run the gamut from a shoe salesman to first vice-president of a large corporation.' The majority of on-the-job training programs cover white-collar jobs such as 'clerk, salesman, installation-service-repairman, beautician, traffic agent, inspector, assistant agency manager, teller, and district manager.' [12] Under these programs the veteran trainee receives the industrial wage rate usual for the work he is doing, plus a subsistence allowance from the federal government. Total receipts, however, are not supposed to exceed $175 a month for a single, and $200 for a married, veteran, as is also the case in the apprentice training programs.

The official attitude of the states toward these training programs is indicated by the following pronouncement of the New York Labor Department: 'It is the aim of the Labor Department to see that official approval is granted to the greatest possible number of On-the-Job Training Programs, for such programs mean job opportunities and jobs, in turn, mean security to industry, business, and veterans alike.' [13] An appraisal of the true value of these programs, however, is not yet possible. Neither the aggregate number nor the quality of training which will develop under this system can be prophesied.

The situation in the field of apprenticeship is somewhat different since there exists a well-developed organization of federal and state authorities and of joint apprenticeship committees representing management and labor, all of whom have a clear view of their goals. With the cooperation of all these agencies in the effort to absorb increasing numbers of veterans into apprenticeships, the system may be expanded to proportions that would correspond with the size of the skilled labor force.

[12] *Industrial Bulletin* (February 1946), p. 4.
[13] Ibid. p. 3.

XI

Apprenticeship Programs and Standards

APPRENTICEABLE TRADES

INASMUCH as trades originate, develop, change their content continuously, and even expire, as a result of technological change, the concept of an apprenticeable trade cannot be rigidly maintained nor can it be determined by purely rational processes. Trades such as those of the blacksmith, sheet metal worker, or plumber, were in existence long before steam, and electric and gas power were introduced; those of tool and diemakers, jig builders, heat treaters, boilermakers, millwrights, and others, flourished after steam power began to play an important role in production, and an entirely new group of apprenticeable trades was created with the introduction of power-generation and electrically driven machines and gas engines. Thus there are now special mechanics for aircraft, automobiles, Diesel engines, oil burners, and refrigeration, and there are special electricians for outside and inside work, voice, sound, vision, and transmission.

As a result of this development, many modern apprenticeable trades now exist side by side with those old trades that have survived despite changes in the techniques and knowledge required. The fact that certain older trades were formerly regarded as apprenticeable, but are now considered merely skilled occupations, may be explained in part by the great difficulty of operating the earlier machines or the more complicated hand operations required for the production process. On the other hand, new skilled occupations have sprung up, some of which are likely to broaden into apprenticeable trades. The craft of the metal polisher, for instance, is gradually being replaced by the more modern and efficient methods of metal plating, which has recently developed into an apprenticeable trade in the electrochemical field.

In an effort to clarify this rather complex situation, the Apprentice-Training Service published in 1943 a revised list of about 120 apprenticeable trades.[1] Among 46 in the machine and metal industry are those of diemakers, diesinkers, draftsmen, machinists, nine different types of mechanics, three types of model makers, pipefitters, plumbers, shipfitters and shipwrights, steamfitters, tool and jig builders, and toolmakers. Fully aware of the variability in the field, the Service foresees changes in this list, as evidence is found to warrant additions or deletions.

The trades as taught in vocational high schools are, in general, broader in scope than those listed by the Service as apprenticeable, a situation justified by the fact that this instruction, in order to conform to the purpose of in-school education and training, has to be broadly basic. The Service, however, in listing the apprenticeable trades, had to take other factors into consideration. While the work processes to be learned had to be sufficiently diversified to develop all-round skills and flexibility over a wide range of employment opportunities, it was also essential that they should not cover too broad a field to be learned within a reasonable period of time. In addition, the Service had to take into account the lines along which the craft-oriented trade unions are organized, since the successful expansion of apprenticeship depends to a great extent on union cooperation and must therefore recognize traditional union rules, structure, and jurisdictional areas.

An examination of the apprentice programs and standards in the machine and metal trades, as they have been developed according to the provisions of the Fitzgerald Act, will serve to indicate the character of apprenticeship in this country and the status of young workers employed under apprentice agreements. Consideration will be given to certain basic factors of all apprenticeship programs: namely, selection of apprentices; term of apprentice-

[1] U.S. Apprentice-Training Service, *The National Apprenticeship Program* (Washington, 1943), p. 6.

ship; working schedules; related school instruction; compensation; and restriction of apprenticeships.

SELECTION OF APPRENTICES

In view of their long association with an enterprise, and of the rigorous demands of work and training, intelligent and careful selection of apprentices is of primary importance. Items to be taken into account in choosing apprentices are suggested by the topics investigated by the Murray Corporation of America (Detroit): interest and inclination for the trade; ability to learn; previous education and training in the trade; work and general attitude; future possibilities, reliability, and strength of purpose; personality, appearance, poise, and ability to get along with people. Distinction along these lines, however, is prerequisite to success in any career and is not peculiar to apprenticeship.

More concrete standards of selection are based on age, education, physical fitness, American citizenship, and good moral character. In some cases, preference is given to single men, local residents, or children of workers employed in the industry.[2] For example, one contract openly states that 'preferences will be given to sons of employees in the selection of apprentices to the extent of at least eighty (80) per cent of the number employed.'[3] But, in general, the preference accorded candidates on such grounds is tacit rather than avowed.

The minimum age for entering upon an apprenticeship depends on the school-leaving age in the state in which the agreement is made. It is usually between sixteen and eighteen, with the maximum in the early twenties, though occasionally no top limit is set. In actual practice, the age limit is not so rigid as the specifications suggest. In boom times, when the supply of eligible apprentices is small, the restrictions on age are relaxed, while during periods of economic depression the rules are more strictly enforced. Moreover,

[2] Ibid. p. 4.
[3] Elias Lieberman, *The Collective Labor Agreement* (New York, 1939), p. 55.

the agreements frequently allow apprenticeship committees to raise or to waive entirely the maximum age limit for persons with previous experience in the trade—for instance, those who entered the trade as helpers and subsequently decided to learn it by the more systematic means of apprenticeship. Some agreements specifically stipulate a higher age limit for such persons. During the war, high school youth of sixteen and seventeen were encouraged to become apprentices. To make the prospect more attractive, a system of interrelated credits for high school graduation of these apprentices was worked out jointly by the schools and the apprenticeship authorities. Such inducements, however, were promptly withdrawn at the end of the emergency, and efforts to keep youth in school took on renewed vigor.

High school education or its equivalent is referred to in nearly all apprenticeship standards, but with varying degrees of emphasis. The least exacting requirements term high school attendance 'desired but not necessary,' while others presuppose graduation. One of the standards assumes that 'the majority of applicants will have completed high school, but this is not to be construed against the applicant, with mechanical ability, who has been unable to complete high school, due to conditions beyond his control.' [4] Sperry Gyroscope Company is generous in its stipulations with regard to education, accepting in place of four years of high school a grammar school education plus two years of approved trade school education, or 'night school, tutoring, special instruction or such other educational background as shall be considered satisfactory.' [5] The other extreme is exemplified by the Murray Corporation of America, which requires high school graduation 'carrying above average scholastic standing.' There is scarcely any standard, however, in which vocational high school education is mentioned, which indicates how little weight it carries among those whom it would serve best and how loose is the connection between the two

---

[4] U.S. Labor Standards Division, *Machinists' Apprenticeship Standards* . . . (Washington, 1940), p. 6.

[5] U.S. Labor Standards Division, *Apprenticeship Standards of the Sperry Gyroscope Company, Inc.* (Washington, 1940), p. 1.

main types of vocational training, which should be so closely linked.

As a safeguard against errors in judgment on the part of the company in selecting apprentices or on the part of apprentices in choosing a trade, each contract provides for a probationary period, during which the employer or the apprentice may terminate the contract without obligation, either by annulment or on request to the apprenticeship committee. In the machine and metal industry, the period is usually 6 months or 1,000 working hours, but it may be only half that long. Cancellation of the apprenticeship by the employer after the end of the probationary period is subject to the approval of the Federal Committee on Apprenticeship and is limited to such causes as failure to do satisfactory work or infractions of discipline. With regard to the apprentice who wishes to break the contract, it is unlikely that he would be forced to serve the full term against his will. But the sacrifice of the advantages to be derived from a completed apprenticeship is usually enough of a deterrent to any premature withdrawal from the contract on the part of the apprentice.

Apprenticeship Terms and Working Schedules

On the basis of all the considerations that shaped its choice of apprenticeable trades, the Apprentice-Training Service stipulated the number of years required for apprenticeship in each of these trades. The terms can be grouped as follows: 69 trades, 4 years; 16 trades, 3; 15 trades, 2; 15 trades, 5; 2 trades, 7; 1 trade, 2 or 3 (operating engineers); 1 trade, 2 or 4 (bookbinder); 1 trade, 4 or 5 (electrician, building); 1 trade, 5 or 6 (compositor).

In the machine and metal trades the prevailing term of 4 years applies to all 9 types of mechanics and the 3 types of model makers, the boilermakers, machinists, sheetmetal workers, shipfitters and shipwrights, toolmakers, and tool and jig builders. The exceptionally long term of 7 years is required only for diesinkers, while patternmakers (metal), pipefitters, and steamfitters are required to serve 5 years. Very few trades in the machine and metal industry are listed as requiring less than 4 years; metal platers are put down for 3 and metal fitters (aircraft) for 2.

In local and plant agreements the terms of apprenticeship are expressed in years or hours. In the standards, 1,900 to 2,250 hours—or an average of 2,000 hours—are figured as being equal to a year. The currently more frequent stipulation in hours is to the advantage of the apprentice who, if he works overtime, can then finish his term in less time than if it were expressed in years. The situation is, of course, reversed if the apprentice is laid off for a time during his term. The standards of apprenticeship sometimes specify the right of 'promoting an apprentice . . . in less than four years when such promotion is merited on account of outstanding ability or experience.' [6] Credit granted for work experience in the same trade prior to regular apprenticeship may also shorten the term.

One of the main problems in establishing the scope of an apprenticeable trade and the length of the period of training is the choice of the number and kinds of operations and processes to be included and their arrangement in working schedules. Every apprenticeship program has a more or less elaborate working schedule, indicating the subjects which must be covered in shop practice and the time to be spent on each. Study of a number of apprentice standards, however, reveals that the working schedules differ not only among the trades but also substantially within the individual trades, and they differ not so much in respect to the subjects covered as in the time distribution and sometimes even the length of the whole term of apprenticeship.

Although the apprenticeable trades for the most part have been built up on a trade, and not an industrial, basis, the type of production in the industry concerned determines the importance

[6] U.S. Labor Standards Division, *Report on Apprenticeship System of American Airlines, Inc.*, by Oswald L. Harvey, Technical Bulletin No. 4 (Washington), p. 7.

given to each of the operations and therefore the arrangement of the training program. For example, the schedule for a machinist apprentice in the automobile industry is quite different from that for one in the textile machine industry, although it is quite true that with brief additional training, a machinist trained in one industry should be able to apply his skill in another, since the basic operations and problems are essentially the same.

Other differences in standards are due to the size of the enterprise. Training schedules in a large, modern plant differ from those of small shops which have only limited machinery setups for all-round purposes. And still another source of differences in schedules is the variety of opinions among apprenticeship committees with regard to the emphasis, both of time and sequence, to be accorded the subjects covered. There are also specific working conditions and many production processes requiring unique knowledge and skills for which special training schedules for an individual enterprise may have to be drawn up. And one company goes so far as to state that 'so varied are the particular characteristics of each apprentice, indeed, it may be said that each schedule of work progress has to be tailor made.'

Just how the varying conceptions of adequate trade training for apprentices are translated into practice may be demonstrated by examples of working schedules for machinists, one of the most widely distributed occupations within the machine and metal trades. The term 'machinist' may be interpreted in two ways: one refers to the machinist whose main work is in the machine shop; the other to the machinist whose chief job is assembling, fitting, and repairing, or, in general, bench and floor-work. Both types belong to one and the same apprenticeable trade, with the center of gravity shifted according to the needs of the plant and the special branch of work chosen by the apprentice.

In only one of the programs studied was the usual 4-year term for the machinist apprentice shortened to 6,000 hours or approximately 3 years. In addition to the term length, almost all the programs had one other feature in common—the assignment of a very substantial part of the training to work on the engine lathe. Indeed, the engine lathe is probably the most universally used machine and its operation is difficult and complex.[7]

The difference between average programs and those that are either more flexible or more schematic can best be clarified by a comparison of actual work schedules. Probably the best examples of an average training program for machinist apprenticeship are offered by the standards prepared by the local committees of Houston, Texas, and Memphis, Tennessee.[8] These are not intended for specific enterprises but are designed to suggest working schedules for apprentices in those particular areas. The number of months allotted to various work processes by the two programs is shown below. Both standards contain special clauses warning against too rigid adherence to the amount of time suggested for

	Memphis	Houston
Preliminary: assisting in toolroom for acquiring names and uses of hand tools, hack sawing, etc.	1–3	1–3
Drill press, single spindle & radial	1–3	2–3
Engine lathe	9–11	8–10
Turret lathe & screw machine	—	3–5
Planer	2–4	2–4
Shaper and slotter	2–4	3–5
Universal milling machine & vertical milling machine	7–9	4–6
Boring mills, horizontal & vertical	3–5	3–6
Grinding machines—external, internal, & surface grinding	1–3	—
Tool forming, toolmaking, heat treating	1–3	—
Layout	2–4	2–4
Erection floor & bench work	2–4	2–4
Electric & oxyacetylene welding	1–3	3–5
Dismantling and erection in commercial work, etc.	3–5	—

[7] In other countries, lathe hand is treated as an apprenticeable trade.

[8] U.S. Labor Statistics Division, *Houston, Texas, Machinists' Apprenticeship Standards* . . . (Washington, 1940) and *Memphis, Tennessee, Machinists' Apprenticeship Standards* . . . (Washington, 1941).

each of the machines and both concede the necessity for changes in the schedules to suit special enterprises.[9]

For the most part, the programs coincide with regard to subjects included and they are fairly similar in distribution of time. Each program, however, contains subjects that are not included in the other. Memphis, for example, does not include the turret lathe, the operation of which may be learned in a short time, but which presents difficult problems of work setup, maintenance, and repair. Houston omits any reference to grinding, a skilled occupation and an integral part of almost every machinist apprentice's training. Memphis enlarges its program by the inclusion of dismantling and erection in commercial work and, also in contrast to Houston, allots 1 to 3 months to tool forming, toolmaking, and heat treating, the last of which is itself an apprenticeable trade; not more than a smattering of the basic elements of this most complicated of all machinist subjects could be given in so short a period. The time differences for training on milling machines, a subject included in both programs, may well be the result of the character of the local industries and the extent to which these machines are used.

The program of the Bath (Maine) Iron Works Corporation is representative of those schedules distinguished by their flexibility. It provides that for the first 500 hours the apprentice shall act as a helper on different jobs on the floor, bench, and machines. Thereafter he is to be assigned to the machines for small work, such as drilling, milling, shaping, and small lathe work. At the end of 1,000 hours he is to be allowed to operate machines independently and is to be given a variety of work with increasing responsibility. At some time during his apprenticeship he is to be assigned to the drawing room. Beyond this outline all other details of the working schedule are left to the discretion of the employer and the apprentice supervisor.

Another example of flexibility is the program of the Manitowoc (Wisconsin) Shipbuilding Company. This allots 3 to 6 months to

[9] Most agreements contain similar clauses.

both toolroom attendance and bolt cutter and drill press; 3 to 8 months to miscellaneous work, repairs and the like; and 12 months each to lathes and boring mills; shapers, planers, and milling machines; assembling, erecting, bench work, and layout work material; and inspecting and drafting. The program makes it clear that the processes are not 'necessarily to be taught in the order listed, nor will all the time on a single process necessarily be continuous. Furthermore, other processes intended to improve the quality of the apprentice in his trade may be added, if deemed desirable.'

The working schedule of the Griscom Russell Company, Inc., of Massillon, Ohio, exemplifies the highly schematic type. It divides apprenticeship into eight 6-month periods, each devoted to a special machine or group of operations—namely, drill press, engine lathe, horizontal boring machine, vertical turret lathe, small milling machine, horizontal turret lathe, planer, and tool room and (erection) assembly.

The programs of Lockhead Aircraft, Vultee Aircraft, and Sperry Gyroscope Company are also carefully planned in all details (Table 8). The Lockheed program places major emphasis on engine lathes, milling machines, and bench work, these three subjects together accounting for almost 45 per cent of the instruction time. The Vultee program is divided into two 4,000-hour periods, the first consisting more or less of training in operations, while the major part of the second is occupied with advanced machine training. The latter probably includes the more difficult branches, especially engine lathes, which are given only 600 training hours in the first period. At first glance, the Sperry program appears to be less typical of machinist training than the other two, but if the time on turning and on the engine lathe is combined, the importance of the training on this machine assumes its proper place. The greater emphasis laid on milling and profiling is probably demanded by the nature of the product.

The standards of very large enterprises that train machinists are

TABLE 8. DISTRIBUTION OF TRAINING TIME FOR MACHINIST APPRENTICES IN THREE LARGE INDUSTRIAL PLANTS, BY TYPE OF OPERATION

LOCKHEED AIRCRAFT [a]		VULTEE AIRCRAFT [b]		SPERRY GYROSCOPE CO. [c]	
Operation	*Hours*	*Operation*	*Hours*	*Operation*	*Hours*
Bench hand	300	*First 4,000-hour period:*		Misc. (incl. shaper)	320(320)
Drill presses	500	Drill press	350	Drill press	640(160)
Turret lathe	500	Engine lathes	600	Turning (all types)	800(800)
		Turret lathes	250		
Engine lathes	1,800	Milling machines	600	Bench lathe	480
Milling machine	1,000	Planer	250	Hand screw mach. or turret lathe	640
Planer	300	Shaper	250	Precision grinding	1,120(320)
		Tool grinding	250		
Shaper	500	Precision grinding	500	Engine lathe	480
Turret lathe job setter	500	Heat treatment	250	Milling & profiling	1,280(480)
Precision grinding	200	Bench layout	350	Engraving	160
		Inspection	350		
Tool grinding	700	*Second 4,000-hour period:*		Gear cutting	160
Inspection	200	Welding	800	Aeronautical assembly	480
Bench machinist	1,000	Advanced machine trg.	2,250	Other assembly	640
Special work [d]	320	Office system	150	Tool room	320
		Misc. assignments	800	Inspection	320
Miscellaneous [e]	500			Review	160(160)
TOTAL	8,320	TOTAL	8,000	TOTAL	8,000

[a] U.S. Labor Standards Division, *Lockheed Aircraft Apprenticeship Program*, 1939, p. 5.
[b] U.S. Labor Standards Division, *Apprenticeship Standards for Vultee Aircraft, Inc., Nashville Division, Nashville, Tenn.*, 1941, p. 4.
[c] U.S. Labor Standards Division, *Apprenticeship Standards of Sperry Gyroscope Company, Inc.*, 1940, p. 2. Figures in parentheses indicate training in apprentice shop.
[d] Production office, tabulating operation sheets, office system in department.
[e] These remaining hours may be spent on any or all of the above operations, depending on business conditions and the ability

differentiated among themselves and serve to distinguish the several types of machinist. The Ford Motor Company, for example, has the following different work schedules for three kinds of machinist: [10]

(1) Machine repairmen and machinists: shaper, planer, slotter, 1,000 hours; engine lathe, 1,000; milling machine, 1,000; grinding, 1,000; optional, 1,000; bench and floor, 3,000.

(2) Locomotive machinists: locomotive repair, 1,433 hours; crane repair, 1,000; shaper, planer, slotter, 1,000; lathe, 1,000; milling, 900; grinders, 667; pump shop, 1,000; speed reducers, 1,000.

(3) Airframe machinist: lathe, 2,400 hours; milling, 1,300; drill work, 500; grinder, 1,000; bench, 500; heat treating, 300.

Lathe, milling machine, and grinding occur in each of the types, but with special emphasis in the program for the airframe machinists. For the machine repairmen and machinists, bench work is stressed, while all other activities are divided into periods of equal length. The schedule for the locomotive machinists only partially reveals the operations involved; locomotive repair probably includes considerable bench and assembly work, and the same may be true for crane repair. The airframe machinist, trained for only 6,000 hours, in contrast to the 8,000 required for each of the other machinists, emerges as a specialist but with good all-round training except in bench or layout work.

The Tennessee Valley Authority also trains two types of machinist apprentices: construction machinists and gas-Diesel machinists. Both training schedules provide for comparatively little machine shop work, but accord more emphasis to assembling, dismantling, and repair. The Diesel machinists spend no less than 5,000 of their 7,000 hours on gas-Diesel equipment, and only 1,000 on machine shop.[11]

The extent to which working schedules for mechanics may differ from those for traditional machinists is shown in the Ameri-

[10] Ford Motor Co. and UAW-CIO, *Apprenticeship Standards* (Dearborn, Mich., 1943), pp. 7, 8, 18.

[11] U.S. Apprentice-Training Service, *Report on Apprentice-Training Program of the Tennessee Valley Authority* (Washington, 1942), Appendix S.

can Airlines' three-year training program for an airline mechanic apprentice, which is arranged as follows: [12]

(1) Approximately 15 months for line service and line maintenance (line servicing ships—cleaning; spark plug reconditioning; daily major engine and propeller checks; general engine repairs; landing gear major checks; hydraulic systems; general airline repairs; trouble-shooting; servicing de-icer, heating, ventilating systems; instrument and electrical checks and service; accessory and engineering changes).

(2) Approximately 9 months for engine, propeller, and accessory overhaul (engine disassembly—cleaning; cylinder and piston work; clowers and reduction gears; crankshafts and bearings; final assembly—timing-test stand; propellers; mechanical accessories; electrical accessories).

(3) Approximately 10 months for airplane overhaul (metal structure and general metal repairs; interior and unit refinishing and repairs; hydraulic systems—cleaning; control and cable systems; miscellaneous assembly; electrical systems; general repairs; engineering changes).

(4) Approximately 2 months for instrument overhaul (handling and packing of instruments, parts, etc.; general care of shop instrument systems; engine instruments; flight instruments).

Auto mechanics have somewhat less crowded working schedules, as is indicated by the St. Paul, Minnesota, apprenticeship standards.[13] The subjects covered and the time distribution of the 8,320 hours is as follows: brakes, 750 hours; steering and front end system, 770; rear axle, 750; transmission and clutch, 1,500; motor, 2,000; tune-up and electrical (ignition, battery, starter, lights, generator, carburation), 2,000; miscellaneous (springs, frame, rattles, soldering, welding), 550.

It is obvious that training for both types of mechanics is concentrated on the mechanics and functioning of the machinery to be

[12] U.S. Labor Standards Division, *Report on Apprenticeship System* . . . (cited above), Exhibit D.

[13] U.S. Labor Standards Division, *St. Paul, Minnesota, Automobile Mechanics Apprenticeship Standards* (Washington, 1942), p. 2.

served and to a lesser degree on operational skills. Good technical instruction is therefore essential for the success of these training programs.

The following working schedule, based on standards for a five-year plumber's apprenticeship drawn up by the Seattle Joint Apprenticeship Committee, is an example of a detailed outline of the work to be done, in which, however, no indication is given of the amount of time to be spent on learning the various operations. The subjects include: installation of piping for waste, soil, sewerage, vent and leader lines; installations of piping for hot and cold water for domestic purposes; installation of lead pipe, tin pipe, wiped joints, sheet lead, and solder work; assembly in position and connection of fixtures and appliances used in the plumbing and drainage systems; welding connected with the trade; maintenance and repair of plumbing; operation, care, and use of all tools connected with the trade; operation and maintenance of the complete repair service and kit; safety as applied on the job, and local and state laws as applicable to work.[14]

There is little point in analyzing thoroughly and critically the programs cited here; their value lies more in the way they are executed than in the outline of subjects included and the time to be spent on each. But the impression given by most of the programs is that the apprenticeship committees are more concerned with including work on every type of machinery than with giving thorough training on those machines that can be operated only by highly skilled workers. The drill press, shaper, and slotter, for example, are usually run by an operative and could therefore be given less emphasis in apprenticeship schedules, while bench and lathe work could be taught more extensively. The task of apprenticeship is, of course, to provide broad knowledge of the operation of the various machines, but it must not overlook the importance of a complete understanding of some of the machines by which the most difficult and diversified work is done.

[14] U.S. Labor Standards Division, *Seattle Plumbing Apprenticeship Standards* (Washington, 1940), p. 2.

RELATED SCHOOL INSTRUCTION

Whereas schools are well equipped to provide technical instruction related to a trade, but less well equipped for teaching operational skills, the reverse is true of the plants that offer apprentice training. Supplementary classroom instruction in apprentice training has therefore long been recognized as essential. In the days when apprenticeship started at the age of fourteen, after eight or even fewer years of grammar school, the classroom instruction was intended to improve the apprentice's knowledge of such basic subjects as English and arithmetic. Today, however, basic knowledge of these subjects can be largely taken for granted, and the greater part of supplementary classroom instruction need be devoted only to the related technical subjects that have become so important for most trades.

The subjects currently taught fall into two main categories. One is fairly general, comprising blueprint reading, drafting, shop mathematics, and safety regulations, business English (correspondence, minutes of meetings, and reports on job progress). In the other group, the subjects are more closely related to the trade and are planned separately for each occupation. In addition to technical instruction in the narrower sense, they often include some shop instruction aimed at teaching special work processes and the use of special machinery. This part of the instruction is particularly valuable for apprentices in small shops for whom there may be no other opportunity of becoming informed on advanced production methods.

Almost all apprentice standards formulated under the Fitzgerald Act provide for a minimum of 144 hours a year, or about 4 hours a week on the basis of a 38-week school year, to be spent in school. A few standards require 200 hours, while others suggest that school attendance be required only in the first three years of apprenticeship.

The government has promoted related instruction in apprentice training, not only by making provision for it in standards but also by providing financial aid within the framework of the Smith-Hughes Act. In 1940, 62,419 of the 84,000 employed apprentices enumerated by the census—or about 75 per cent—were enrolled in federally aided public vocational high school classes for apprentices.

The introduction of special apprentice classes into the vocational high school system marked the beginning of a program of cooperation between educational authorities and agencies and those responsible for apprentice training. A number of apprenticeship agreements now advise the local and plant apprenticeship committees to arrange with local vocational education authorities for special apprentice classes. Such cooperation is also in evidence at the state level; the Connecticut State Apprenticeship Council, for instance, reports that 'arrangements have been made through the Secretary of the Council and the State and local departments of Education to provide this related instruction. This entailed a complete canvass of all of the local boards of education in communities where approved programs were in existence. In contacting each board of education, the program of the State Council was explained and the assistance and cooperation of the local school authorities was enlisted. Schools were then designated in each community to handle this related instruction.' [15] The New York State Apprenticeship Council has established a similar relationship.

Corporations training groups of apprentices large enough to warrant the establishment of classes of their own frequently make independent arrangements with the local education authorities, which permit plant personnel to instruct apprentices on a part-time basis and to be paid out of Smith-Hughes funds.

Another means of providing related instruction is the union trade school, an example of which is the one operated by Local 3 of the International Brotherhood of Electrical Workers in New York City. But even this school leans heavily on the public school system, with which it has arranged for related instruction of ap-

[15] U.S. Labor Statistics Division, *Report on the State Apprenticeship System in Connecticut* (Washington, 1941), p. 16.

prentices at Stuyvesant High School, thus bringing this aspect of its apprentice-training program within the jurisdiction of the Board of Education of the City of New York.

The courses of the International Correspondence Schools are also often used in apprentice schools. Where regular schools are not easily available for related instruction, enrollment in the ICS courses may even be substituted for school attendance. This institution has played an important role in providing related technical instruction and its influence should by no means be minimized, though it can be assumed that with the expansion and improvement of vocational high school education the need for correspondence courses is likely to lessen.

The cost of related instruction is seldom borne by the apprentices. It is generally covered either by public funds or by employers.

COMPENSATION

Unlike the apprentices in Europe, apprentices in this country are not expected to consider the opportunity to learn a trade their main compensation for the labor they contribute. Boys of eighteen —the average age at which apprenticeship is entered upon here— are physically and mentally mature, and capable of working at full capacity. They are therefore held to be workers rather than students, and, as such, entitled to remuneration almost as great as that of other workers of their age.

This acknowledgment is expressed in the standards of the National Apprenticeship Program, which provides for 'a progressively increasing scale of wages for apprentices that should average approximately 50 per cent of the journeyman's rate over the period of apprenticeship.'[16] In accordance with this stipulation, wages are usually below 50 per cent at the start and above 50 per cent at the end of the apprenticeship term. Individual contracts may define the apprentice wages either in terms of percentages of jour-

[16] U.S. Apprentice-Training Service, *The National Apprenticeship Program* (cited above), p. 2.

neymen's wages or in absolute amounts, that is, cents per hour. The following examples of both methods illustrate their application. They are, however, representative only of registered apprentice agreements arrived at by collective bargaining. When agreements are made with shops that are neither registered nor unionized, the apprentice wage scales may be lower.

The national standards for apprenticeship in the electrical construction industry deal with the wage problem in rather general terms, stipulating that in the first years the wages should be low, but not less than 25 per cent, and in the last two years, high enough to average at least 50 per cent, of a journeyman's wage for the whole period.

In other agreements the wages are expressed partly in cent values and partly in percentages of journeymen's wages. Thus the Lockheed Aircraft Corporation agreement sets its wage scale partly in terms of journeymen's wages and partly in cent values; the starting wage is not less than 30 per cent of the journeyman's or senior mechanic's rate and increases 6 cents per hour every 6 months. The reverse policy is followed by the Pattern Makers' Standards of Chicago. Here the scale is given in terms of cents per hour for the first 18 months and in terms of an ascending percentage of the journeyman's wage rate for the next 2½ years, each increase occurring after a 6-month period.

The diemakers and sinkers who serve a seven-year apprenticeship have an exceptionally liberal wage scale. Diemaker apprentice wages range from 32 to 58 per cent of journeymen's wages, while for diesinkers the range is from 64 to 96 per cent, so that the latter, by the end of the term, are getting compensation almost equal to that of the journeymen.

Apprentice wage schedules for eight groups of enterprises may be compared in Table 9. Most of these standards were approved in 1940 or 1941 and may therefore have undergone considerable change since then, in line with the general trend of wage adjustments. For the most part, the wages for the first year of apprenticeship were less than those of an unskilled helper, while in the later years they rose considerably, and in the last year, at least, were exceeded only by those of skilled workers.

Increases are usually on a semiannual basis, but some agreements provide for more frequent raises, especially during the first two years when the wages are relatively low. Most standards state that wage increases should not be automatic but that they should depend on the successful completion of examinations, that apprentices may be required to repeat certain parts of their training, and

TABLE 9. HOURLY WAGE SCALES FOR APPRENTICES
(SIX-MONTH PERIODS OVER FOUR YEARS)
IN REPRESENTATIVE INDUSTRY GROUPS, 1940–41 [a]

Industry Group	1st	2nd	3rd	4th	5th	6th	7th	8th
I [b]	$.30	$.35	$.40	$.45	$.50	$.55	$.65	$.75
II [c]	.40	.45	.50	.55	.60	.65	.70	.80
III [d]	.30	.35	.40	.45	.55	.60	.70	.80
IV [e]	.40–45 [f]	.50	.55	.60	.65	.70	.75	.80
V [g]	.50	.56	.62	.66	.70	.74	.80	.86
VI [h]	.42	.44	.46	.48	.51	.55	.60	.65
VII [i]	.30	.32	.35	.38	.41	.45	.50	.55
VIII [j]	.38	.45	.52	.59	.66	.73	.80	.87

[a] Enterprises operating under agreements with National Apprenticeship Program.

[b] Auto truck mechanics apprenticeship standards for truck mechanics of Philadelphia, approved in 1941.

[c] Manitowoc Shipbuilding Company, approved in 1941; Griscom-Russell Company, Massillon, Ohio, approved 1940; Vultee Aircraft, Nashville, Tenn., approved 1941.

[d] Memphis machinist standards, approved 1941.

[e] St. Paul auto mechanics standards; periods of increase are 1,040 hours instead of 1,000 hours.

[f] The lower figure applies for the first 500 hours (probationary period).

[g] Bath iron workers, approved 1941.

[h] American Airlines, Inc., approved 1941.

[i] Kearney & Trecker Corp., Allis, Wis., 1941.

[j] Seattle plumbers' apprentices.

that time lost by absence must be made up before transfer to the next higher wage bracket can be made. Some agreements also allow credit for previous experience in the trade. In these circumstances the term of apprenticeship is shortened and the apprentice starts with the wages in the bracket commensurate with his advanced rating. These credits are not given indiscriminately, however, and in most instances are based on a proration of time.

Apprentices are frequently paid for the time spent in related classroom instruction, while in other cases they have to attend these classes without compensation. There are also instances in which half the related instruction time is paid for by the employer, while the apprentices attend without remuneration during the other half.

APPRENTICE-JOURNEYMAN RATIOS

In each of the apprenticeship programs provision is made for the ratio of apprentices to journeymen according to the needs of the trade or of the individual enterprise. This is done in order to avoid overtraining in specific trades, with a resultant imbalance in the labor market, and to equalize the opportunities for work by eliminating undue competition between journeymen and apprentices. It is also necessary in order to guarantee adequate and proper training, which would be jeopardized by an excess of apprentices.

The regulations governing ratios vary considerably. In many cases they allow much latitude and their interpretation is left to the apprenticeship committee; thus at Vultee Aircraft and also at Sperry Gyroscope, the plant committees set the ratio on the recommendation of the factory or apprenticeship superintendents. The Ford Motor Company standards assign to the apprenticeship committee the task of working out a plan for the establishment of a suitable ratio to be mutually agreed upon by the company and the union. The national standards program for the electrical construction industry maintains that 'the ratio of apprentices to journeymen varies, but should be determined by collective bargaining.' [17]

There are also many instances in which ratios are prescribed. A

[17] U.S. Labor Standards Division, *National Apprenticeship Standards for the Electrical Construction Industry*, Bulletin No. 50 (Washington, 1942), p. 4.

flat 1:10 ratio is frequent, especially among machinist, tool and die-makers, and auto mechanics. There are also higher ratios. The mechanics agreement of American Airlines provides that the number of apprentices shall not exceed 30 per cent of the total number of chief mechanics, inspectors, lead mechanics, senior mechanics, and mechanics—in other words a ratio of 1:3.3. The Memphis and Houston committees for apprentice machinists have established a ratio of 1:5 and an additional apprentice for each shop. The Seattle plumbers' apprenticeship standards and those for the auto mechanic apprentices in St. Paul call for the same ratio; 4 apprentices, however, are the ceiling, and in the St. Paul standards it is also stipulated that enterprises with less than 3 mechanics or specialists may not hire an apprentice. A ratio of 1 apprentice per employer, plus 1 per 7 journeymen, is found in the machinist, tool and die-making standards of Philadelphia; 1 per employer, plus 1 per 8 journeymen, is introduced by the patternmakers of Chicago. At the Kearney & Trecker Corporation of West Allis, Wisconsin, 9 per cent of the men engaged in skilled trades are apprentices.

These individual ratios are, on the whole, not unfavorable to apprenticeship, indicating that the provisions contained in these agreements do not restrict apprenticeship unduly. The number of enterprises, however, which employ apprentices is very small. These few, therefore, would have to employ an excessive number, quite out of proportion to their training facilities and beyond the limits imposed by the ratios, in order to make up for the deficiency in the labor force as a whole.

Most of the standards contain provisions for proportionate reductions in the number of apprentices if it becomes necessary to reduce the number of journeymen in a plant. But provision is also made in many standards to protect apprentices against undue hardship in these circumstances, which involve not only the loss of employment but also a break in the continuity of the learning process. Arrangements are often made to transfer an apprentice to another company without interruption of training; other agreements foresee the maintenance of seniority rights in the event that the

apprentices are re-employed when the original number of journeymen is reinstated. These are moves in the right direction,
since layoffs of apprentices require more consideration than those
of other workers.

A more direct solution for all these problems may be found in
the growing practice of organizing apprenticeship for a trade, as
a whole, rather than for individual plants. Over-all ratios of apprenticeship to journeymen allow for greater flexibility; if one
plant employs no apprentices, another may then be permitted to
exceed the number stipulated for an enterprise of its size. The
ultimate effect of this broader planning may well be an increase
in the total number of apprentices, which would be highly desirable.

XII

Attitudes of Management and Labor toward Vocational Education and Training

VIEWS ON APPRENTICESHIP

BECAUSE of its direct bearing on the supply of workers—especially, skilled workers—both management and labor have a stake in occupational training. Whereas management generally welcomes a vast, and therefore cheap, labor force, labor finds itself in a stronger position when the number of workers in a given trade is restricted. Throughout the nineteenth century these opposed interests repeatedly led to mutual accusations: employers complained of the restrictive influence of union policies on apprentice training, while unions accused employers of apprentice breeding and of using apprentices as cheap labor under the pretext of giving them all-round training. Nevertheless, both groups have always been in fundamental agreement that good apprentice training is highly desirable and that cause for complaint lies only in the abuse of the system or its undue restriction.

Reviewing the numerical development of apprenticeship during the last century, it is difficult to understand precisely what either group found to protest. Unions, it is true, insisted on apprentice-journeymen ratios, but as the industrial system developed, the actual number of apprentices fell consistently below the level permitted. That fact alone should have removed grounds for both management and union charges. Confronted with this paradox, Paul Douglas explains it by saying that union complaints were justified in part by local overcrowding in certain trades and that, moreover, they were aimed at the increase of industrial child labor rather than at the number of bona fide apprentices.[1]

Obviously, some of the dying hand trades were bound to become overcrowded even without the entrance of many new trainees into the field, especially since immigration continuously furnished a great number of skilled workers for contracting as well as for expanding industries and trades. More generally, it must be remembered that American industry has moved in cycles. In times of depression and large-scale unemployment it is only natural that labor should consider any training activity excessive, no matter how limited it may be. On the other hand, in prosperous times employers have been quick to deplore the scarcity of skilled labor.

Despite the fact, however, that a preoccupation with economic considerations has always dominated the workers' stand on systematic in-employment training, labor has generally supported the idea of apprenticeship, and in recent years has cooperated actively in establishing apprentice standards. But this same concern with economic factors has caused labor to maintain an unfavorable attitude toward learnership, at least in the craft trades, since it considers this kind of training a mere dilution of skills and a threat to the standards set by apprenticeship programs.

Views on In-School Training

The attitude of management and labor toward in-school occupational training has usually been expressed on a different level. Successful individual manufacturers and businessmen, in establishing private trade schools for industrial education, gave concrete expression to their belief in the practical and educational value of manual training. With the steady decline of apprenticeship these schools became more and more numerous, a circumstance that aroused the concern of the unions who suspected these institutions of being sources of cheap and subservient labor. When, after 1900, the National Association of Manufacturers strongly supported the

[1] Paul H. Douglas, *American Apprenticeship and Industrial Education* (New York, 1921), p. 74.

expansion of privately financed and privately controlled trade schools, unions grew even more suspicious.

Organized labor's attitude toward industrial education, however, was never merely negative. Indeed, its partial obstructionism can be truly evaluated only in the light of its long and intense interest in an improved general education for the masses of the working force.

American labor has played an important role in the democratization of education since the 1830's. Its spokesmen, backing the movement for more and better schools, were among the most enthusiastic supporters of progressive education. Convinced that its expansion would prevent poverty, preserve the free institutions of the republic, maintain the natural equality of man, and generally raise the standard of living,[2] labor demanded educational reforms, competent teachers, a ladder system of free public schools, and school boards chosen by the people and responsible to them.[3]

During the early years of the last century, the agitation for the inclusion of manual training in education aroused no particular interest among the workers; they were far more concerned with the larger problems of general education. Nevertheless, certain labor groups endorsed manual training as a school subject and others recommended that young people be enabled to combine gainful work with continued study.

When the Morrill Act was passed in 1862 it was regarded by the Knights of Labor as a fine precedent for the extension of public aid to schools for mechanics.[4] This organization, which dominated the labor movement during the 1870's and 1880's, did not, however, pledge itself to the unqualified support of vocational and technical education. Like its predecessors, it was primarily concerned with general education and especially with the extension

[2] Horace M. Kallen, *Education, the Machine and the Worker* (New York, 1925), pp. 4-5.

[3] American Federation of Labor, *Report of the Proceedings of the 64th Annual Convention . . . 1944*, p. 219.

[4] Ellwood P. Cubberly, *Public Education in the United States* (New York, 1919), p. 280; Philip R. V. Curoe, *Educational Attitudes and Policies of Organized Labor in the United States* (New York, 1926), pp. 8-9, 14-21.

of school attendance. Nevertheless it supported the inclusion of practical training in school programs, and took a sympathetic interest in the revival of the manual training movement. But unlike other groups, it drew a sharp distinction between manual and vocational training, favoring the former for its development of the hands and arms, but opposing the latter as specific trade training that would disturb the labor market.[5]

The American Federation of Labor shared not only the Knights of Labor's enthusiasm for education and its fight for extended compulsory school attendance, but also its suspicion of the role of vocational training in schools. When, however, the industrial education movement got under way early in this century, labor felt the need to develop a firmer, more positive stand on the matter of vocational education. Accordingly, it evolved a philosophy shaped by two main considerations: on the educational side, by its conviction of the high value of education and of vocational education as the task of the public school; on the economic side, by the conviction of the need for our educational system to devise an equivalent for apprenticeship.[6] Its support of vocational education, however, was contingent on the continued maintenance of a 'fair and proper apportionment of the supply of labor power to the demand for labor power in every line of work.'[7]

For more than ten years, investigations were carried on by the committee on education of the AFL, and annual conventions repeatedly weighed the educational value of vocational education against the possible economic disadvantage to labor. From these studies and discussions there evolved a generally favorable attitude toward public vocational education. In 1910, the year in which the work of the National Society for the Promotion of Industrial Education began to arouse national attention, the AFL committee

[5] Curoe, op. cit. p. 280.
[6] American Federation of Labor, *Report of the Proceedings of the 29th Annual Convention* . . . 1911, p. 109.
[7] Samuel Gompers, 'The Attitude of the AFL toward Industrial Education,' an address before the National Society for the Promotion of Industrial Education, Richmond, Va., 10 December 1914.

crystallized its views on industrial education and was prepared to make concrete recommendations to the annual convention: 'We favor the establishment of schools in connection with the public school system at which pupils between the ages of fourteen and sixteen may be taught the principles of the trade, not necessarily in separate buildings but in separate schools adapted to this particular education . . . [the] course of instruction in such a school should be English, mathematics, physics, chemistry, elementary mechanics and drawing, mechanics, physiological and biological science applicable to the trade, the history of that trade, and a sound system of economics, including and emphasizing the philosophy of collective bargaining . . . there should be local advisory boards, including representatives of the industries, employers and organized labor . . . Industrial education should be a public function, conducted by the public . . . at public cost.' [8] In this brief statement the Federation established a policy to which it has, in the main, adhered.

Four years later, before the eighth annual convention of the National Society for the Promotion of Industrial Education, the Federation, through its president, Samuel Gompers, officially joined the Society in its efforts to gain federal legislation in support of vocational education. [9] The role of the AFL in securing the passage of the Smith-Hughes Bill was far from negligible, [10] and in the years following the bill's passage, organized labor kept a vigilant watch over its administration. The school curriculums were of particular interest and the variety of trades taught were under the constant scrutiny of the committee on education.

In 1919 the AFL committee on education urged more diversified training for school youth, with the expressed aim of insuring democratic equality of opportunity for all children to prepare for 'the

[8] American Federation of Labor Committee on Industrial Education, *Industrial Education* (Washington, 1912), p. 21.

[9] Gompers, op. cit. pp. 4–8.

[10] Lloyd E. Blasch, 'Federation Cooperation in Agricultural Extension Work, Vocational Education and Vocational Rehabilitation,' U.S. Office of Education Bulletin 1933, No. 15, pp. 60–61.

calling of their choice.' [11] This cannot, however, be construed as an unconditional demand for free admittance, according to individual preference and regardless of labor market conditions, to any of the various types of schools, especially vocational high schools, because at the time the problem was more or less theoretical and remained so until public vocational high schools had gained considerable ground. A noticeable change in the attitude of organized labor occurred in the thirties, when the expansion of public vocational education coincided with the economic depression and threatened the balance of labor supply and demand. Labor continued to support the idea of in-school vocational training, but began to subordinate the educational aspects to economic considerations. The shift in emphasis became clearly evident for the first time in 1935 when the AFL committee on education voiced its protest against what it termed abuses in the use of federal funds, charging that financial aid had been granted to schools located wholly within private industrial plants and operated in a manner that tended to overcrowd certain skilled trades and to lower wages.[12] At the Federation convention in the following year the committee presented its detailed formulation of conditions under which a public school system would be justified in establishing training programs within a private industrial plant.[13] It also recommended that 'State Federations of Labor and Central Labor Unions take steps to set up local advisory committees to advise on all plans of vocational education.' [14] This, of course, was not a new phase of labor's support of vocational education; it merely served to accent its already established policy with regard to these committees and its own participation in them, in order to exert greater influ-

[11] American Federation of Labor, *Report of the Proceedings of the 39th Annual Convention* . . . 1919, p. 431.

[12] American Federation of Labor, *Report of the Proceedings of the 55th Annual Convention* . . . 1935.

[13] American Federation of Labor, *Report of the Proceedings of the 56th Annual Convention* . . . 1936, p. 181; *American Federationist* (March 1936), pp. 242–3, 251–5.

[14] American Federation of Labor, *Report of the Proceedings of the 56th Annual Convention* . . . 1936, p. 409.

ence in the administration and promotion of vocational education.

Organized labor's agitation for better, more vigilant supervision of vocational education reached a peak in 1937 when the George-Deen Act, increasing the amount of federal aid to vocational education, was presented for approval by the Congress. Despite the explicit negative provision in the bill barring the use of training programs in industrial plants unless they provided bona fide vocational training, labor's opposition to the increased appropriation was so strong that on signing the bill President Roosevelt called for an investigation of the whole vocational setup.

The committee appointed by the President published a comprehensive study, to which was appended the report on the experience of labor with vocational education, prepared by the committee's labor members. This report contained the sharpest criticism of vocational educational practices ever voiced by organized labor, and presented recommendations that would have meant the virtual abolition of vocational education at the secondary level and severe restriction of vocational training in all other fields. The stand taken by the report was neither approved by the entire membership of the Federation, nor was it accepted as official policy. The Federation did, however, insist more strongly than before on reforms in vocational education practices and administration, and on more widespread labor representation on advisory committees for vocational education. Its attitude has, on the whole, continued to be favorable to the expansion of public vocational education, subject, however, to constant adjustment of educational ideals to economic needs.

Prevailing Support

The foregoing opinions of representatives of management and organized labor were stated mainly at national conventions, and being couched in general terms, they did not touch on everyday, practical problems; they offered, therefore, little ground for specific opposition. The views of individual employers and trade union leaders, who cope with these specific problems in the course of their jobs, are much more difficult to elicit and to evaluate. A report of the New York Regents' Inquiry,[15] for instance, states flatly that a questionnaire sent to the Central Labor Council in 1936 evoked so few answers that no conclusions could be drawn. Any investigation, however, made at that time, when the effects of the long depression were still being felt, especially by the building trades, could hardly have met with success. In those circumstances, unions were scarcely eager to hear anything about the training of new workers; from their vantage point it appeared that the oversupply of labor would last indefinitely. At the same time, no leading union representative cared to go on record against vocational education, since such a stand would be in contradiction to labor's national policy.

In the meantime, of course, conditions have greatly changed. Not only has unemployment given way to a scarcity of labor, but the position of most unions has definitely improved. The fear that in-school vocational training could be used to undermine the strength and bargaining powers of unions has been virtually dissipated. The active participation of unions in the establishment and conduct of vocational and technical high schools is more frequent, though still the exception rather than the rule. In general, the relations between a union and a vocational high school depend more upon the personalities in both bodies than on general union principles.

Though outspoken hostility on the part of union leaders toward vocational high schools has become exceedingly rare, the immediate occupational value of in-school training is not so highly esteemed by organized labor as one might like to think. The craft unions do not admit that vocational high school attendance can take the place of one or two years of apprentice training, and even unions composed mainly of operatives hesitate to give schools much credit for the development of really marketable skills. They do, however, regard the vocational high schools as an effective medium for interesting young students in the development of their chosen trade

[15] Thomas L. Norton, *Education for Work* (New York, 1938).

or industry, in the technical principles underlying production, and in the social history of the industry and of organized labor. Indeed, many unions feel that the teaching of labor relations and union principles has at least as much bearing upon the well-being of future workers as the technical and manipulative skills they obtain in such schools.

Employers, of course, do not lay such stress on the teaching of labor relations, but neither do they demand that this problem be excluded from vocational high school programs or that the instruction be weighted against trade unionism. Managerial interest is expressed in the demand for instruction that will develop 'good work habits, dependability and the ability to get on with their fellows.' [16] It is true that some employers are less tolerant of union influence than others, but, on the whole, the divergent interests of management and labor have ceased to be a serious obstacle to the cooperation of both groups in the development of vocational education.

With respect to direct occupational aims, representatives of many large corporations lay more stress on the teaching of technical knowledge than of manipulative skills. Owners and operators of small workshops, however, are not so definite in their stand on this more theoretical education; they usually need definite skills and would be only too glad if schools would provide them. To what extent schools are prepared to do this, they hesitate to judge. Indeed, inquiries made by this study indicate that most employers do not feel that they have had enough experience in hiring vocational school graduates to be able to evaluate the quality of their training fairly.

Some employers, however, are openly critical of vocational high school graduates, not because of any deficiencies in the education and training provided by the school, but simply because they assume that vocational high school students are of lower caliber than those in academic high schools. This stricture is implied even in

[16] Donald S. Bridgman, 'Education for Work and Citizenship,' in *Yale Review*, vol. 28, no. 1 (September 1938), pp. 93–110.

their praise of a few selected vocational high schools for admitting and graduating only "good" students.

But outspoken and well-founded adverse opinions are rarely encountered among either labor or management representatives. The greatest obstacle to the more effective contribution of these groups to in-school vocational education and training lies in their unfamiliarity with the actual work of existing institutions. Wherever and whenever their interest and participation have been enlisted, they have become loyal supporters of this branch of vocational preparation.

XIII

Vocational Education and Training: Problems and Recommendations

IN the foregoing chapters this study has offered an analysis of the occupational structure of the country and what it implies in the way of desirable, if not absolutely essential, education and training for the worker—particularly, the manual worker—if the interests of the individual and of the economy as a whole are to be best served. The study has endeavored also to outline what forms of occupational education and training are available to the worker and to what extent they are being utilized. In the light of the data assembled, it is inescapably clear that, despite the progress of the last few decades, both in-school and in-employment training still fall far short of our educational goals and our industrial requirements. The problems inherent in both our system as a whole and the details of its functioning are challenging and persistent, but if this nation's economic and social vitality are to be maintained and if the highest level of productivity and a high standard of living for all are to be achieved, solutions for these problems must be found.

THE PLACE OF THE VOCATIONAL HIGH SCHOOL

There is no question that the achievement of the secondary public school in incorporating vocational education and training in its sphere has been notable. But it is equally true that the vocational high school has not attained in all parts of the country the social recognition or the educational prestige of the general high school. This circumstance not only hampers the expansion of a sound vocational high school system but is entirely contrary to the ideals of a free society, in which functional, not social, differences between manual and intellectual labor should prevail, and in which educational opportunities for all the youth of the nation should be equal. Blame for the situation must be divided between the inflexibility and prejudice of public opinion and the defects in the vocational high school system itself.

Too often, in the past, the vocational high school has been regarded as a dumping ground for children whose academic record in the elementary grades gave little or no promise of success in clerical and commercial fields, to say nothing of the professional world. This attitude, however, disregards the fact that the evolution of industrial processes during the last century has been such as to require an increasing amount of mental ability and general education on the part of labor. An understanding of the technical aspects of industry has become as important as manual dexterity for the mastery of many jobs in the economy, and while it is true that not all workers are required to have wide technical knowledge, advancement lies ahead for those who do. The choice of a vocational or technical, rather than a general, high school should therefore be based not on the negative assumption that the student is not good academic material, but rather on the grateful recognition that he has, in addition to a capacity for mental development, an aptitude for manual and technical work. This imposes on those who guide the student's choice of secondary schools an obligation to adopt a more positive attitude toward the vocational high school.

The differentiation among students of varying mental abilities should then be made within each school, and not by segregation in different types of schools. An adequate distribution of mentally gifted children throughout all branches of the school system, and subsequently throughout the producing branch of society, is required by the technical demands of the economy. It would also go far to offset the undemocratic cleavage between the manual worker and the professional and semiprofessional, to raise the standards of the vocational high school, and to heighten its prestige in the eyes of students, teachers, and the public at large.

The failure of the vocational high school to establish its proper standing as an institution of general education may be laid to certain features of its program and pedagogical approach. Obviously, the vocational high school has to provide the basic manual, technical, and intellectual preparation for specific occupations, but it must, at the same time, infuse this preparation with the characteristics of general education if it is to be regarded as being on a level with the academic high school.

To some extent, all in-school vocational education and training includes fields that are considered the province of general education, such as mathematics and science. All occupations in the metal, machine, and electrical industries, for example, involve applied science and presuppose a knowledge of mathematics. Preparations for these occupations, if conceived in broad terms, must therefore accord these subjects at least the same emphasis given them in general education. Indeed, for these and a number of other trades, it would even be desirable to extend such instruction beyond the limits set by the general high school, in order to meet the student's interests and to establish a direct connection between his particular field of study and the general development of science and technology.

These ends, however, cannot be attained without revising the standards set by the Smith-Hughes Act which, by stipulating a maximum, but no minimum, limit on the time to be devoted to general education subjects, permits the cessation of general education for fourteen-year-olds who plan to become workers in the manual and technical occupations. Fortunately, only a small number of the vocational high schools have so far made use of this opportunity to exclude general education from the curriculum, but the opportunity for them to do so without forfeiting federal financial aid must be regarded as a threat to the unity of the whole secondary school system. And it cannot be accepted as a proper basis for the organization of vocational education.

With regard to the subjects that constitute related instruction, current vocational high school practice often follows the rule that teaching in these fields should serve nothing but vocational goals. Such a narrow utilitarian approach may help to solve certain immediate teaching problems, but it does not open the student's mind to the vast complex of which his work is a part, as would the more theoretical approach of the academic high school. Moreover, the application of two fundamentally divergent conceptions of teaching the same subjects to students, all of whom are just beginning to develop a capacity for abstract thinking and higher understanding, whatever type of school they attend, is not compatible with our one-school system. If the future manual or technical worker is to be given the same educational opportunities as the future professional or semiprofessional, a broader interpretation of related instruction is essential.

Another threat to the unity of the American educational system lies in the disruption of continuity between the vocational high school and institutions of higher learning, inherent in the fact that most vocational high schools make no provision for those of their students who might want to go to college. The vocational high school can never achieve equality with the general high school, if its students have to renounce a college education because there is no curriculum designed to meet college entrance requirements. Moreover, there is no justification for forcing on a fourteen-year-old a premature decision regarding the extent of his future education and the nature of his career.

In these circumstances the vocational high school has not been able to realize fully its potential usefulness to industry. Although in-school vocational and technical education cannot be considered either an alternative to apprentice training or a substitute for training on the job, it undoubtedly constitutes the soundest foundation for both. Even if apprenticeship and systematic training on the job were available to a greater extent than they are now, vocational and technical high schools would still be urgently needed to provide the educational background. As it is, these schools now offer

almost the whole of the great body of workers their only opportunity for systematic vocational preparation, and it is not likely
that this situation will be radically altered within the foreseeable
future.

The statistical comparison of the percentage of the high school
population attending vocational high schools with the percentage
of the total labor force engaged in manual and technical pursuits
makes it abundantly clear that the vast majority of persons working
in the trades and industry have had no systematic in-school preparation. The number of persons enrolled in vocational high schools
and preparing for the craft trades far from meets replacement
needs in the field of craftsmanship, which remains so vital a factor
in modern production. As for the training of operatives, only
pioneer work has been done in a few limited fields. Thus, the task
of providing workers with the broad basic training requisite for
mobility in their occupational careers lies ahead.

In the light of the occupational distribution of the labor force
and its implicit educational requirements, it is reasonable to expect
that vocational or technical high schools should command half the
secondary school enrollments. Obviously, such expanded vocational education will always tend to increase the supply of labor for
occupations commanding the greatest amount of learning, skill,
and income. As a trend, this in no way conflicts with economic
needs or with the aims of vocational education, and should not be
discouraged. And since it would increase the productivity of the
nation as a whole, it is consistent with democratic ideals as well.

CONTENT AND LEVEL OF INSTRUCTION

The closer the approach of the vocational high school system to
its proper dimensions, the more care will have to be exercised in
the analysis of the individual occupations, and in the direction of
students into the various trades, in order to avoid an imbalance of
labor supply and demand. Within the vocational high school system, however, there can be no question of adhering too strictly
to the demarcations between individual trades and occupations,

and of distinguishing sharply between the preparation of foremen, supervisors, craftsmen, and operatives. If it is agreed that what the vocational high school can offer most advantageously is basic training, in-school preparation for craftsmanship should not be built around narrow labor market standards.

The fact that, through increasing division of labor in industry, many individual jobs require a smaller range of skills does not mean that in-school vocational education should also become more narrowly specialized. This study has found constant fluctuations in the occupational status of foremen, craftsmen, and operatives. The boundaries are fluid and it would be a mistake to assume that the 12 per cent of jobs requiring the highest skills in manufacturing industry, for example, are held by the same employees throughout their working lives. Thus the function of the vocational high school is to prepare not only for an initial occupation but for the future advancement of the worker as well. This situation calls for basic preparation of a larger student body for craft and technical careers than is immediately suggested by the statistics for any given period, and it requires broader technical education and more widely extended basic training for the manual trades.

Vocational and technical school programs will always concentrate on the traditional apprenticeable trades, but should not be dominated by them at the expense of trades and technical pursuits that have developed only recently or that do not enjoy the prestige of commonly recognized skilled work. The incorporation of a vast area of vocations, old and new, remains a goal for vocational education planning.

For the future operative, appropriate in-school preparation has always posed a serious problem. It is clear from what has been said above that for a considerable number this problem should not exist, since many of them are potential craftsmen and should be trained as such. Moreover, there is no reason why, in such fields as the metal and machine industry, the preparation of students who may remain operatives should not closely approach the training of those who will become craftsmen. There are, however, a number of alternatives to basic training for a craft, which would serve the operative well in his occupational life. For future workers in industries like the textile, clothing, and shoe, which rely mainly on operatives, the most effective and fruitful instruction is that which combines chains of operations and elements of planning and management in an integrated industrial curriculum. Another acceptable approach is the teaching of job families, involving different work in similar materials or the handling of similar machinery in different industries. The educational yield of this last-mentioned type of preparation is admittedly not wholly satisfactory, because adjustment to work is only part of the broader pedagogical objective. But since these programs of study usually require less emphasis on related subjects, their deficiencies may be remedied by allowing for a wider choice of electives in the field of general education. These curriculums, therefore, should not be rejected on principle.

Although basic preparation for work must remain an essential element of secondary vocational education, the other important educational requirements must also be met. To this end, the amount of shopwork in the curriculum should be neither rigidly stipulated nor unduly extended. A minimum of 15 shop hours or 20 periods a week is not necessarily an optimum; it should be regarded as an average, rather than an absolute, requirement. Moreover, shopwork should be offered on a graduated scale, such as the following: 10 shop periods in the 9th grade and 15 in the 10th, in place of the 15 and 20 periods, respectively, in current schedules; 20 periods in the 11th grade, as is now common; and 25 periods in the 12th, in contrast to 20. The reduction of total shopwork hours from 3,000 to 2,800 (2,250 clock hours to 2,100) would not substantially affect the breadth or intensity of basic preparation for a trade. It would, however, leave for nonshop activities 25 of the total 35 weekly periods in the 9th grade, and, of the 40 weekly periods in each of the last three years, 25 in the 10th, 20 in the 11th, and 15 in the 12th. Such an arrangement would make more time available during the first two years for the traditional general education subjects and would give the vocational high school a better chance to achieve its dual purpose. This kind of flexibility would also enable the school better to adjust a student's program to his individual needs.

The proposed schedule would, of course, make for greater similarity of all secondary education, especially in the 9th year, thus easing the student's shift between vocational and academic programs and giving the instructor more opportunity to discern the student's particular abilities and interests. The same ends might be served by requiring junior high school attendance of all pupils and deferring their choice of special schools and programs until after the 9th year. In a great many communities, however, there are no junior high schools. Moreover, the junior high school as it exists today gives no promise that even with extensive reorganization it would be able to explore satisfactorily both the mental and manual aptitudes of the student. In general, they are not much better equipped than elementary schools to provide shopwork facilities that would adequately serve exploratory purposes. For the future manual and technical worker an exploratory 9th year in a vocational school would be far more valuable. It would seem advisable, therefore, to lay stress not on the unified 9th year in a junior high school, but on sufficient similarity in the work of the 9th year in all schools, to facilitate the transfer of students from one type of school to another.

Such transfer will be made easier by the growing acceptance of English, social studies, mathematics, and science, as essential components of all high school curriculums. On this common ground the vocational high school is enabled to move closer to the center of the high school system and to assume a position of full equality with the general high school. With the total of 85 periods for subjects other than shopwork, as suggested above, a typical vocational high school curriculum could offer a 4-year course in English, a 3-year course in social science, a 4 or 3-year course in mathematics, a 3 or 4-year course in scientific and technical instruction (both general and applied), and 2 or 3 weekly periods of health education, leaving 5 periods for electives in the 11th and 12th grades.

In this connection, it is well to repeat what has already been briefly noted as a basic problem in the relationship of the vocational to the general high school: equality presupposes an equal standard of teaching as well as common subjects. This does not, however, preclude differences in the approach to the material. For the vocational high school it implies an abandonment of the idea that facts, rules, or formulas in the fields of mathematics and science should be taught as mere instruments of shopwork, without any theoretical explanation, but it does not demand that the inductive method of teaching be rejected entirely in favor of the deductive system, toward which the general high school leans. Either approach is justified, if its ultimate objective is the student's true knowledge and understanding. With regard to social studies, the general content of the course in the vocational high school should not vary substantially from that of the general high school, but the former may prefer to introduce these subjects as the social and technical history of various industries, proceeding from there to general political and social history. By starting at the point of the student's immediate interest, and interpreting first the growth and functioning of a society within the range of his experience, a much sounder comprehension of the historical background may be achieved.

In any case, whatever the approach, the standards of teaching in both the vocational and general high schools should aim at equal success in developing the mental facilities of their students and preparing them for intelligent citizenship. The educational issue can, of course, never be wholly resolved by discussion of either the content of school programs or the teaching methods to be applied for effective results. Development of the human personality depends as much on the atmosphere of the school, the quality of the teachers, and on an infinite number of other factors—even imponderables. These, however, raise problems for general, as well as vocational, education and are not the special concern of this study.

Desirable Adjustments in School Programs

Various other adjustments in the vocational high school program should be permissible. In a vocational-technical course requiring mainly technical information, shop hours might well be further reduced. Conversely, in courses preparing for trades that demand little related knowledge, the usual related subjects should be replaced by more shopwork or more general education. It should always be possible to make revisions in favor of one subject at the expense of another, according to the particular trade or the student's special requirements.

Adjustments should also be directed at preparation for college. Normally, of course, the vocational high school would continue to prepare for immediate gainful employment in agriculture, industry, or the service occupations. Nevertheless, it should provide an opportunity to prepare for further education at an advanced level by offering a course of study acceptable for college entrance.

Most vocational high school students who aspire to college are likely to be interested in engineering careers, for which the technical high school or a high school of science would generally offer the best preparation. But vocational high school would serve these ends as well, if the curriculum were reorganized to offer less shopwork in the first two years and to teach mathematics and science at the same level as in the general high school. The flexibility and scope of the vocational high school would be further increased if it were to include more vocational-technical classes, a development that is highly desirable in view of the increasing importance of technical knowledge in production.

Indeed, such a development might eventually lead to a definition of the role of purely technical education within the high school system. If the vocational high school should assume the vocational-technical role for which it seems destined, the purely technical high school could then concentrate on preparing only for the engineering professions and for the technical vocations—drafting, designing, laboratory work, and the like—that require familiarity with manual skills only in so far as they further technical understanding. The technical high school would thus become a modern school of applied science in the strictest sense. It would seem advisable to encourage the establishment of more such schools; to outline uniform basic curriculums that would prepare qualified students for their role in the technical world; and, since the need for technical aptitudes and abilities is not confined exclusively to industrial areas, to seek federal aid for a more coordinated development of technical high schools on a national scale. At the same time, the distinction between purely technical, vocational-technical, and purely trade careers should be fluid and mainly a question of degree; no rigid differentiation between technical and vocational high schools should be allowed to develop.

Within a system in which technical instruction would be so widely expanded at the secondary level, the future of the technical institute would depend on its assumption of specific tasks. It is somewhat doubtful that a realistic solution to the problem as a whole can be found in the recent plans for technical institutes of post-high school grade, which are to be attended as an extension of high school. This stricture should not be construed as a negation of the value of such institutions in specific and local cases. New York and certain other cities may offer conditions that favor technical institutes in the form of a 13th and 14th high school year. If the collaboration of management, labor, and educational authorities is secured, and if curriculums are built around the needs of local industries, the handicaps which have hitherto barred the expansion of technical institutes may be overcome in more than exceptional instances.

But, in general, the logical institution for preparation for technical pursuits should be the technical high school. The transition to work for those students who do not go on to engineering college should not be deferred by attendance at a technical institute. There is a time limit beyond which it is simply not efficient to keep a student at the school level in his practical preparation for a job. If the student has been wisely guided in his progress through vocational and technical courses, he should be ready to benefit by training within industry more than by extended in-school preparation.

The future of the great majority of technical institutes therefore depends on a clear separation of their task from that of the technical high schools, and on the recognition that as mere post-high school institutions they cannot play an important role. If, on the contrary, they are conceived as adult education institutions for the further training of experienced workers in vocational-technical fields, they have a definite place. By specializing in the various production methods of individual industries, and by teaching more advanced and more specific technical material than either the technical high school or the engineering college would be willing or able to provide, the technical institute can render invaluable service to the worker bent on advancement and to the producer intent on improving his production techniques.

BREADTH OF TRAINING IN OPERATIONAL SKILLS

One of the most critical and most complex questions in the entire field of in-school vocational education and training is what constitutes proper breadth of training in operational skills. It has repeatedly been established by this study that narrow training for a single job is undesirable from every point of view. The wider limits, however, are far more difficult to define. Any number of factors—the interest of the student, the facilities of the school, the demands of the economy, the attitude of organized labor—must be given due consideration in attempting to reach a sound and reasonable conclusion on this subject.

In many of the schools within the vocational high school system, shopwork is arranged in such a way as to give the student an opportunity to work with widely different materials, tools, and machines, in the first year or two, and to permit concentration on the chosen trade only in the last half of the course. The traditional craftsman is, of course, extremely skeptical about the practical value of any plan that offers introductory training covering a variety of fields. The craft skills and apprenticeship are focused on a single trade, and the higher the craftsman's skill, the greater his skepticism. Nevertheless, for in-school vocational education and training, the broad approach is the most valid. In so far as it is education, it aims to introduce the student to as wide a segment of industrial production and processes as possible. Moreover, it gives him a sound basis for making a wise final choice of vocation.

Multiple trade experience also enables the student to try his hand at several unrelated industries, even if only as a semiskilled worker or an operative. Such flexibility makes him less dependent on any one industry for a livelihood, and it is directly in line with the demands of modern technology, which has so greatly expanded the need for capable operatives in a wide range of industries. And finally, familiarity with a variety of materials, work processes, production methods, machinery, and apparatus must be regarded as an asset, even for the worker who clings to one trade. It is for this last reason that the Brooklyn Technical High School, for one, requires all students to take shopwork in patternmaking, foundry practice, forging and welding, sheet metal and elementary machine shop, as part of an integrated technical training course. The experience in the different workshops is not viewed as unrelated exploratory work, but rather as an essential part of a continuous course of study preparing for work in a single trade.

Vocational high schools would do well to pursue a course that lies somewhere between the strictly integrated one-trade curriculum and that of exploratory work in several unrelated industries. The 9th grade might well offer prevocational training in only loosely related industries, for the purpose of teaching initial skills as well as characteristics of materials and production processes. Work in the 10th year could more closely approach the content of the chosen occupation while still offering broad basic training. For example, shopwork for all the metal trades would be essentially the same. The last two years would be concerned with a more definite occupational area and would include large projects requiring extensive work in the field. This is especially necessary since the task of the vocational high school is by no means achieved by teaching isolated skills under laboratory conditions. It consists rather of teaching the skills in conjunction with their application to a given piece of work. In other words, the planning of the work, determining the materials and production processes, and making decisions on other broad phases of the procedure as a whole, are essential components of shopwork and its related instruction.

This matter of work projects poses one of the gravest problems in the whole vocational education system. Actual production on a commercial basis is, of course, neither the province nor the aim of the vocational high school. It is precisely this freedom from commercial requirements that enables the schools to plan courses that permit extensive demonstration and explanation and give the student a chance to learn more operations than industry requires of a single worker. Suitable work projects are, nevertheless, vitally important, since operational skills can be learned only by doing, and serious pedagogical difficulties are encountered when students are not given tasks that tax their full capacities and command their whole attention. The Connecticut trade schools offer one of the best examples of adequate work projects, for the major part of their programs consists of actual labor, ranging from minor repairs through the production of small parts and machinery to the building of complete houses. Such a system brings to the vocational high school an atmosphere of reality and has enormous advantages for training the student, provided that it is not stressed at the expense of cultural and related trade instruction.

So far as this study was able to determine, most schools do not have enough work projects to enable the students to practice extensively the required basic operations. Although shop facilities are usually entirely adequate, the schools are forced to resort to the making of small exhibition objects, which strongly suggest the avocational activities of the general education program.

Since the provisions of the Smith-Hughes Act require shopwork to be 'on a useful basis,' the vocational high schools hesitate to admit openly the need to employ practice work in the absence of suitable work projects. This is a negative attitude that should be overcome. In the academic schools virtually all work is done in the form of exercises, though it might be preferable to do mathematical computations or engage in creative writing for practical purposes. On the same basis, vocational schools should either be permitted to give extensive practice training without subordinating systematic step-by-step teaching of basic operations to the idea of 'useful work,' or they should be granted greater freedom to obtain actual productive work from city departments, state and federal agencies, and industry. Many schools now rely on students, teachers, or friends of the staff to supply them with work projects, but this is too casual a solution and for the study of many trades not really feasible. Cooperation with official or industrial groups offers a more satisfactory answer.

Whatever objections industry or labor might have on this score can be easily met: the amount of production by schools would, at best, be too small to constitute a threat to either element. And with regard to labor alone, the more adequate the vocational high school, the more likely will be a prolonged school attendance on the part of those very boys and girls whose early entrance into the labor market would be real competition.

Arrangements for getting suitable work projects might well be facilitated by the vocational high school advisory committees. Composed, as they are, of educators and representatives of management and labor, these bodies not only have the ideal background for studying the subject, but they are also in a strategic position to act fairly in the best interests of all concerned—the school, industry, and organized labor.

If, however, vocational high schools are to handle entire work projects successfully, their teaching staffs must be adequate to the task. That means that the faculty must include not only academic instructors and craftsmen, but also technicians, engineers, architects, or other trained persons capable of organizing and executing the projects—in other words, a staff composed somewhat along the lines of plant personnel.

The inclusion of entire work projects within the vocational high school range implies a greater emphasis on technical knowledge, and thus brings the goals of the vocational and technical high school closer together. This is a trend to be encouraged. Since schools are really better equipped to cultivate understanding than they are to teach operational skills, they should make the most of that advantage. At all events, every effort should be made to keep at a minimum the division between those students who can plan a production process and those who can perform only a few operations. It is true that a sizable number of students in the vocational high school may have difficulty in keeping pace with the technical instruction, and that they will have to be grouped according to their capacities in this direction, but this is a problem common to all schools and should not be permitted to lower vocational high school standards as a whole.

If the vocational high school is to participate actively in promoting the intellectual mobility required by the skilled crafts and trades, and the technical and semitechnical positions reached through them, the vocational-technical course will have to be the rule rather than the exception, especially in regard to the metal and electrical trades and some of the building trades. The practical value of this recommendation is supported by the fact that many companies that conduct elaborate apprenticeship programs give preference to technical high school graduates in selecting their candidates. The trades for which these programs prepare require extensive operational skills, but the companies act on the theory that they can, and would rather, teach the necessary skills to students who already have an ample technical background.

Were there any likelihood that apprenticeship in this country would expand to the proportions it has attained in Europe, the vocational high school might consider concentrating its educational activities on technical information, and its operational activities on demonstration. But since the probability of wide expansion of organized trade training in industry is slight, the vocational high school is still faced with the task of teaching operational skills and supporting, but not supplanting, this teaching with technical and scientific instruction.

THE ROLE OF APPRENTICESHIP

Placing the burden squarely on the vocational high school by no means solves the problem of providing craft skills adequate for our industrial needs. Industry, itself, must assume its share of the training task, both by improving the character of the instruction and by expanding apprenticeships and the less formal systematic training programs.

For example, apprentice training might well be expected to include not only a succession of work opportunities, but also positive elements of teaching. Actually, however, the training includes little systematic demonstration, teaching, and explanation; the best the apprentice can anticipate is the opportunity of seeing how craftsmen do their work and of being allowed to do the same sort of work in proper surroundings. Related instruction constitutes the one exception to this rule, but this occupies only a very limited time and does not affect the prevailing character of apprentice training.

Thus, despite the apprentice's advantage over the in-school trainee in having the chance to observe a number of well-trained journeymen at work, the almost total limitation of his training to operational skills is constricting. The minor role accorded technical training usually prevents the apprentice from getting a broad understanding of production as a whole. The situation could be remedied with relative ease by having vocational education and training in school precede apprenticeship. With the expansion of vocational-technical training at the high school level, the apprentice could be equipped with a much broader understanding of all vocational-technical problems before he enters on his formal in-employment training, and the related instruction given during his apprenticeship could then be carried on at an advanced level.

Schooling, however, should not end with the expiration of apprenticeship. The young journeyman, for whom many opportunities for advancement exist, should avail himself of further part-time education and training in vocational or technical high school; for study in specialized fields he should attend a technical institute.

The figures on apprenticeship show how dismally this type of training fails to supply the necessary replacements for the craftsmen who withdraw from industry each year. According to the 1940 occupational classification made by this study, the number of positions for which apprentice training should be considered logical preparation was approximately 6.5 million—that is, 5.7 million craftsmen, some 600,000 foremen, and at least 200,000 independent producers for whom the possession of operational skills is prerequisite to successful self-employment.

In order to calculate the number of apprentices to be trained annually for such occupations, it is necessary to have an approximate idea of the annual dropout rate. A National Industrial Conference Board study, made in 1935,[1] estimated that 5 per cent of the skilled workers were lost to the labor force every year, as a result of death, retirement, or change of occupation. On this basis, the average occupational life expectancy would be only 20 years —a very low estimate, indeed. The Apprentice-Training Service, on the other hand, based its estimates of the required number of apprentices on a much lower annual dropout rate.

In analyzing apprentice-journeyman ratios, the authors of this study proceeded on the assumption that average tenure for a craftsman is 28 years. The annual dropout rate in this case would be 3.6 per cent, which can hardly be considered an excessive estimate, at least for the near future, in view of the fact that the median age of skilled workers is comparatively high. If, therefore, the annual openings in the ranks of craftsmen are to be filled by workers who have had apprentice training, 234,000 would have to enter apprenticeships every year. This figure presupposes, of course, that the majority of those who start apprenticeships complete their train-

---

[1] National Industrial Conference Board, *Wanted: Skilled Labor,* Studies of the National Industrial Conference Board, No. 216 (New York, 1935).

ing and become members of the skilled labor force. The Apprentice-Training Service, however, estimates that, in the past, less than half the apprentices graduated into skilled labor classifications. If this situation prevails in the future, the annual number of new apprentices must be correspondingly higher.

The total number of apprentices who should be in training at any given time depends on the number entering apprenticeship and on the average length of training. According to the standards formulated by the Federal Committee on Apprenticeship, the average term is three years and nine months, so that on the basis of 234,000 new apprentices annually, there should be about 877,000 in training at any given time. This figure, however, appears to be out of all proportion, not only to the potential technical expansion of apprentice training, but also to the actual training requirements of the economy. It might well be desirable to have 234,000 youths absorbed annually into a systematic program of training for skilled work in industry, but it would be an exaggeration to say that all of them would require a formal four-year apprenticeship to qualify for those positions that have been included in the estimates of the number of craftsmen, especially if in-school preparatory training is extended. But if only half this number were to serve a regular apprenticeship, even that figure would amount to four or five times the number of all apprentices enumerated in the 1940 census.

A shorter and less formal apprenticeship (learnership) might be sufficient to fill the other craft positions. These, together with the regular apprenticeships, might then absorb 234,000 annually, without raising the total number of trainees for crafts beyond a reasonable level. According to the composition of the gainfully occupied in crafts and technical pursuits, about 210,000 of each year's group would be boys. This constitutes about 17.5 per cent of the males leaving school, and corresponds to the average percentage of craftsmen, foremen, and self-employed in the labor force. The figure can therefore hardly be considered too high.

The needs of the economy, however, may not be satisfied by a system of in-employment training restricted to the replacement of craftsmen only. A number of industries rely mainly on workers who are classified as operatives, but whose occupational skills can be acquired only over a long period of training and work experience. Among the 8 million operatives there are many, especially in the textile, clothing, and shoe industries, whose work approaches craft standards, although only in a limited field, and for whom some kind of systematic introduction to work would also be desirable. A sound training policy might well include an extension of learnership programs, lasting about a year and designed primarily for these operatives. Assuming that some 100,000 youths would be given such training every year, the annual systematic introduction to industry would then involve a total of approximately 334,000 young persons.

ORGANIZED TRANSFER FROM SCHOOL TO INDUSTRY

The whole task of occupational training would be greatly facilitated by the organized annual transfer of school-leaving youth into industry. Such a project would, of course, be a formidable undertaking, and could be accomplished only with the cooperation of schools, management, and organized labor, working through the medium of the advisory boards. It would, however, go far toward solving the serious educational and social problem of launching youth on an occupational career without an interruption of years spent in dead-end jobs or possibly without employment. It would also enable the worker to derive the fullest advantage from his vocational preparation, and to develop his abilities and knowledge during the years when his flexibility and capacity for learning are at a peak. And beyond that, the probability of a promising job immediately after the completion of schooling would give meaning and inspiration to vocational education and training in school.

The expansion of vocational and technical high schools along the lines suggested in earlier portions of this study would be an essential step in the direction of unifying educational and industrial life. Undeniably these schools can contribute the kind of intellectual preparation and vocational training that would render the students extremely desirable as apprentices or learners. During the contact with the students over a four-year period, teachers and guidance counselors have unexcelled opportunities to judge their aptitudes, qualities, skills, and interests, and to guide them accordingly in their selection of an occupation and their later transition into the working world. Indeed, the best testing ground for future apprentices is the vocational high school, where the student's qualifications can be checked against the requirements of a particular trade. If industry were to make full use of this advantage, errors in the choice of apprentices could be virtually eliminated.

Cooperation of this nature between schools and industry would also enable the former to assemble useful data on the quantitative and qualitative demands and the general working conditions of the local plants into which their students would probably be absorbed. They could then, to a certain extent, adjust their programs and teaching accordingly. The practical benefits to be gained from such cooperation are obvious, but they should not be allowed to blind the schools to their primary function of education. Vocational and technical high schools must always be intensely conscious of their tasks in the field of general education, and of their obligation to prepare future workers for advancement by providing them with broader operational skills and technical knowledge than local industries may regard as adequate.

The employers' main contribution to the systematic transfer of youth from school to industry would be to create annually the number of openings that would be needed. To a large extent, these openings would depend on business and labor market conditions, which are partly beyond the control of the individual employers. In times of growing unemployment, the absorption of new workers, though they may be only trainees, would naturally be opposed by management, as well as by those persons already employed. The problem of transferring students to industry cannot be solved independently of general employment policy. For its part, any full employment policy would evade one of its most urgent tasks and would substantially lessen its chances of success, by failing to provide for the absorption of school-leaving youth into the economic world, and for their initial occupational training within industry.

The willingness of management, however, to expand the number of apprenticeships and to enter into more apprenticeship and learnership agreements depends not only on the level of employment. The persistent scarcity of skilled labor, which we cannot reasonably expect to be mitigated by a renewal of the immigration of European craftsmen, may induce management to recognize the need for more systematic training than there has been in the past. But other persuasive factors are bound to modify the employer's readiness to expand his training programs. Long indentures are manifestly repellent to the entrepreneur, especially when business conditions are unsettled and thus not favorable to long-term commitments. This resistance could, of course, be overcome by expansion of the system of apprenticing to a trade rather than an individual employer, which shifts the responsibility for continuous employment from the single employer to the joint apprenticeship committee of the trade.

The set wage rates of the apprenticeship standards also pose a problem in some quarters. Big corporations that are in need of specially trained workers may be willing and able to comply with advanced standards, but the small shop owners, who should rightly play a major role in the training of craftsmen, are likely to have difficulty in meeting these stipulations, and may therefore be more inclined to employ helpers and other workers for whom there are no strictly regulated wage scales or training requirements. It would seem then that if the yearly transfer to industry of several hundred thousand graduates of the various types of high schools is to be efficiently organized, there will have to be more flexibility, in general, and certain specific adjustments in apprenticeship standards.

Another consideration in the potential expansion of apprenticeship is the willingness of school-leaving youth to commit themselves to an additional four-year course of training. Boys of eighteen may hesitate to enter such long-term agreements, despite the advantages to be gained thereby. To date, however, all available information indicates that there have usually been more applicants for apprenticeship than there have been openings. This may be ascribed partly to the fact that the courses have usually been offered either by big corporations, in which promising careers seemed possible, or in trades with comparatively high wage rates. With the expansion of opportunities this situation may change, but in the near future, at least, the number of candidates is likely to exceed the number of openings.

Labor's stand on apprenticeship will, of course, always be governed by labor market conditions. It is entirely justifiable that organized labor should make every effort to safeguard jobs and wage standards. But in order to prevent undue restriction of the opportunities for entering a trade, all standards and regulations bearing on the actual number of apprentices should be determined first by management and labor alone, and then subjected to public examination.

As this survey indicates, the groups concerned with apprenticeship inevitably have diverse views and interests. Economic conditions, however, seem so strongly to urge more systematic occupational training that the common welfare of management, employed labor, and school-leaving youth may be expected to cause them to reconcile their conflicting theories and to shape an integrated educational and industrial training system comparable to that which has developed for the professions.

CONCLUSIONS

A truly comprehensive system of vocational education and training, then, should include the following elements: elementary school education, including a few hours weekly of manual work or practical arts; four years of in-school vocational education, starting with an exploratory 9th year offering work of a prevocational character, and providing in the next three years an increasingly specific education and training in trade school, vocational-technical high school, or technical high school. Graduates of these schools should then be enabled to make an easy and systematic transfer to apprenticeship or some less formal type of in-employment training. All apprentices should continue to receive supplementary instruction, while other trainees should also have access to such instruction. Beyond that, any worker should have the opportunity to obtain trade extension training in part-time or evening classes. Full-time training of a specialized and advanced nature should be available in technical institutes. Since college preparatory courses would be included in vocational education programs, college would also be open to those desirous of pursuing their studies at the level of higher education. Such a system would have the advantage of securing technical mobility without sacrificing the opportunities for work on a craft level, and it would, in addition, overcome the rigid separation between craft, technical, and managerial positions—a result that must be regarded as desirable from technical, social, and political points of view.

This broad outline and the preceding proposals for specific reforms and adjustments in our vocational education and training system are neither unrealistic nor impracticable. Indeed, the conduct of this study has been motivated throughout by the conviction that all recommendations should aim not merely at changes that would be theoretically desirable, but rather at improvements that would be solidly grounded in the underlying educational philosophy of the nation and, at the same time, capable of achievement in the light of the social and economic conditions of today and of the foreseeable future. It is for these reasons that so many technical details of both the occupational structure and the educational system have been examined and weighed with regard to their place in a precise definition of satisfactory vocational education goals and the means of attaining them.

Important as the resultant conclusions may be for the furtherance of vocational education, they are by no means irrelevant to the vast and complex problem of general education. In fact, their greatest importance lies in their applicability to the focal task of education as a whole and not in their bearing on a specific phase of education.

In the recent spate of literature on educational issues, the proponents of the liberal arts have launched a vigorous offensive in support of their particular educational aims. A dominant theme in all discussions is the warning against vocationalism and specialization. With these warnings we can find no fault. It is true that vocational education implies a certain degree of specialization, which is essential to the realization of its goal of practical occupational preparation. But a sound vocational education program does not prevent a student from getting a balanced general education. The danger of vocationalism exists only when the principles and aims of a fully rounded education are neglected. Indeed, if vocational education in its future development conscientiously assumes the duties of any truly organic education, its work may well proceed on a sounder basis than that of certain liberal arts programs which too, in their own way, run the risk of being dangerously narrow. Neither such programs nor any others can claim to be an integrating force unless they help the student to find and fill his proper niche in the social and economic life of our time.

Since college requirements mold the character of the institutions from which their students are drawn, the statements made by liberal arts educators have an influence that penetrates far beyond these colleges. Thus any overemphasis on their part on the humanities, the social sciences, or the physical sciences has direct bearing on the secondary schools and, in fact, contains a threat to the unity of the public secondary school system. The high schools cannot possibly nullify their significant achievement in having incorporated vocational education and training in their sphere. The need is too great to permit their withdrawal from the field. Liberal arts educators should therefore accord to vocational education its rightful place in a unified educational program, in order to avoid a definite cleavage among the secondary schools.

There is nothing in the pedagogical situation as such to cause such a cleavage. The recommendations made by this study, in rejecting vocational extremism, are based on a search for a synthesis of educational aims and therefore contain no threat to this favorable circumstance. As here conceived, vocational education does not compete with the goals of a truly humanistic education; on the contrary, it embodies some of the latter's oldest and soundest principles—learning by doing, preparation for life, and the integration of education with the actual social process.

Thus the reinterpretation of the ever-recurring interest in vocational preparation, evidenced throughout the history of American pedagogical thinking and practice, should be a current pressing concern for our educators, economists, and statesmen. It may well be that a workable fusion of vocational and general education, and the recognition of the equal value of both, will be one of this country's major contributions to a new concept of democracy in education the world over.

Notes on General Education
in Selected European Countries

GERMANY

O F ALL European educational systems, the German may be
regarded as the most conservative. Throughout the nineteenth century and the first decades of the twentieth, the institutional structure remained essentially unchanged. Education was ad-
ministered by the individual states, but the kinds of schools, the
curriculums, and the teaching methods were more or less uniform
throughout the Reich. With very few exceptions, elementary and
secondary schools were public schools, with the former category
divided into Catholic and Protestant institutions in the majority of
the states.

In general, full-time education was compulsory for children six
to fourteen years of age. Terminal elementary education was provided by the *Volksschule*, the backbone of the German educational
system. The *Mittelschule*, an elementary school augmented by a
ninth year, and occasionally a tenth, also offered terminal education. Secondary education was provided for children from nine
to eighteen. Under the monarchy, most of the secondary schools
had their own three-year preparatory classes (*Vorschulen*). Thus,
children who planned to enter secondary schools were, from the
very start, educated separately from the great mass of children
who attended the *Volksschulen*. Under the Weimar Republic,
however, these special preparatory classes were abolished; a uniform elementary education for all children six to ten years of age
was established, thereby deferring the separation into two groups

until after four years of common schooling. In line with these changes, the age limits for secondary education were set at ten to nineteen.

In the course of time, secondary education, which had long been confined to the classical *Gymnasium*, with its heavy stress on Latin and Greek, achieved a certain diversity.[1] Other types of schools were established: namely, the semiclassical *Realgymnasium;* the *Realschule*, with a six-year curriculum designed to follow immediately after three (subsequently four) years of elementary schooling, and to prepare especially for commercial pursuits; and the *Oberrealschule*, which was the same type of school as the *Realschule*, but extended the course by three years, laid special emphasis on modern languages, and science, and, like the *Gymnasium* and the *Realgymnasium*, prepared students for admission to a university. After 1918, attempts were made to open secondary education to students who had completed seven years of elementary school, and thereby to ease their access to universities, by establishing a special six-year secondary school (*Aufbauschule*). These schools, however, remained few in number.

Under the National Socialist government, German schools became channels of Nazi ideology and propaganda, but with few exceptions, the structure of the educational system remained unchanged. A Reich Ministry of Education was created to unify the system throughout the nation. At first, the individual states were permitted to retain their autonomy in the administration of education, but, as the Nazi regime developed, the state ministries gradually became subordinate agencies. In 1938, the nine-year secondary education program was reduced by a year to meet the growing demand for manpower imposed by the expanded preparation for war. The secondary school system was simplified by reducing the principal types of schools to only two: the *Oberschule* became the main type, with one branch specializing in mathematics

[1] Adolph E. Meyer, *The Development of Education in the 20th Century* (New York, 1939), pp. 312–36; Rudyard K. Bent and Henry M. Kronenberg, *Principles of Secondary Education* (New York, 1941), pp. 392–3.

and science, and the other in languages (Latin, English, and a second modern language); the *Gymnasium*, stressing Latin, Greek, and English, survived as a less prevalent type. The few *Aufbauschulen* also continued in existence.[2]

The distribution of pupils among the various types of schools in 1931–32 may be seen in Table 1. The high percentage of school attendance among children under fourteen, and the sudden decline in attendance in the older age groups, indicate that the bulk of the population attended only elementary school. Together with the *Mittelschule*, the elementary school absorbed almost 80 per cent of all ten to thirteen-year-olds, and 87 per cent of the total school population in the ten to fourteen age group. Only some 12.6 per cent of the fourteen to sixteen-year-olds attended secondary schools. Since many students left school at sixteen to enter on commercial

TABLE 1. PERCENTAGE OF POPULATION (GERMANY) IN VARIOUS AGE GROUPS ATTENDING VARIOUS TYPES OF SCHOOLS, 1931–32 [a]

Age [b] Group	Total Pop. (in thousands)	% in All Schools	% in Elementary Schools	% in Mittelschulen	% in Secondary Schools
10–13	3,489	91.0%	75.0%	4.0%	11.0%
13–14	651	81.0	65.0	4.8	13.0
14–15	624	19.5	3.0	3.9	12.0
15–16	698	16.0	0.4	3.0	12.5
16–17	930	6.4	—	—	6.0
17–18	1,194	4.4	—	—	4.4
18–19	1,212	3.9	—	—	3.9

[a] Computed from official figures in *Statistisches Jahrbuch für das Deutsche Reich*, 1932 (Berlin, 1932), pp. 421–9.

[b] The number of students in each age group has been estimated from data on the number of students in the different grades, using as criterion the normal age of children in each grade. In secondary schools, therefore, the later age groups include students who were one, or even two, years older than indicated, since all children are not automatically promoted from one class to another because of age. The difference in the sizes of the groups may be accounted for by the low birth rate during World War I.

[2] H. Burmann and C. Schmölder, *Handbuch des gesamten Jugendrechts*, vol. 1, section 3, pp. 32–7.

or technical careers, those who completed the course required for admission to a university comprised less than 4 per cent of their age group. Even of those who were qualified for university entrance, only a part actually enrolled.

The content of elementary education included the usual subjects: the three R's, drawing, singing, gymnastics, and the rudiments of history and science. Instruction was directed toward early entrance into occupational life, with the result that arithmetic was heavily stressed while such subjects as civics were neglected. Workshop instruction, however, was virtually unknown, though a few progressive schools under the German Republic developed some programs in this field. In sharp contrast, secondary education was scarcely influenced by practical considerations; indeed, this was more true in Germany than in most other European countries.

An important feature of the German school system was that while elementary school instruction was tuition-free, all secondary schools required payment of fees. This largely accounts for the virtual exclusion of the whole working population from secondary education. Scholarships granted under the Weimar Republic helped a small number of children to surmount this obstacle, but, as we have seen, these left small impress on the system as a whole. The length of secondary and university education, with its tuition costs and the implied deferment of earning, rendered such advantages available only to the small minority that could afford them. With this line of demarcation imposed by economic factors, the secondary schools and universities became institutions for the benefit of only selected social strata as well.

Since the end of the second world war, educational policy and school administration have again become the responsibility of municipal and state governments. Inspired by the social changes effected by the war, discussion of educational reform is rife in all parts of Germany. The chief topics under consideration are the introduction of a compulsory ninth school year, the extension of common primary school attendance from four to six or eight years, the abolition of secondary school tuition fees, at least for the needy, and revision of secondary school curriculums toward a reduction of the classical content and an adjustment of teaching to the more practical requirements of modern society.

The outcome of these discussions is still in doubt, but in any event it is likely to vary widely among the states. For example, some industrial areas of northern Germany are virtually certain to accept the compulsory ninth year, whereas southern Germany appears hesitant to endorse this reform.

ENGLAND AND WALES

The English school system, like the German, gives evidence of a distinct barrier between primary and secondary education. More devices have been developed, however, to level this barrier. In addition, the classical type of secondary education is less pronounced, and practical considerations are given more weight. Character-building, rather than learning as such, is recognized as the principal task of education.

As may be seen from Table 2, the pattern of English school attendance in 1938 was not wholly unlike that of Germany in 1931-32. The sharp decline from an enrollment of 93 per cent of the thirteen to fourteen-year-olds to 36 per cent of those in the fourteen to fifteen group, and then to only 17 per cent of those in the fifteen to sixteen group, is eloquent. Schooling at that time was compulsory for all children between the ages of five and fourteen. Obviously, the majority of the children were leaving school on the completion of their elementary education.

In England, as in other European countries, attendance at secondary schools is not the logical 'next step' after elementary school that it is in the United States. Students who intend to enter secondary school are transferred from elementary school between the ages of eleven and twelve. That the great majority of the school population between eleven and fourteen or fifteen remain in elementary schools is evident from the fact that these schools claimed 86 per cent of the twelve to thirteen-year-old school population, and 85 per cent of the thirteen to fourteen-year-olds. In many

TABLE 2. PERCENTAGE OF POPULATION (ENGLAND AND WALES)
IN VARIOUS AGE GROUPS ATTENDING VARIOUS
TYPES OF SCHOOLS, 1938 [a]

Age Group	Total Pop. (in thousands)	% in All Schools	% in Elementary Schools	% in Grant-Aided Secondary Schools	% in Junior Tech. Schools
5–6	558.0	84.9%	84.7%	.2%	—
6–7	578.0	92.6	92.2	.4	—
7–8	590.0	94.1	93.7	.5	—
8–9	592.0	92.9	92.2	.7	—
9–10	594.0	93.5	92.3	1.2	—
10–11	598.0	93.3	91.3	2.0	—
11–12	614.0	94.7	87.1	7.6	—
12–13	630.0	94.5	81.4	13.0	0.2
13–14	642.0	93.3	79.2	13.2	0.9
14–15	658.0	37.0	22.8	12.3	1.0
15–16	581.0	17.0	3.1	12.3	1.4
16–17	727.0	6.9	0.3	6.1	0.5
Over 17	2,577.0	1.1	—	1.1	—

[a] *Education in 1938*, Report of the Board of Education and Statistics of Public Education for England and Wales (London, 1939), Table 2, p. 91.

towns, elementary schools are themselves divided into junior sections for the first five age groups, and senior sections for the next four. But about half the older elementary school pupils, especially those in small communities and thinly populated areas, are taught in elementary schools common to all age groups.

Elementary school instruction is generally confined to reading, writing, and arithmetic, the rudiments of physics, history, and geography, and some work in industrial arts. Thus, the bulk of the school-leaving population enters the working world with only limited general education, a little manual training, and no vocational education at all. Actually, with so low an age level for school-leaving youth, little more could be accomplished in the way of occupational preparation.

The Education Act of 1936 raised the age limit at which children were permitted to leave school to fifteen, effective as of September 1939. Exemption was made possible, however, for those who had found 'beneficial' employment. Because of the outbreak of the war, enforcement of the act was deferred. School attendance up to fifteen years of age was then made compulsory, with no exemptions, by the Butler Act of 1944, which became effective on 1 April 1947.

Secondary schools in England are mainly private schools, most of which are publicly inspected; if deemed 'efficient,' they receive public aid. The 1938 census enumerated the secondary school enrollments only in such grant-aided schools; in addition to the 470,000 so counted, there were more than 100,000 students in publicly inspected, but not grant-aided, secondary schools, and in others that were neither inspected nor grant-aided.[3] The total number of enrollments in secondary schools was therefore somewhat higher than indicated by the census.

In the matter of secondary school instruction, more importance is attached to local initiative and to the development of the individual school than to uniformity of teaching practice and courses of study. Board of Education recommendations with regard to the curriculum are therefore quite general. The course of study is mainly academic: English is regarded as the prime subject, foreign languages occupy a prominent place, and science and mathematics rank next in importance. All London secondary schools teach Latin, and about 20 per cent of them offer Greek as well. Other subjects suggested by the Board of Education are history, geography, music, drawing, and the Scriptures. The curriculums also include manual arts, physical education, organized games, and sports.[4]

The transfer to secondary schools is conditional on the passing of an examination. But since secondary schools charge tuition, the selection of their student body does not rest on competence alone. The Board of Education, however, requires that each year 25 per cent of the students be chosen independently of their ability to

[3] Exact figure not ascertainable.
[4] Bent and Kronenberg, op. cit. pp. 400–01.

pay the prescribed fees. This percentage is frequently exceeded, and fewer than half the pupils pay full tuition. Nevertheless, a large part of the student body is chosen from those who, in addition to their ability to pass the examination, can be expected to pay the fees; thus many children with greater aptitudes, but less fortunate financial status, must forego an extended education. It is true that some progress has been made in remedying this situation: in 1913, the ratio of all secondary school pupils twelve to fourteen years of age to elementary school pupils in the same age brackets was 1:14; in 1926, it was 1:9.3, and in 1937, 1:5.3.

Secondary school careers in England are frequently not completed. Indeed, the attendance figures show a high rate of dropouts among fifteen-year-olds, and an even higher rate among sixteen-year-olds. In 1938, enrollments in grant-aided secondary schools were made up of 84,900 thirteen-year-olds, 71,290 fifteen-year-olds, and 44,686 sixteen-year-olds. The apparent dropout rate of more than 40 per cent over a period of four years in such a selective group seems rather high.

SWITZERLAND

Though Switzerland contributed many great educators—Pestalozzi, Fellenberg, Zellweger, Wehrli, and others—the school system of their day was surprisingly poor. Swiss schools of the early nineteenth century did not meet with even modest educational requirements; the teaching profession did not exist as such, and school instruction was rather like a sideline engaged in by men who had a few spare hours from their regular business pursuits. Not until after the revolution of July 1830 in France, which acted as a signal to all progressive forces in Europe, did the impulse for more and better education gain ground. This period of 'regeneration' in Switzerland witnessed the development of a public school system worthy of the name.

During these decades, one after the other of the twenty-five Swiss cantons and municipalities took over the organizations of schools and developed them to remarkably high levels. The result of cantonal initiative was a colorful variety in the school system. Proud of their achievements, the cantons fought hard to maintain their independence in educational matters, and they won their point when the Federal Constitution of 1874 declared schools to be a cantonal responsibility.

One restriction, however, was imposed by the Constitution on the cantons' freedom of choice. The principle of compulsory primary school attendance, to be given free of charge in public schools, was laid down as binding on all cantons. In 1902, constitutional provision was made for an annual federal contribution to the cantons for the maintenance of their public schools, but no further restrictions of cantonal independence were imposed. In addition to the prescribed free instruction, free school materials are provided by most of the cantons; the more progressive cantons also guard the physical welfare of the children by providing, whenever necessary, food, medical care, and vacations.[5]

School attendance is compulsory in most cantons for the eight years between six and fourteen or seven and fifteen. Some few, however, require either seven or nine years.[6] The primary school is common to all children for six years in most cases, though in some cantons it is five, and in a few only four. The majority of the children complete their required formal education in other primary schools; the rest enter one or another of the various types of schools established by the different cantons.

The *Sekundarschulen* or *Bezirksschulen,* set up in many cantons, may best be compared with the German *Mittelschulen.* These schools start with the fifth, sixth, or seventh primary grade and extend through a ninth or tenth year. The curriculum includes more mathematics and science than are offered in primary schools, and a second 'national' language. Since there are four national lan-

---

[5] Otto Wettstein, *Die Schweiz* (Aarau, 1934), pp. 150–51; Georges Werner, *Suisse,* in 'La Vie juridique des peuples,' ed. by H. Levy Ullmann and B. Mirkine-Guetzévitch (Paris, 1935), pp. 64–7.

[6] Walter Guyer, 'Die Volksschule der deutschen Schweiz,' in *Erziehungsgedanke und Bildungswesen in der Schweiz* (Frauenfeld and Leipzig, 1936), pp. 95–114.

guages in Switzerland—German, French, Italian, and Romanch [7]—each spoken by a part of the population, the mastery of a second language has special importance.

Students who neither remain in primary school, nor enter a *Sekundarschule* or *Bezirksschule*, transfer after four or six years of primary school attendance to a secondary school proper, which, in Switzerland, is called a *Mittelschule*. These schools are often divided into separate institutions for the upper and lower grades. Graduation usually takes place when the student is between eighteen and twenty, and it is a prerequisite for admission to a university.

Secondary schools are either cantonal or municipal; in either case, supervision is exercised by a cantonal educational director. Annual meetings of these directors serve as a unifying element in the administration of school matters. Another influence for uniformity is the regulation by the Federal Council of 1925 of the educational requirements for students planning to enter medical, dental, veterinary, or pharmacological professions. Admission to these faculties, or to the Federal Technical University in Zürich, the only school of its kind in Switzerland, is dependent on observance of these federal requirements.

As a result of these influences, curriculums are fairly rigid. There are, however, three distinct types of secondary schools: the classical, with the main emphasis on Greek and Latin; the semi-classical, featuring Latin and modern languages; and the scientific, with mathematics and science constituting the core. Graduates of the scientific school must pass supplementary examinations in Latin for admission to medical and allied faculties.[8]

The distribution of pupils among primary and secondary schools in 1939–40 may be seen in the following figures.[9] Assuming that each age group contains about 65,000 children, and that there are

[7] Spoken in some parts of the Canton Grisons.
[8] E. L. Bähler, *Die Organisation des öffentlichen Schulwesens der Schweiz* (Zürich, 1932), pp. 4–7.
[9] Computed from *Statistisches Jahrbuch der Schweiz*, 1940 (Berne, 1941), pp. 306–9.

	Primary schools	Bezirks-schulen	Lower secondary schools	Upper secondary schools
Boys	230,863	24,928	14,051	12,073
Girls	224,698	24,381	9,602	3,279
TOTAL	455,561	49,319	24,103	15,352

eight grades in the average primary school, it may be surmised that almost the whole of the potential school population attend the lower grades, and about 80 per cent the higher grades, of the primary school. The figures for secondary school attendance are correspondingly low, showing that the vast majority of Swiss children receive only primary education. Only 10 per cent of the twelve to nineteen-year-olds attend secondary schools, and yet this is the best showing of all European countries, with the exception of Denmark and Norway.[10] Less than 20 per cent of each appropriate age group is enrolled in *Bezirksschulen* or lower secondary schools, and only 6 per cent in upper secondary schools. Graduates of upper secondary schools account for about 3 per cent of the proper age group.

U.S.S.R.

Though the system of education and training in the Soviet Union has an important place in any comparative survey of Europe, it cannot be described and analyzed with the accuracy that is possible in the case of other countries, because of Soviet curbs on the freedom of research and publication. Official statistical data are available, but they are so carefully selected that the real trends, aims, and results can be discovered only after considerable sifting, and then not too accurately.

The Soviet task of education and training was, of course, shaped by its revolutionary context. Its main objective was to convey to an illiterate people the rudiments of knowledge and sufficient general education to enlist their cooperation in the transformation of the political structure of their society and in the industrialization of an almost completely agrarian economy; in the final analysis,

[10] Guyer, op. cit. p. 97.

education was to enable the Soviet regime to function successfully and to endure.

Between the twenties and the thirties, the character of the educational system altered considerably. Dominated in its early stages by the principle that 'life must teach,' the system produced interesting, and in some cases confusing, experiments, which, however, have long since been abandoned. The inauguration of the first Five-Year Plan in 1928, and even more definitely that of the second Five-Year Plan in 1932, marked the start of a new era in education.

Education is the responsibility of the Commissariat of Education in each of the republics; there is no central Commissariat of Education for the entire Soviet Union. Actually, however, there is a high degree of centralization. In the first place, there is a central committee which deals with the problems of higher education in the Soviet Union as a whole. Furthermore, the Central Planning Commission of the U.S.S.R. has a cultural section which decides on the number and kinds of schools to be built, the number of teachers to be employed, the number of libraries to be established, and sums to be appropriated from the central treasury to each republic for educational purposes. And finally, the Commissariat of the Russian Socialist Federated Soviet Republic (which includes the greater part of the population of the Soviet Union) exerts a strong influence on the work of the commissariats of the other republics in such matters as textbooks, curriculums, and length of the school day.

The rapid expansion of school attendance between 1914 and 1939, both in absolute numbers and relative to the entire population, may be seen in the following figures.[11] It is also clear how much of the expansion was concentrated in the latter part of the period between the two world wars. This was the decade in which

---

[11] Compiled from *Socialist Construction in the USSR*, Statistical Abstract, ed. by the State Planning Commission of the USSR, English translation (Moscow, 1936), p. 397, and *Socialist Construction . . .* in Russian (Moscow and Leningrad, 1939), p. 116.

	Total population	School enrollments	School enrollments in % of total pop.
1914	139.3 million	7.8 million	5.6%
1928–29	154.3	12.1	7.9
1930–31	—	17.7	—
1933–34	165.7	22.1	13.3
1935–36	—	25.5	—
1938–39	170.5	31.4	18.4

universal school attendance became really effective in the Soviet Union.[12]

General education is provided on a full-time basis by primary schools, preliminary secondary schools, graduating secondary schools, and institutions of higher learning. In addition, there is the special secondary school called the '*technikum*' which has no exact parallel in other European systems, and is, according to a competent Soviet author, on a lower level than the American high school.[13] Primary schools and both types of general secondary schools all start with the first grade. They are, therefore, parallel schools with regard to the grades they have in common, and are differentiated only by the number of grades included: the primary schools have four, the preliminary secondary schools seven, and the graduating secondary schools either nine or ten. The preliminary secondary schools correspond to American elementary schools; for the eleventh and twelfth grade of the American high school there is no equivalent in the secondary school system of the Soviet Union.

The Soviet school system is a ladder system. Students in primary schools can transfer to the corresponding grades of the preliminary secondary or of the secondary schools; after completion of a preliminary secondary school course, students may transfer to the eighth grade of a secondary school. Initially, the Soviet Union did

[12] At the same time, much was accomplished in the field of adult education, in which Communist party institutions played a large part.
[13] A. Pinkevitch, *Science and Education in the USSR* (London, 1935), p. 51.

away with social class distinctions within the school system and the restriction of secondary education and higher learning to the wealthy. Then, contrary to the Soviet Constitution of 1936 (Art. 121), however, which provided for education free of charge on all levels, an order of the Council of People's Commissars of 2 October 1940 introduced rather high tuition fees for the upper grades of secondary schools, *technikums*, and universities.[14] The Constitution, as amended in 1947, legalized this situation and restricted free education to the first seven grades.[15] Another innovation of the war years was the introduction, at the beginning of the school year of 1934–44, of separate classes for boys and girls in seventy-two large cities.[16]

It is to the prodigious growth of the primary school that the rapid decrease in illiteracy [17] may be largely attributed. Starting at the relatively advanced age of seven (before the outbreak of the German-Russian war, at eight), compulsory school attendance is required for seven years. The shift in distribution of pupils among various grades between 1932 and 1939 may be seen in the following figures.[18] Substantial progress was made in this interval toward a much greater absolute and proportional attendance in the fifth to tenth grades. But even in 1938–39 the limited secondary education provided by the Soviet schools was extended to only a small percentage of the population. Whereas there were an average of

[14] *The Soviet Union Today*, ed. by the American Russian Institute (New York, 1943), pp. 50, 54; *American Review on the Soviet Union* (February 1941), p. 67. John Somerville, "Educational System," in *USSR, A Concise Handbook*, ed. by Ernest J. Simmons (Ithaca, 1947), p. 326.

[15] Embassy of the Union of Soviet Socialist Republics, Washington, D.C., *Constitution (Fundamental Law) of the Union of Soviet Socialist Republics* . . . (December 1947), p. 34.

[16] *The Soviet Union Today* (cited above), pp. 52–3; Somerville, op. cit. p. 327.

[17] In 1914, 28 per cent of the population over nine years old could read and write; the census of 1939 reports 81.2 per cent of the population of and over school age as literate (90.8 per cent of the men and 72.6 per cent of the women), figures which disclose marked accomplishment but also show that the Soviet Union is still behind other European countries. *See* Beatrice King, *Changing Man* (London, 1937), p. 17; *The Soviet Union Today* (cited above), p. 54.

[18] *Socialist Construction* . . . Russian ed. (cited above), p. 118.

	1932–33		1938–39	
	Attendance (in thousands)	% of total attendance	Attendance (in thousands)	% of total attendance
Grades 1–4	17,674.6	83.2%	21,202.4	67.5%
Grades 5–7	3,515.2	16.5	8,780.0	28.0
Grades 8–10	67.1	0.3	1,403.9	4.5
TOTAL	21,256.9	100.0	31,386.3	100.0

5.3 million pupils in each grade of the primary schools, there were no more than 468,000 or 8.8 per cent of that figure in each of the three top grades; in terms of the potential school population for these grades, the proportion would be still lower. Assuming that the 30 million pupils in the first to seventh grades constituted the total potential school population [19] (after the deduction of the small percentage who in every country do not attend school for various reasons), and assuming equal distribution, there would have been 4.3 million in each grade. Instead, there were 5.3 million in each of the grades from the first to fourth, and only 2.9 million in each grade from the fifth to seventh. This indicates that millions of children in the Soviet Union had no opportunity of proceeding to the upper grades, and had to spend the required education period in primary schools.

This imbalance, which on the basis of past progress may be expected to decrease, was more pronounced in rural than in urban schools. This is the more serious, because in 1939 the Soviet Union was still predominantly agricultural, with a population 67.2 per cent rural and 32.8 per cent urban; 22.1 million pupils, or 70.4 per cent of the total, attended rural schools and only 9.3 million, or 29.6

[19] These figures must be interpreted with caution. Whereas they show about 30 million children in the first seven grades in 1938–39, *Izvestia* of 29 April 1940 reported that, according to the census of January 1939, there were 13.8 million in the five age groups, ten to fourteen; *see* Gregory Bienstock, Solomon M. Schwarz, and Aaron Yugow, *Management in Russian Industry and Agriculture* (New York, 1944), p. 123, note 21. If this figure was correct, school attendance in the first to seventh grades could not have been above 20 million.

per cent of the total, were in urban schools. No less than 72.3 per cent of the total rural school population were enrolled in the first to fourth grades; the number of enrollments in the eighth to tenth was negligible. In urban schools, there were 1.3 million pupils in each grade from the first to fourth, 1.1 million in each grade from the fifth to seventh, and 285,000 in each from the eighth to tenth. In the towns, therefore, a normal seven years' school attendance spread over the seven grades was not far from being a reality when the war broke out. Secondary education, on the contrary, in the limited sense of the term in the Soviet Union, was only for a minority even in the towns; the number enrolled in each of the upper grades was only 26 per cent of those attending each of the lower.

During the war and the occupation, many young people were unable to obtain normal schooling. For them a broad system of schools is scheduled to be put into effect. By 1950 the number of pupils in all elementary and secondary schools is to be raised 'to a total of 31,800,000, universal compulsory education being extended to all children from the age of seven both in town and country.' [20]

Teacher training in the Soviet Union is not yet adequate. The primary classes are conducted by teachers who received their education and training in a *technikum*.

It appears then that much has been accomplished toward providing a general school education for the mass of children, who, under the czarist regime, had grown up illiterate; much has also been done to give the adults some rudimentary education. On the other hand, until 1928 the majority of the potential school population in the Soviet Union got no schooling, and from then until about 1936, the majority of the children attending school were enrolled in four-grade primary schools. Only a small minority of the children attended the eighth to tenth grades, and most left school at fourteen or fifteen years of age after seven years' at-

[20] Embassy of the U.S.S.R., *Information Bulletin*, Special Supplement on the Fourth Five-Year Plan (Washington, June 1946), p. 17.

tendance. Elementary and secondary education still fall far below the level in other European countries and the United States.[21]

Curriculums are centrally approved by the People's Commissariats of Education of the constituent republics and are the same everywhere, except for minor differences between urban and rural districts, and between Soviet Russia proper and the other republics. For one thing, the school year in the towns is generally 40 to 42 six-day weeks; in rural districts it runs 36, 37, and 38 seven-day weeks for the low, middle, and upper grades respectively—a pedagogically unfortunate arrangement.

The regular curriculum for urban schools in the prewar years[22] laid great stress on the mother language (Russian, in Soviet Russia proper) or on the native tongue and Russian, in addition, in the other republics. It also accorded strong emphasis to mathematics and scientific subjects, such as nature study (botany, zoology, and biology), physics, and chemistry. History was amply represented, especially in the upper grades, but the more than 90 per cent of the students who left school at the completion of the seventh grade or earlier, received no instruction in modern history, since the syllabus for the fifth to seventh grades included only ancient and medieval history, ending with the English Revolution. In line with European practice, instruction in one foreign language started in the fifth grade. Physical culture was granted little time, but, like military studies, this was more strongly stressed during the war, especially for boys.

In building up a common public school covering all grades, and in stressing the mother language, mathematics, and scientific subjects, the Soviet system resembles the American. It differs, however, from the American structure in its strong centralization, and

[21] With regard to preschool education in kindergartens, which took children from three and one-half to seven years of age, the Soviet figures likewise indicate a great increase. In 1934–35, however, 1.2 million children (689,000 of them in cities), or less than 10 per cent of the approximate number of children in each age group, attended kindergarten. The number of children accommodated in kindergartens in 1950 is to be increased to 2.26 million or double the 1940 figure (Embassy of the U.S.S.R., op. cit. p. 17).

[22] See King, op. cit. p. 312.

in not granting the pupils any choice of subjects; there are no electives except the choice of one of several foreign languages.[23]

Soviet propaganda is an ever-present element and pervades all subjects. With regard to the quality of the instruction, the home environment of illiteracy from which most of the children come, and the probable lack of thoroughly trained teachers, which is not surprising in view of the vast and rapid expansion of schooling, serve to explain why the level of general education appears to be below that of schools in other countries. These shortcomings, however, may disappear in the course of time.

The 'polytechnical' side of education and training in the Soviet Union deserves particular mention. Frequently emphasized by Soviet educators and writers, it aims to 'acquaint the pupil with the basic principles of all processes of production'; at the same time it is designed to 'give the child and adolescent habits of handling the simple tools of all production.' [24] The term 'polytechnical' includes all the courses referred to in the body of this study as manual and industrial arts, and certain other prevocational activities with modern machinery. Soviet educational administrators facilitated a broader application of the manual training idea by making each school an annex of a shop, thus furnishing opportunities for contact between schools and factories, for the use of machinery, and for visits to workshops.

The curriculum bears witness to this interest by including one hour a week of 'handwork and manual work' in each of the four lowest grades, and two hours a week in each of the middle and upper grades. According to Russian terminology, 'handwork' is work done in a workroom with such materials as paper and cardboard, using scissors and knives, while manual work is done in school workshops with wood and metal, using lathes, benches, machines, and the like. Handwork is done in the lower and middle grades, while manual work, including the use of machinery, is

[23] It is interesting to note that since November 1945 Latin and Greek have been added to the languages offered.

[24] Quoted from Karl Marx and Friedrich Engels, *Collected Works*, vol. 18, in *The Soviet Union Today* (cited above), p. 50.

reserved to the upper grades.[25] It is likely, however, that only in exceptional cases can school workshops be adequately equipped for such work, and excursions to factories furnish the pupils only occasional opportunities to observe work there and to handle certain tools. These rudiments of 'polytechnical' training can nevertheless be considered an interesting and promising start.

[25] Since the suppression of coeducation in the large towns, girls usually do needlework instead of 'manual' work.

Notes on In-School Vocational Education and Training in Selected European Countries

GERMANY

EARLY in the nineteenth century, when the average school-leaving age in Germany was still lower than the current level of fourteen, and even later when the minimum age for leaving school was set at fourteen by most German states, it was recognized that the education of children had to be prolonged for several more years. The result of this awareness was the development of the continuation schools. In their earliest form these were Sunday schools confining themselves to religious education. Gradually they undertook to repeat and supplement the elementary instruction of children who, after somewhat irregular school attendance in rural areas, entered employment in urban centers. For example, boys who entered on apprenticeships were required to know reading, writing, and arithmetic, and employers were required to see that they received adequate instruction in these subjects.

Following the foundation of the German Reich in 1871, federal legislation authorized the municipal authorities to enforce attendance at continuation schools of all male journeymen and apprentices under eighteen years of age, and to compel employers to grant employees the time necessary for attendance at these schools. Thus the continuation schools emerged as part-time day schools.

With the changes in technology and in the economic structure, instruction in the German continuation schools reached beyond the bounds of general education to include subjects that were directly useful to young workers. Eventually, separate industrial and commercial continuation schools were created, and several states ruled that apprentices or other young workers might attend these institutions instead of a general continuation school. The most progressive continuation school policy was conducted by the state of Württemberg which in 1906 required that all localities, in which at least 40 boys below the age of eighteen were employed in industrial or commercial enterprises, had to establish industrial or commercial continuation schools.

As industry developed, and education in vocational and related fields became increasingly important, more and more schools became training centers for industrial, agricultural, mining, and other vocational pursuits, instead of general education institutions. Accordingly, the continuation school or *Fortbildungsschule* changed its name and became known as a *Berufsschule* or vocational school.

The Weimar Constitution (1919) made the continuation school a part of the general school system for the entire Reich, by ruling (Art. 145) that all children between the ages of fourteen and eighteen had to attend continuation school, if they were getting no other schooling in that interval. But since no federal law was adopted to implement this article of the Constitution, the German states continued to regulate continuation school attendance and organization rather independently. The number of pupils increased considerably; in 1931, enrollments totaled more than 1.2 million, one-third of whom were girls.

The industrial vocational school (*Gewerbliche Berufsschule*) constituted one of the main divisions of this branch of education. In the large cities almost every major trade had at least one school of this type. There were also private vocational schools called *Werkschulen*, conducted, for the most part, by large plants but, like the municipal schools, operated under the supervision of state educational or economic authorities.

Courses in these schools were generally three years in length, except those leading to agricultural occupations, which were only two years. Apprentices in industry and crafts had to attend for the full term of their apprenticeship which was, in most cases, four years. Before World War I, instruction occupied four hours a week; under the Republic it was extended to six, and in a few states or municipalities one hour or even more were added to this prevailing number.

Despite many minor differences among the states, the programs and courses of the various branches of vocational schools achieved a certain uniformity throughout the country. Subjects were classified as vocational, managerial, and civic. In Prussia, an average of three hours weekly were devoted to vocational subjects, two to managerial, and one to civics. States or towns which set up schedules of seven or eight hours usually extended the instruction time devoted to vocational subjects. In some of the smaller states, instruction in civics was sometimes reduced to even less than the scant amount given in Prussia.

Vocational subjects included drawing, modeling, geometry, algebra, science, characteristics of materials, use of materials, and some shopwork, which was especially valuable for apprentices in small shops equipped with only limited machinery. Managerial subjects were written and spoken German, bookkeeping and accounting, and home management. As is demonstrated by the negligible time devoted to it, civics was slighted almost as much as in the elementary schools.

Prior to World War I, the Munich vocational schools, under the direction of Georg Kerschensteiner, whose work attracted worldwide attention, developed an exemplary program of vocational subjects and civics. On the whole, however, despite the undeniable progress of the part-time vocational schools under the Weimar Republic, the success of this type of school was limited, mainly because of insufficient instruction time.

The National Socialists made very few changes in the vocational schools. Instruction time was slightly increased and apprentices were required to spend from six to ten hours a week in school, depending on the trade. Attempts to impose a uniform technical curriculum throughout the Reich met with little success, but the civics courses were widely used for Nazi indoctrination. The factory schools were not regarded with favor by the National Socialists, with the result that many of the leading firms abandoned these projects and sent their apprentices to the city-operated vocational schools.

A highly developed system of school training was that provided by the German technical institutes (*Fachschulen*), which were designed to enable experienced and gifted workers to acquire additional technical education. This type of schooling, which these workers availed themselves of after an apprenticeship and a year or two of journeyman's work, was necessary, since the majority of workers had had only eight years of formal education which provided no adequate preparation for technical work. Technical institutes were first established in the 1880's when it was recognized that industry could not be effectively promoted without a more elaborate technical training.

A great number of technical institutes in the metal and building industries were created as state institutions; others were set up for textiles, crafts, and commerce by municipalities, but were, for the most part, subsidized by the state and conducted according to the same directives. Mining schools were established by the associations of entrepreneurs in the field of coal mining, but since Prussia was the largest owner and entrepreneur of coal mines, it exercised a notable influence on the development of these schools too. In other states, similar developments took place. Accordingly, the influence of public officials on these schools was substantial, especially in the fields of agriculture, industry, and crafts.

The main branches of technical institutes in industry and commerce were: machine and metal institutes (*Metallfachschulen*); schools for the building trades (*Baugewerksschulen*); textile institutes (*Textilfachschulen*); mining institutes (*Bergschulen*); the institutes for crafts and applied arts (*Kunstgewerbe und Handwerkerschulen*), which offered a great variety of courses; and commercial schools (*Handelsschulen*). This by no means exhausts the list. There were also a great many other institutes or *Sonderfachschulen*, specializing in such fields as woodworking, chemical work, papermaking, ceramics, leather work, and shoemaking. Other specialized institutes were created to serve local industries or enterprises. For example, an institute for opticians at Jena served the Zeiss Company; Saxony, Württemberg, and Baden had institutes for watchmakers. All these special institutes were smaller in number than those included in the large industrial groups, but even so not negligible. Their real importance, however, lay not in their number, but in the services they rendered to local industries or crafts, which were sometimes essential to the economy of the region or even the nation.

Unlike the continuation or vocational schools, the technical institutes offered full-time training. Only those schools which were attended on a voluntary basis, and which trained for a specific vocation by full daytime instruction for a period of at least one year were to be considered *Fachschulen*.[1] In actual fact, these stipulations were not always strictly observed, and even evening schools were not denied classification as technical institutes if they complied with the other requirements.

In general, admission to technical institutes demanded the completion of both elementary school and an apprenticeship; in some cases, vocational activity of several years' duration was considered an acceptable substitute for apprentice training. In several fields, however, technical institutes were set up on two different levels with different admission requirements. There were, for example, institutes of advanced instruction in the metal and machine trades, textiles, commerce, and agriculture. Admission to these was confined to persons who had successfully completed six years of secondary school, that is, a total of ten school years, and at least two years of apprenticeship. Access was made possible to applicants, with only eight years of schooling but four years of apprenticeship, by giving them a full-year preparatory course.

Thus the institutes could take for granted a common vocational background and could plan curriculums and instruction accord-

[1] According to a resolution of the *Reichsschulkonferenz*, a meeting of educators and administrators of the highest authority, held in 1920.

ingly. In some mining schools there existed a cooperative system whereby part of the time was devoted to school attendance and the rest was spent on practical work. Students enrolled in the institutes for the building trades often worked during the summer to earn the money for school attendance extended over several winters.

The number of students attending all public technical institutes in 1931 was 170,320. What proportion of these were male students cannot be ascertained precisely, since the figures for the largest state, Prussia, were not divided by sex. It can be assumed, however, on the basis of detailed Prussian figures for 1926 and of the 1931 figures for other states, that at least 100,000 were male. The total number of students attending public technical institutes for industries and crafts was 67,000, of whom about 55,000 can be assumed to have been male. Among the 43,000 students in the schools for commerce and transportation, on the other hand, the majority (about 26,000) were female.

No exact data are available on students of private technical institutes. Figures for private institutes in Prussia in 1926 show that they were then unimportant in the fields of industry and crafts, numbering not more than 4,000. In later years the enrollments grew, because for a long period all state and municipal institutions were filled to capacity. The value of many of the private industrial and craft institutes was contestable, however. The private commercial schools played a bigger role, with enrollments of 13,-072 in 1926, among whom 6,175 were female.

Among the largest branches of the public technical institutes for industry and crafts were the institutes for the building trades and the machine industry, each group enrolling about 10,000 students, the institutes for the textile trades (more than 6,000), and the institutes for the metal industry (about 5,000). In order to give some idea of the teaching in these schools, typical curriculums of technical institutes for machine and advanced machine construction are reproduced in Table 3. The former covers four terms of twenty weeks over a period of two years, the latter, five such terms over a two-and-a-half-year period. The six-day week with seven periods a day is a heavy program, requiring great energy and application on the part of the student.

In many subjects, especially those devoted to machines and technology, the instruction includes both theory and practice. The two curriculums differ in a number of ways, mainly because that of the advanced institutes presupposes a body of knowledge which students in the other schools have still to acquire. Thus German is

TABLE 3. WEEKLY HOURS OF INSTRUCTION IN TYPICAL CURRICULUMS OF GERMAN TECHNICAL INSTITUTES FOR MACHINE AND ADVANCED MACHINE CONSTRUCTION [a]

Subject	Machine Construction [b]				Advanced Machine Construction [c]				
	Terms: I	II	III	IV	Terms: I	II	III	IV	V
German	4	—	—	—	—	—	—	—	—
Econ., civics	2	1	1	2	2	2	1	1	—
Mathematics	14	5	2	—	8	6	4	—	—
Physics	4	2	—	—	4	2	—	—	—
Chemistry	4	—	—	—	4	—	—	—	—
Prep. Drawing	11	—	—	—	—	—	—	—	—
Mechanics	—	5	4	2	6	6	6	—	—
Descript. Geometry	—	—	—	—	7	—	—	—	—
Machine parts	—	16	4	4	6	12	12	—	—
Power machines	—	—	9	11	—	—	—	13	14
Hoists, cranes, etc.	—	—	2	3	—	—	—	9	8
Electricity	—	4	4	4	—	2	4	4	12
Construction, plant	—	—	—	3	—	—	4	6	—
Technology	2	6	9	8	3	10	7	3	2
Lab. exercises	—	2	4	4	—	—	2	4	4
Physical culture	2	2	2	2	2	2	2	2	2
TOTAL	43	43	43	43	42	42	42	42	42

[a] Compiled from Rudolf Horstmann, 'Die Metallfachschulen,' in Alfred Kühne, Handbuch für das Berufs- und Fachschulwesen, 2nd ed. (Leipzig, 1929), p. 339.
[b] Four terms of 20 weeks, over 2 years.
[c] Five terms of 20 weeks, over 2½ years.

taught only in the lower institutes, which also offer more mathe-matics (including arithmetic) than the advanced schools, and teach it in a more elementary way. Preparatory drawing also is taught only in the lower schools, while descriptive geometry is offered only in the advanced institutes. The broader background of the students attending the advanced institutes and the five-term cur-riculum allow more time for mechanics, and for work on machines, and on machine and plant construction. Students who graduate from the institutes for advanced work have, of course, technical skills and knowledge that enable them to take more complicated technical jobs than graduates of the lower institutes.

The work of the German technical institutes has played an im-portant role in the total system of occupational training and techni-cal education. Whereas graduates of technical universities were educated mainly for research and experimental work, the graduates of technical institutes were usually entrusted with the planning and supervision of production, and they comprised the great body of technicians, draftsmen, designers, supervisors, and foremen. Since the number of persons who attended the technical universi-ties was extremely small (under 10,000 in 1937–38), the German system of drawing on the rank and file of skilled labor for the prac-tical engineering positions furnished the only possible solution of the production problem.

GREAT BRITAIN

Full-time in-school vocational education is but slightly de-veloped in Great Britain. It has no place, of course, at the elemen-tary level, where it would be out of order in view of the age groups involved, or at the secondary level. Since 1904, however, efforts have been made to introduce a type of vocational school into the educational system; the result of these efforts is the junior technical school.

Junior technical schools developed from the daytime technical classes, which from 1904 to 1912 were conducted within the frame-work of the secondary schools; they became separate institutions only in 1913. Their rise from then on was slow. In 1935, there were 194 schools with 24,000 pupils; in 1938, the number of pupils had increased to 28,000.[2] Enrollments in these schools in percentages of the potential school population were as follows: 0.8 per cent of the thirteen to fourteen-year-olds; 1.6 per cent of the fourteen to fifteen group; 1.4 per cent of the fifteen to sixteen group; and 0.4 per cent of the sixteen to seventeen group. The junior technical schools are not a part of any ladder system. For the most part, they are entered at the age of thirteen or fourteen, though in exceptional cases at twelve. Students are admitted by entrance examinations in English, mathematics, drawing, and sometimes handicrafts. Most courses are two years in length, for children from thirteen to fifteen; some are three years, for twelve to fifteen-year-olds; very few schools offer three-year courses to those entering at thirteen. The junior technical schools do not prepare for university entrance.

There are four types of junior technical schools: preapprenticeship schools, which prepare for specific industries; junior technical trade schools, which prepare for specific occupations; junior housewifery schools preparing for household management; and junior commercial schools leading to careers as 'shorthand typists' and clerks of various kinds. In 1938, excluding the housewifery and commercial schools, only 17,771 boys and 2,177 girls were receiving this kind of in-school vocational preparation for entrance to industry.[3] Nearly one-third of the preapprenticeship schools, as well as three-fourths of the trade schools, were located in the metropolitan area; about half of the two groups had less than 100 pupils each, and 97 out of a total of 124 had less than 200 pupils each.

Of the preapprenticeship schools, which had an enrollment of 16,500 in 1938, the great majority prepared for the metal and ma-

---

[2] Computed from Appendix I, Table 2. The enrollments listed there include schools of nautical training and junior departments of art schools.

[3] Computed from *Education in 1938*, Report of the Board of Education and Statistics of Public Education for England and Wales (London, 1939), Table 59, p. 155.

chine, and building industries, a few for the chemical or mining industries. A small number of schools, comparable to the American vocational high schools of the general industrial type, prepared for unspecified industrial occupations. As for the trade schools, in which enrollments were very low (only 3,300 in 1938), the occupations taught were mainly cabinetmaking, printing, tailoring, the needle trades, boot and shoe manufacturing. Hardly any trade was taught in more than two schools in the country.

The preapprenticeship and trade schools require no final examination for graduation, nor are they operated according to any uniform standards. Teachers are selected according to their experience in the occupations for which the schools prepare. Contacts are established between the schools and industries through industry representatives who serve on advisory committees or on the Board of Governors, or by close relationships between the head teachers and the local and regional firms.

The hours of instruction per week in an average preapprenticeship school curriculum are as follows: English, history, and geography, 6; mathematics, 6; science, 6; technical drawing, 4; physical training, 2; and craftwork, 6.[4] The time distribution in an average junior technical trade school curriculum is somewhat different: English, history and geography, 5 hours a week; science and mathematics, 5; drawing, 4; craftwork, 14; physical training, 2.[5] General education subjects are not wholly lacking, but are less dominant in the technical trade school curriculum; science and mathematics, offered in the technical schools for 40 per cent of the instruction time, are accorded only 17 per cent in trade schools. Craftwork, on the other hand, occupies almost half the instruction time in trade schools, but is less heavily stressed in the technical schools.

On the whole, the junior technical schools have made a promising start in providing all-day vocational education, but they have

---

[4] *A Review of Junior Technical Schools in England*, Board of Education Educational Pamphlets No. 111 (London, 1937), p. 18.
[5] Ibid. p. 20.

not gained much strength or popularity and, as the Board of Education put it, are almost unknown to the general public.[6]

Aside from junior technical schools, the only other full-time vocational education institutions in Great Britain are the larger technical and commercial colleges and schools, which prepare for employment in building, engineering, commerce, art, and domestic crafts, with courses lasting a year or more. A large proportion of the 19,000 students, nearly half of whom are women, range in age from sixteen to nineteen, and enter these schools after completing secondary school programs.

In continuation schools, students up to eighteen receive instruction for three to six hours a week in either general education or vocational subjects. Schools and employers sometimes work together in planning the supplementary theoretical instruction for employees.

Though the record of vocational education as a part of the regular school system is far from impressive, the number of persons who voluntarily take additional general or vocational courses is important. In 1938, about 1.2 million students were enrolled in almost 3 million part-time classes, an average of 2.5 classes per student. As a rule, the classes are held three times a week during evening hours from September to March or April. They include all kinds of trade preparation, trade extension, or general education courses, given either as junior courses, two years in length, for boys and girls who have just left elementary school, or as senior courses for those sixteen years of age and over.

The junior evening classes are attended by about one-third of the graduates of elementary schools. The courses cover industrial, commercial, agricultural, domestic, and general subjects. In the industrial classes, boys who have already entered industry learn workshop calculations and blueprint reading, written and spoken English, and the intelligent use of tools. 'The aim of the courses is to continue the pupils' elementary education and to prepare them for more advanced courses in technical schools, but, as the Board

6 Ibid. p. 14.

has put it, "no high efficiency can be claimed for junior evening arrangements as an educational system." ' [7] Thirty-five per cent of the students, indeed, do not go beyond the first year, and 40 per cent of the remainder do not go on to take the advanced courses.

The senior courses, attended by 900,000 in 1938, of whom 55 per cent were over 21 years of age, provide opportunities for persons engaged during the day in industry and commerce to increase their theoretical and practical knowledge, their general education and vocational background. English, languages, and social science are offered, as well as mathematics and science, industrial, professional, and commercial subjects, art, music, and physical training. Among the industrial subjects are mining, chemical trades, engineering, and the metal trades, textile trades, clothing trades, food and drink trades, book printing and paper trades, building, woodworking and furniture trades.

In view of the miscellaneous character of the instruction it is difficult to determine the exact contribution of these schools to the vocational training of the gainfully occupied population. Some skepticism about their value has been expressed.[8]

The British educational system has provoked much criticism, and various proposals for reform. Outstanding are the suggestions made during the war by the New Fabian Research Bureau in London and the Nuffield College Social Reconstruction Survey at Oxford.

These groups opposed in-school vocational education and training at the secondary level, but recommended compulsory part-time continuation education, including vocational subjects, until workers reached the age of eighteen. They further suggested that in view of the strain of 'night school,' a considerable amount of the daytime should be released for purposes of study, and that employers should so arrange the work schedules that trade apprentices

[7] Barbara Drake and Tobias Weaver, *Technical Education,* New Fabian Research Bureau (London, 1936), p. 9.
[8] Ibid. p. 10.

up to the age of eighteen could devote half their work time to education, including vocational education, and a smaller proportion of working time thereafter.

The rapid development of junior technical schools was also proposed by both groups. The Fabians wanted them to become technical secondary schools admitting pupils at the age of eleven and offering an advanced course leading to a university or higher technical college. The Nuffield College Survey insisted on facilities for an easy transfer from one type of school to another and expressed a preference for junior technical schools that would not be narrowly vocational, as opposed to specialized trade schools. It stated, however, that direct trade training should be the main goal of apprentice training in industry, but should be largely supplemented by part-time education.[9]

SWITZERLAND

Vocational in-school education in Switzerland stems from the work of Philipp Emanuel von Fellenberg, who was the first to see the connection between a democratic government and an intensive, well-planned, and purposeful vocational education. Following the suggestion of Pestalozzi, early in the nineteenth century he founded on his estate near Berne an institution for the poor, in which general education was combined with work in agriculture. Other similar schools developed, for the crafts as well as for agriculture. Craftsmen and businessmen also created Sunday schools in which drawing and modeling and other subjects pertinent to the enlargement of vocational knowledge were taught. In connection with local crafts and industries, special vocational schools developed in urban centers, among them schools for drawing and modeling at Basel, for industrial arts at Lucerne, for furniture and weaving at Zürich, for watchmaking at Geneva and Neuchâtel. While most of these were born of the initiative of economic and vocational associations, others were founded by individual enter-

[9] Nuffield College, Oxford, *Industry and Education* (Oxford and London, 1943), pp. 31-8.

prises in order to build up a steady supply of skilled workers.

Much more systematic was the growth of the continuation schools, which were originally designed to review and supplement primary school education for employed persons, by means of instruction on a part-time basis. Continuation schools were matters of cantonal discretion until 1930 when federal law created the term *Berufsschule* (vocational school) for industrial and commercial continuation schools and made attendance at these schools compulsory for all apprentices. The cantons remained free to regulate attendance of nonapprentices.

The continuation schools increasingly developed from refresher institutions for general education into schools for specialized vocational training. The following figures reveal the size of enrollments and the distribution of students among the various types of continuation schools during a recent decade.

	Gen.	*Indus.*	*Comm.*	*Agr.*	*Home Econ.*
1928–30	31,629	49,804	21,060	4,697	35,440
1934–35	25,529	52,468	16,380	8,792	43,378
1939–40	18,122	48,468	16,248	9,937	47,391

The slight absolute decline from total enrollments of 142,630 in 1928–29 to 140,166 in 1939–40 constitutes a proportional increase, since the average potential continuation school population was smaller in 1939–40 than in the earlier periods because of the lower natality. The figure of 140,000 indicates that more than half the potential school population (including a majority of all boys and a minority of all girls) between fourteen and eighteen attend continuation schools. Special continuation school attendance increased at the expense of general continuation school attendance. The number of students in agricultural continuation schools more than doubled; in home economics it increased by more than 30 per cent; the number of those enrolled in industrial continuation schools remained stable.

Federal law, enacted in 1930, provides that apprentices must attend continuation school for 200 to 300 hours a year, or, if drawing and practical instruction are not required, 160 to 240 hours, for the duration of apprenticeship. Theoretical and practical instruction related to each trade is prescribed; subjects include drawing, shop mathematics, commercial correspondence, bookkeeping, civics, and economics. The cantons are free to include additional electives. Federal officials established standard schedules, adherence to which, however, is optional.

In addition to the part-time continuation schools, Switzerland has full-time vocational schools for skilled and intermediate occupations. Attendance is on a voluntary basis. In 1939–40, the highest attendance was at commercial schools (4,687 boys and 3,368 girls) and the schools for home economics and women's work (8,704). The 38 trade and industrial schools, in contrast, had only 2,612 students, and the 6 *technikums* (technical institutes) 1,816—figures that do not suggest a strong position for these institutions in the training system of the country.

An interesting feature of the in-school training system is the 41 public apprenticeshops (*Lehrwerkstätten*), which function under the supervision of the federal government. Apprenticeship training in these shops is similar to that given by a commercial enterprise. The students receive the practical instruction prescribed in the apprentice programs and, in addition, more theoretical instruction than the usual apprentice program affords. K. I. Boeschenstein, a Swiss authority on vocational education, asserts that an apprenticeship shop has a series of advantages which cannot be offered by a practical apprenticeship with related instruction in a continuation school. There are apprentice shops for mechanics, watchmakers, metalworkers, electrical workers, woodworkers, clothing workers, and others. Although they operate on a semicommercial basis, offering for sale the products made by the students, they cannot subsist without the contributions they receive from municipalities, cantons, and the federal government.

The ample opportunities for vocational training in large cantons may be illustrated by the example of Zürich Land, which includes the territory around Zürich but not the city itself. There are, first of all, continuation classes for specific trades (painting, carpentry, gardening, and the like). The training for each trade is concentrated in a different locality and the students from all over the canton gather there for instruction.[10] A big continuation school is located in Winterthur, the main town of the canton. It offers training in the following fields: mechanical-technical; construction; diverse trades (printing, baking, shoemaking, clothing, and the like); and it gives free courses in languages, business, trade economics, and other similar subjects. A separate section is devoted to home economics and women's vocations. The same town contains a *technikum*, subsidized by the federal government and designed to convey by theoretical instruction and shopwork essential knowledge for technicians in intermediate jobs in trades and industry. There are sections for architects, chemists, technicians (machine work, electrical work, underground construction), and for commerce. The courses, for which fees are charged, last six terms; a minimum age of fifteen, nine years of school attendance, and a year or two of work experience are prerequisite to admission. Graduation includes the right to the legally protected title of 'technician.' A metalworker's school, also in Winterthur, has sections for mechanics, precision work, electromechanics, auto mechanics, and patternmaking. School attendance is a substitute for apprenticeship, and cantonal apprentice examinations are held at the end of three years. Admission is granted on examination to fifteen-year-olds who have had nine years of school attendance. Fees are set according to the financial status of the student. This school also offers additional courses of one to two years' duration, composed mainly of shopwork and intended for students of secondary schools and institutions of higher learning, and for trade extension training of young mechanics.

U.S.S.R.

The rapid progress of industrialization in the Soviet Union, with its attendant shift of population from rural to urban areas,

[10] E. L. Bähler, *Die Organisation des öffentlichen Schulwesens der Schweiz* (Zürich, 1932), pp. 21–6.

created a need for centers of training that would build up the body of skilled workers, technicians, and engineers demanded by the new economic structure. The institutions that grew out of this need are the *technikums*, the factory apprentice schools, and the trade and industrial schools. There are also a limited number of engineering colleges.

Boys and girls who complete the seventh grade (last year of a preliminary secondary school) [11] have the choice of proceeding either to the upper grades of a secondary school or to a *technikum*. The latter may best be described as special vocational schools for future semiprofessional personnel. Actually, they are old Russian institutions adjusted to the new conditions in the Soviet Union and not restricted to technological instruction in the narrow sense. There are *technikums* for medicine, pedagogy, art, agriculture, industry, and transportation. Nurses and other medical aides are trained in the *technikums* for medicine, teachers for primary schools in the *technikums* for pedagogy, foremen and technicians, managers and accountants in the *technikums* for industry and transportation. The *technikums* do not constitute the top rung of an educational ladder; transfer to universities or engineering colleges is possible from them as well as from secondary schools.

The *technikums* have played a big part in providing the speedily trained manpower for intermediate jobs, so greatly needed for the rapid industrialization of the country. Their expansion was linked to the policy inaugurated in 1928 of training a great body of specialists. Training was accelerated and the period of study was shortened, the 'workers' nucleus' in the *technikums* was strengthened, and numerous scholarships were granted. But by the middle thirties, and even earlier, these measures were recognized as failures—extreme specialization and acceleration had seriously lowered the level of technical training. Orders were therefore issued to lengthen the instruction period, revise curriculums, and introduce a general system of strict entrance examinations.[12]

[11] *See* Appendix I.
[12] Gregory Bienstock, Solomon M. Schwarz, and Aaron Yugow, *Management in Russian Industry and Agriculture* (New York, 1944), pp. 106–12.

Admission to, and graduation from, the *technikums* training for industry and transportation are reflected in the following figures. These show a rather stable number of graduations, although, except in 1938, the number of admissions declined steadily as a result of the more rigid entrance requirements. Thus, on the whole, the proportion of graduations to admissions improved. But even in the second half of the thirties, graduations never equaled half the admissions. The average length of *technikum* attendance was therefore below two years, which means that most students did not complete the four-year course. The expansion of the Soviet economy, however, absorbed the available manpower so easily that all these students found jobs in which they were able to utilize their training, incomplete though it was.

	Admissions	Graduations
1932	124,000	33,600
1933	77,600	31,400
1934	70,800	29,200
1935	65,700	31,900
1936	58,800	27,900
1937	58,100	27,100
1938	69,200	30,500

A four-year course in a *technikum* included general and specialized training. All *technikums* offered Russian language and literature, one foreign language, economics, dialectic materialism, and a group of scientific subjects including mathematics, physics, chemistry, and biology. General education subjects had a sizable place in the curriculum, since the knowledge carried over from the seventh grade of a preliminary secondary school was necessarily imperfect and needed improvement. Professor Pinkevitch indicates that 18 per cent of the instruction time was devoted to general education, 47 per cent to scientific and technological subjects, and 32 per cent to special subjects determined by the student's future vocation.[13] This last group was taught mainly by practical work in

[13] A. Pinkevitch, *Science and Education in the USSR* (London, 1935), p. 58.

a Soviet enterprise, the instruction being given by a specialist and supervised by an educator.

During the first two years, theoretical instruction was given in the form of the usual class lesson, supplemented by independent study, discussions, and excursions. For the last two years, the method of the university lecture system was employed, together with group work and discussions. At the end of the course, a thesis had to be written and publicly defended; only then was a diploma issued confirming the qualifications of the applicant for one of the many positions for which the *technikums* prepare. With regard to the level of education in a *technikum*, Pinkevitch holds that it was below American academic and technical high school standards, but on a higher level than the German schools for skilled workers and in some ways comparable to the German *Polytechnikums*.

The expansion of engineering colleges was not unimpressive during the thirties. Whereas before the first Five-Year Plan was inaugurated only 20,200 engineers were employed in the whole of Soviet industry, between 1932 and 1938, 147,300 students graduated from engineering colleges. During the years of the first Five-Year Plan, 1929–32, only 22 per cent of the students newly admitted to engineering colleges were graduated, but from 1935 on, graduations were not far behind admissions. The Soviet regime has coped with the task of securing trained manpower for top and intermediate positions with increasing success.

The task of training skilled workers for the rapidly expanding Soviet industry first devolved upon the factories. All larger plants created factory apprentice schools in order to meet their manpower needs. Under the first Five-Year Plan, and even later, general education was still so little developed that the requirements for admission to these schools had to be incredibly slight; thus only two years of primary education were required. Only with the improvement of school education was the qualifying period lengthened.[14]

In these circumstances the factory schools found it advisable to devote half the instruction time of the two-year course to gen-

[14] Beatrice King, *Changing Man* (London, 1937), p. 172.

eral education and only half to actual training for industry. The apprentices learned to handle tools, to know the structure of machines and how to operate them, and to read blueprints. The factories supplied suitable workshops, materials, and instructors for the training, which was given in a 40-hour work week.

The emphasis on general education in the apprentice schools aroused so much interest in academic subjects that many of the apprentices wanted to transfer to institutions of higher education, access to which was easy at that time, instead of preparing to work in the factory. In view of the urgent need for industrial manpower, this tendency could not be encouraged. In fact, the need was so great that the government decided in 1933 to reorganize the factory apprentice schools. The training period was reduced from three years to six months, or, in some cases, to a year.[15] The greater part of the training—four to six hours a day—was devoted to preparing for industry; theoretical subjects were offered for only two or three hours a day. (By that time, of course, young people entering factory apprentice schools had a somewhat improved general education.) Though the apprentices were not in principle prevented from later attending institutions of higher learning, they had to complete three years of work in the factory first. It is obvious that so short a training period as six months does not allow for apprentice training in the usual sense; this schooling was comparable to the preparatory training given to operatives, or possibly learners, supplemented by some theoretical instruction. The factory apprentice schools were not considered educational institutions, and therefore operated under the control of the Commissariats of Industry.

By a decree of 2 October 1940 the Soviet Union abolished the whole apprenticeship system and announced a policy of establishing vocational schools to be annexed to factories and to supersede the factory apprentice schools.[16] The plan provided for different

[15] Pinkevitch, op. cit. p. 54.

[16] The decree is reproduced in *American Review on the Soviet Union* (February 1941), pp. 67–8.

kinds of training for skilled workers and operatives, who, when trained, were then to be drafted for compulsory labor for a number of years.

Trade schools, railway schools, and industrial training schools were projected, with the aim of creating labor reserves of 800,000 to 1 million persons annually. Trade school and railway school courses were to be two years in length. In the former, skilled metal-workers, metallurgists, chemists, miners, oil workers, river transport and communications workers, and the like, were to be trained. The latter were to furnish skilled railway workers, assistant loco-motive engineers, locomotive and car repairmen, boilermakers, crew leaders for track repairs, and others. In the industrial schools, six-month courses of study were to be organized for the training of operatives in the coal, mining, metallurgical, and oil industries, and the building trades.

The facilities of the former factory apprentice schools were taken over for the new trade, railway, and industrial training schools. About 45,000 experienced teachers, industrial training experts, and other personnel are said to have been selected to staff them. Boys who had completed at least the seventh grade were eligible for admission to a trade or railway school; no educational requirements were set for entrance to an industrial training school. In the trade and railway schools about one-third of the instruction time was set aside for theoretical subjects; training in industrial schools was mainly on-the-job training in mines, oil fields, and the like, preceded, in some instances, by some theoretical instruction.[17]

In order to secure a sufficient number of trainees, the chairman of each collective farm was called upon to designate two male youths fourteen and fifteen years of age for the trade and railroad schools, and two sixteen and seventeen-year-olds for the industrial training schools, for every hundred members of the collective farm, counting men and women between the ages of fourteen and

[17] New York *Times,* 7 April 1943; Embassy of the U.S.S.R., *Information Bulletin,* 18 December 1943.

fifty-five. The number to be drafted by the city soviets was fixed annually by the Council of the People's Commissars. The pupils were maintained free of charge. Those who graduated were regarded as mobilized and were obliged to work for four consecutive years in state enterprises at prevailing wage rates, but were exempt from draft into the army or navy.

It is not ascertainable to what extent these measures, designed to provide a sufficient number of trained workers for industry and to distribute them according to planned production, were actually applied. When the Soviet Union was invaded only seven or eight months after the first enrollments, many schools were put out of operation and others had to work under the most abnormal conditions. According to published figures, there were, at one time or another, some 500,000 or 600,000 enrollments in these schools; in 1943 there were 600 trade schools, 120 railway schools, and 800 industrial training schools, and in Moscow from the beginning of the war until the end of 1943, some 30,000 boys between the ages of fourteen and sixteen were trained in 55 such schools.[18] There is no information available on the curriculums, or on the results achieved in teaching practical skills and theoretical background. The system itself is apparently considered successful since it is to serve the fourth Five-Year Plan also. In the law on this plan, adopted on 18 March 1946, it is proposed 'to improve the training of cadres for industry by extending the labor reserve system and the training of new workers on the job.' [19]

[18] See articles cited in preceding note and *Anglo-Russian News*, 18 October 1943.
[19] Embassy of the U.S.S.R., *Information Bulletin*, Special Supplement on the Fourth Five-Year Plan (Washington, June 1946), p. 4.

APPENDIX III

Notes on Apprenticeship
in Selected European Countries

GERMANY

AS in most European countries, apprenticeship in Germany was well developed long before industrial production prevailed in the economy, but for many reasons, this form of occupational training persisted and spread in this country to a far greater extent than elsewhere. For one thing, small workshops, which have always been the backbone of apprentice training, continued to flourish in great numbers beside the growing industries. According to the census of 1933, of 1.9 million manufacturing enterprises, 1.7 million were small shops, employing one to five persons and accounting for 3.1 million workers out of a total of 9.2 million in manufacturing industries. With certain legal rights vested in their organizations, which can be traced back to the medieval craft guilds, the small shops maintained a leading position in training apprentices, and in that field enjoyed a semipublic status. Industry, too, because its production methods only slowly grew away from the old techniques and continued to require a great percentage of highly skilled workmen, undertook to train apprentices.

One of the most persuasive factors, however, in the maintenance of large-scale apprentice training was the prevailing brevity of schooling for the masses, and the concomitant early transfer of young people to employment. The following figures reveal how high a proportion of the thirteen to twenty-year-olds were employed in 1933.[1]

[1] Statistik des Deutschen Reichs, *Berufszählung* (Berlin, 1937), p. 60.

	MALE		FEMALE	
	Population (in thousands)	Gainfully employed	Population (in thousands)	Gainfully employed
13–14	641.0	10.5%	617.0	8.7%
14–16	654.3	62.8	630.4	46.3
16–18	723.7	84.6	703.4	70.8
18–20	1,177.9	92.4	1,166.8	78.6

How many of these young persons were employed under apprentice agreements is revealed in Table 4. Of the total number of apprentices, 676,997, or more than 75 per cent, were boys. This figure represents about two-thirds of all the gainfully occupied males between fourteen and eighteen and about half the total number of males in these age groups. Boys also accounted for 88 per cent of the 607,200 craft apprentices, but for only half the 273,000 commercial and clerical apprentices.

A study of the number of apprentices in relation to the size of establishment shows how much greater a role the smaller firms play in apprentice training than the larger. The average over-all ratio of 1 apprentice to 15.5 other employees may suggest that not enough apprentices were employed to replace the labor force, but it must be remembered that that number of employed included skilled as well as unskilled workers, and the managerial and clerical staffs. Indeed, if one compares the number of male apprentices with the number of male skilled workers employed in these industries, whose total was only 2.2 million, the average ratio was 1:4.1. In the small industrial shops employing from two to five persons the ratio was about two apprentices to every three skilled journeymen. It is true that small shops in Germany did use apprentices for cheap labor, but the 2:3 ratio gives a somewhat unfair picture of this situation. In the first place, the widespread unemployment in 1933 naturally affected apprentices less than journeymen, and in the second, these apprentices ultimately had to replace journeymen in both the small and larger establishments, and also the many self-employed, whose vast number may be guessed from the fact that, as mentioned above, there were 1.7 million industrial establishments employing only one to five persons.

TABLE 4. COMPARISON OF TOTAL EMPLOYEES AND APPRENTICES IN GERMAN INDUSTRY, 1933, BY SIZE OF FIRM [a]

Size of Enterprise (No. Employed)	Total Employees	Total Apprentices	Craft Apprentices Male	Craft Apprentices Female	Commercial & Clerical Apprentices Male	Commercial & Clerical Apprentices Female	Ratio of Apprentices to Non-Apprentices
			(in thousands)				
1	1,789.7						
2–3	2,720.7	216.2	150.2	23.4	17.9	24.7	1:11.6
4–5	1,273.7	180.7	119.8	19.3	20.1	21.6	1:6
6–10	1,146.1	151.5	89.2	13.8	25.9	22.5	1:6.6
11–20	912.7	85.5	42.3	5.6	21.5	16.0	1:9.7
21–50	1,186.3	76.8	38.3	3.5	20.2	14.9	1:14.4
51–100	1,059.7	49.5	24.6	3.0	12.3	9.7	1:20.1
101–200	1,045.1	38.0	20.0	1.8	8.7	7.5	1:26.5
201–1,000	2,217.5	58.1	33.1	1.3	11.7	11.9	1:37.2
Over 1,000	1,223.2	24.1	17.6	.5	3.5	2.5	1:49.7
TOTAL	14,574.6	880.5	535.1	72.2	141.9	131.3	1:15.5

[a] Statistik des Deutschen Reichs, vol. 462/3, Gewerbliche Betriebszählung, Part 3, 'Die gewerblichen Niederlassungen im Deutschen Reich,' pp. 24–5. This industrial census enumerates all establishments and the number of employed persons, according to occupations and positions within manufacturing industries (Industrie und Handwerk), commerce, and transportation. It excludes all unemployed (of whom there were as many as 4.5 million in these sections of the economy even in 1938), practically all agriculture, and all public and domestic services.

The traditional apprentice training given in small shops concentrated on manual skills. A training schedule for such shops did not exist, but masters and journeymen had long experience and a good general idea of what apprentice craftsmen in the field ought to learn. On the other hand, the machinery used in these shops was fairly limited, thus precluding any training in advanced production methods as such. The training each apprentice received depended largely, therefore, on the work his particular shop engaged in and on the master's willingness to teach his craft.

What uniformity of training existed was mainly the result of the requirements for passing the journeyman's examinations. These examinations were conducted by boards set up by the chambers of craftsmen (Handwerkskammern), representing both masters and journeymen. Failure to pass such an examination reflected not only on the apprentice, but also on the master who trained him; masters with a number of failures against their records could, on occasion, be barred from further training of apprentices. The examination usually involved: (1) a designated piece of work (*Gesellenstück*) to be produced by the candidate entirely unaided; (2) performance of certain work in the presence of the examining board, and (3) testing of the candidate's theoretical knowledge of the technical aspects of the trade.

Apprentice training in industrial corporations was, on the whole, not so very different from that in small shops. But even before World War I, some of the outstanding industrial firms had developed programs of systematic apprentice training, which called for a year or more of training in special apprentice training shops before the apprentice was admitted to production in the general plant. In connection with such programs, detailed training schedules (*Berufsbilder*), outlining the main skills to be acquired for each occupation, were also developed. This kind of systematized training was strongly promoted by the German Committee for Technical Schools (Deutscher Ausschuss für Technisches Schulwesen, known as DATSCH), which was formed in 1908 by the leading associations of machine manufacturers and engineers.[2]

Nevertheless these programs were the exception rather than the rule and the special value of industrial apprenticeship resided in the opportunity for the apprentice to observe modern production methods, the preparation and development of tool and jigs, and even of special machinery, and to acquire thereby a technical knowledge far superior to that of the apprentices in small shops. This opportunity expanded when the plants developed their own vocational schools (*Berufsschulen*),[3] which were enabled by their

[2] Re DATSCH, see Adolf Heilandt, 'Apprenticeship Training and the German Executive of the Technical School System,' in *Year Book of Education* (London, 1939), and R. Harm, 'Berufsausbildung in der mechanischen Industrie an Hand der Lehrmittel des deutschen Ausschusses für technisches Schulwesen,' in *Reichsarbeitsblatt* (1925), *Sonderheft* 32.

[3] *See* Appendix II.

comparatively close contact with the factories to teach systematically the technical principles of the respective industries.

The examination of industrial apprentices was not so well developed as that of craft apprentices. Indeed, the majority of the industrial apprentices became journeymen without any special examinations. Wherever examinations were held, they had to be organized in collaboration with the *Handwerkskammern*, who, because they alone had the final word on master examinations, reserved the right to recognize or not recognize a journeyman's examination.

The length of training was legally limited to four years, which the apprentice usually served between the ages of fourteen and eighteen. The remuneration was accordingly low, being considered not a real wage but rather a payment to make it easier for parents to maintain the boy during his apprenticeship. For example, in 1930 the Zeiss optical firm paid wages that for the whole apprenticeship term averaged only one-fourth of a journeyman's wage and, even in the last year, amounted to not more than a third. And this was relatively high remuneration. Trade union influence on remuneration of apprentices, and indeed, on number and training, was small, and extended to only a few crafts.

National Socialism from its inception paid great attention to the registration, classification, channeling, and general control of labor, especially with regard to the occupational training of youth. In line with its preparation for war, it aimed at a substantial increase in the number of apprentices. As early as 1936, an official estimate put the number of craft apprentices alone at 780,000, which suggests a total for all apprentices of more than 1 million. In the single year of 1938, 330,000 boys, or almost two-thirds of all boys entering gainful employment in this year, started apprenticeships. The shift to war production is emphasized by the fact that of these 330,000, not less than 130,000 entered apprenticeships in the metal industries. By 1940, there were 1.1 million male, and 0.3 million female, apprentices, with 484,000 in the metal industries.

This expansion of apprentice training was facilitated by an expansion of the vocational guidance services, which had gained some prominence in the interwar period. In 1938 the national employment service made it compulsory for all school-leaving youth to register for vocational counseling, and for all employers to report the number of apprentices wanted. This centralization made it possible to distribute the available labor supply in accord with the needs of the economy. Counseling was based on an elaborate system of conferences, detailed registration cards, school reports, medical examinations, and, in some instances, aptitude tests. Acceptance of the vocational advice was not compulsory, but since no apprenticeship agreement could be entered into without the consent of the employment office, the net result was the same. On the basis of the employer's application for apprentices and the assurance from chambers of industry and commerce or of handicrafts that the employer was equipped to train the number of apprentices he requested, students were directed by the employment office to the individual plants for final selection and negotiation of the apprentice agreements.

For the leading industrial firms, this procedure represented a preliminary sifting of applicants. The firms then made their final choice by various methods, including psychological and work performance tests, examinations in general education and theoretical knowledge, and graphological analyses. The test given by the central psychotechnical office of the Reichseisenbahn was fairly representative of those generally employed for the selection of apprentices in the metal trades. This consisted of an examination in school knowledge, general thinking, technical thinking, space and form conception, manual dexterity, practical technical aptitude, and concentration. As the war progressed, the employment offices sent fewer and fewer applicants, thereby depriving the individual firms of a choice in the matter of apprentices.

The German Labor Front not only propagandized actively for the expansion of apprentice training and vocational guidance but sought to inject into its program the political ideology and military views of the National Socialist party. Moreover, it attempted to mold the form and content of the technical training—a move that was strongly contested by industrial management, the *Handwerks-kammern*, the chambers of industry and commerce, and by DATSCH. All these organizations predated National Socialism and considered occupational training their proper function. In this conflict between the German Labor Front, the representatives of handicrafts, and DATSCH, the last-named, because of its long experience and close cooperation with industry, gained more and more influence and eventually was entrusted with the task of re-organizing all apprentice training. It became the official advisory board to the Reich Minister of Economics and was known as the Reich Institute for Occupational Training in Commerce and Trades.

The ensuing reorganization of apprenticeship included the enumeration of all apprenticeable trades, with the result that there-after training programs for only the enumerated occupations were recognized and entered in the apprentice rolls of either the cham-bers of industry or of handicrafts. When the number of such rec-ognized apprenticeable trades had reached a total of 320, it was as-sumed to be complete. Another innovation was the introduction of semiapprenticeable trades (*Anlernberufe*) thought to be necessary and advantageous because of the increasing specialization and divi-sion of labor in industry. The list of such trades eventually enumer-ated not fewer than 260 occupations. For the apprenticeable trades the term of apprenticeship was generally reduced from 4 to 3 or 3½ years; for the semiapprenticeable occupations it was set at 1 to 2 years.

The enumeration of the trades was supplemented by a descrip-tion of the skills that should constitute the various occupations. Whereas such occupational training specifications had formerly been merely guides for training directors, they now became bind-ing rules and were incorporated in the various apprentice agree-ments. Their number was greatly increased with the aim of provid-ing a complete occupational picture of each enumerated trade.

The specifications stated the field of work, the required skills, and the desirable skills. For example, the specifications for a 3½-year apprenticeship for toolmakers, as decreed by the Minister of Economics on 18 February 1939, described as the *field of work* of the toolmaker the following: cuts, punches, fixtures, molds, cutting and holding tools and gauges, equalizing and testing, conditioning and reconditioning of tools. The *required skills* to be learned by the apprentice during his term of training were: measuring, marking, center punching; filing, scraping, chiseling, sewing; fitting, grinding, polishing; drilling, reaming, sinking, thread-cutting; truing, bending; riveting; spring-winding; forging of simple parts and tools; soldering and brazing; simple work at lathe, planer, milling machine, and grinder; tempering and heat-treating of parts and tools; assembling of tools, fixtures, and gauges, and controlling and testing; and reconditioning of tools. *Desirable skills* were considered to be the following: simple welding and torch-cutting; making of divisions; undercutting; and work at file and saw machines, form and die planers and gauge-bore machines.

This brief enumeration is supplemented by a plan of training, which describes each skill in great detail, provides a training timetable, and contains references to training material, also published by DATSCH, that provides full drawings for practice work. The training curriculum for the various occupations is therefore rather complete and standardized. Only during the latter part of the training term does the apprentice do work that is dependent upon the type of production of the company that employs him.

In addition to the occupational specifications and the training plan, DATSCH stipulates the educational and physical requirements an applicant should meet in order to be admitted to a given trade, and also lays down the rules for the journeyman's examination, stating in broad terms what such an examination should comprise.

Semiapprenticeable trades are similarly described. This group of workers is expected to obtain intensive training, but of a narrower range. The training program for a machinist, for instance, may include extended training at the work bench and at the various machines, but a semiapprentice training program will concentrate on work at a planer, or milling machine, or grinder. Training agreements of the latter type, however, have not been very popular; fourteen-year-old boys usually prefer to prepare for a 'full trade' rather than become such specialized workers.

Most of these training and trade specifications would probably have remained dead letters, had it not been for the various institutions that help to vitalize and enforce them. Outstanding among these agencies are the apprentice shops, the systematically prepared journeymen's examinations, and the Reich occupational contest.

Apprentice shops and apprentice corners were, of course, in existence before 1933, but at that time there were only 50 or 60 such training centers. By 1941 their number was estimated at several thousand. An apprentice shop is a separate division of an industrial plant, set apart exclusively for the training of apprentices. It may range from a small room installation to a sizable industrial plant with all the required machinery. An apprentice corner, on the other hand, usually consists of only a work bench and a few arrangements permitting the demonstration and practice of some of the basic skills in a given trade.

The training in these shops is systematic, and is given by teaching individual skills. Practice jobs, requiring the various skills, are designed and performed in a prescribed order. Of equal importance with the types of work done by the apprentice are the method and quality of performance. The apprentice works under the constant supervision of journeymen trainers, or, in the larger shops, under masters and engineers.

Systematic training in an apprentice shop usually lasts for one year, but sometimes for two, and occasionally for the entire term of apprenticeship. It varies somewhat from trade to trade, but mainly from plant to plant. During the first six or twelve months the apprentice may perform only practice work, but in the latter part of his apprenticeship he is usually required to participate increasingly in the production of the plant. Nevertheless none of the great corporations consider their apprentice programs paying propositions, though they concede that they are a necessary measure for providing a trained labor force for the future.

The training outside the apprentice shop inevitably loses something of its systematic character. But here, too, great care is taken that the apprentice should have an opportunity to be employed in the various divisions of the plant, working always under the supervision of a journeyman to whom he is specially assigned. Moreover, he never completely loses touch with the apprentice shop, to which he has to report monthly for an examination task. Such tasks are carefully designed and, together with the material for basic training, provide an integrated curriculum for the whole term of apprenticeship.

Good apprentice-shop training also provides a certain amount of technical instruction pertaining to such matters as characteristics of materials, proper use of machine tools, and the interpretation of work specifications and blueprints. All further technical education is entrusted to trade schools, which the apprentice is obliged to attend for six to ten hours a week.[4]

The apprentice completes his period of training with a journeyman's examination, which is virtually compulsory. These examinations are now independently organized by the various local chambers of industry and of the craft trades, and conducted in cooperation with the local trade schools. Only in Berlin will unified examinations be reintroduced.

The examination consists of two parts: one on acquired skills, and the other on related trade knowledge and, to some extent, civics. The examination of skills has always been the core of the journeyman's examination. Formerly the apprentice chose his piece of examination work himself, and produced it in his training shop, but since 1938, a uniform examination task, designated in each district by the respective trade chambers for production by all apprentices of a given trade, has become common practice. Toward the end of the National Socialist regime, attempts were made

[4] *See* Appendix II.

to have unified examination pieces, not only for a given city or state, but for the whole Reich. The evaluation of the examination work on a prescribed point system is also established in advance. This method of grading is reported to be uncommonly objective and leads to practically identical evaluations of the same work piece by various members of the examining boards.

The second part of the journeyman's examinations, dealing mainly with related trade knowledge, is also carefully prepared. The written examination refers to technical questions of the trade, to trade arithmetic (*Fachrechnen*), and to technical drawings. All apprentices of a given trade have to solve the same problems, and the individual examination boards are provided with answers regarded as acceptable. Only the oral examinations vary, and depend on examiner as well as apprentice.

The final grading of the apprentice takes into consideration not only the examination but also the records of his work kept by the apprentice during his whole term of apprenticeship. Grades received in the monthly training shop examinations are not given direct consideration, but they are, of course, reflected in the report the apprentice receives from his employer. The chambers of industry and of handicrafts have the right to grant the journeyman's certificate (*Gesellenbrief*).

One final unifying factor in German apprenticeship training remains to be mentioned—the Reich vocational contests inaugurated by the German Labor Front in 1934, which boasted 3 million participants by 1938. Since the tasks set for the contesting apprentices were increasingly developed by the very persons who directed the leading apprentice shops and who had written the trade specifications and developed the training materials, they inevitably corresponded closely to the prevailing content and methods sponsored by the larger industrial firms. Smaller shops, in their effort to compete with apprentices from these firms, naturally copied their training programs as closely as possible, with the result that apprentice training throughout the Reich became increasingly uniform.

The defeat of Germany in World War II brought apprentice training virtually to a standstill. Many industrial training shops were destroyed and industrial production is at a low ebb. Nevertheless, great effort is being expended in all parts of the country toward the restoration of occupational training along established lines. Employment offices have resumed occupational guidance and placement of apprentices; former training specifications are being further developed, and the chambers of handicrafts and of industry are again conducting journeyman's examinations. It is unlikely that any substantial changes will be introduced into the system.

GREAT BRITAIN

The status of apprenticeship in Britain is largely governed, as in most European countries, by the extremely early age at which the majority of the children terminate their schooling. In 1931, 54 per cent of the fourteen to fifteen-year-old boys, 75 per cent of the fifteen to sixteen-year-olds, and 88 per cent of the sixteen to seventeen group had already entered employment. The corresponding figures for girls were lower, but the majority of those employed had also started to work at fourteen.[5]

A study of the occupational classification of gainfully employed youth in 1931 [6] reveals that among the 450,000 boys, fourteen and fifteen years of age, the four largest groups were messengers and van boys (120,500), agricultural workers (46,000), distributors in commerce or delivery boys (45,550), and general and unskilled labor (44,000). Together these accounted for about 60 per cent of the total. In contrast, hardly more than 20 per cent had entered manufacturing or construction industries, and only 7 per cent were in mining.

The four largest occupational groups among the 356,000 girls of fourteen and fifteen were domestic service (82,000), textile

---

[5] *Census of England and Wales for 1931* (London, 1933).
[6] John Gollan, *Youth in British Industry* (London, 1937), pp. 309–10.

trades (73,000), distributors in commerce (40,000), and general and unskilled workers (32,100), amounting to 64 per cent of the total.

Shifting to the sixteen and seventeen-year-old boys, we find a very different picture. There were 54 per cent more employed than in the lower age groups, but 50 per cent less in jobs as messengers or van boys. The increase in the number of boys employed in manufacturing industries was proportionally higher than the general increase, with the metal and machine trades claiming the largest group. Of the whole age group, 36 per cent were employed in manufacturing, construction, or mining. Among the 600,000 girls of sixteen and seventeen years of age, domestic service, trades, and distribution in commerce were still among the four leading groups; third place was held by clerks and typists.

The implication of this more distinct vocational stratification among the older boys is that many of them took dead-end or other temporary jobs at fourteen and fifteen, and found their way into skilled work only after a year or two. The reluctance of employers to hire the youngest boys for anything but menial work, and the understandable lack of decision on the part of youngsters with regard to their future vocations may have contributed equally to this situation. In any case, the premature curtailment of school education and the lack of any systematic transfer of youth into employment were obviously disadvantageous both educationally and vocationally.

The British *Census of Occupations* gives no usable information on the number of apprentices since it includes them with the labor force as a whole in each of the separate trades. Our most recent source of information, therefore, is the extensive inquiry into the subject made by the Ministry of Labour 1925–26,[7] which discloses to what extent apprenticeship and learnership were instrumental in leading youth into skilled occupations. Since then, it is true,

[7] British Ministry of Labour, *Report of an Enquiry into Apprenticeship and Training for the Skilled Occupations in Great Britain and Northern Ireland*, 1925–26, Parts 1–6 (London, 1928).

total apprentice figures may have declined, but the whole process of absorption of youth into industry has not been basically affected.

The Ministry Report is divided into seven parts, each covering one important industry. The part dealing with the entire machine and metal industry stated that the number of apprentices was not so great in 1925–26 as formerly, and that, as a consequence of the progressing division of labor and the increasing use of machinery, many of the old skills based on hand operations had disappeared. The Report stated further that new methods of production had 'undoubtedly introduced what might almost be described as a new class of operatives into industry,' but it nevertheless maintained that 'for the more skilled occupations which are still the mainstay of the industry, apprenticeship remains the normal method of recruitment.' [8]

Total employment of males in the machine and metal industry was estimated at 1.6 million, the number of apprentices at 72,000, and that of learners at 25,000.[9] This estimate was based on a sample inquiry in reply to which 1,573 firms reported 43,923 apprentices and 58,647 trainees (apprentices and learners combined); total employment in the firms reporting apprentices was about 500,000 male workers (Table 5).

The over-all ratio of other workers to apprentices was 11.4:1, and to trainees, 8.5:1. If this had been the journeyman-apprentice ratio, the number of trainees would not have been high enough to replace the skilled labor force. Since, however, it included all unskilled and semiskilled workers, the clerical staff, and others, this ratio may well have served to maintain apprenticeship as the usual form of recruitment of skilled workers.

The table shows, moreover, that the small firms trained a proportionately larger group of apprentices and learners than did the big corporations. There was an almost consistent mathematical relationship between the size of the firm and the number of em-

[8] Ibid. Part 6, p. 4.

[9] Learners are obviously not strictly definable; most of them work under contract for several years and their training is similar to that of apprentices, though it may be less systematic.

TABLE 5. TOTAL EMPLOYEES, TRAINEES, AND APPRENTICES IN VARIOUS MACHINE
AND METAL INDUSTRIES, GREAT BRITAIN AND WALES, 1925–26, BY SIZE OF FIRM [a]

Size of Firm (No. Employed) [b]	No. of Firms	Total Male Employees	Total Trainees [c]	Total Apprentices	Employees per Trainee	Employees per Apprentice
1–4	38	109	56	47	1.9	2.3
5–10	56	378	126	111	3.0	3.4
11–20	129	1,854	455	384	4.1	4.8
21–50	260	8,565	1,672	1,307	5.1	6.6
51–100	245	17,445	3,184	2,509	5.5	6.9
101–200	313	44,529	6,551	5,268	6.8	8.4
201–500	286	89,489	12,364	9,518	7.2	9.4
501–1,000	136	93,250	10,036	7,482	9.3	12.5
1,001–3,000	90	141,519	15,513	11,820	9.1	11.9
Over 3,000	20	103,389	8,690	5,477	11.9	18.9

[a] British Ministry of Labour, *Report of an Enquiry into Apprenticeship and Training for the Skilled Occupations in Great Britain and Northern Ireland*, 1925–26, Part 6 (London, 1928), p. 4. Table includes engineering, shipbuilding, and ship repairing industries.

[b] Includes all trainees and all salaried workers and clerks, as well as manual workers.

[c] Includes all apprentices and other types of learners.

ployees and trainees—the larger the firm, the smaller the proportion of apprentices.

Apprenticeship terms in the machine and metal industries were quite extended, as may be seen in the following figures on the percentage of apprentices with various periods of training. Hardly

Years	Per cent
4	1.6
5	47.7
5–7	17.9
6	6.7
7	26.1

any apprentices served less than five years, and more than a quarter were under seven-year agreements. The age at which apprenticeship starts is indicated by the following figures.

14 years	28.4%	15 or 16 years	4.5%
14 or 15 years	6.0	16 years	34.7
14 to 16 years	16.0	16 to 18 years	.9
15 years	8.7	18 and over	.3

Approximately 99 per cent of all apprentices begin their terms between the ages of fourteen and seventeen. In view of the common school-leaving age, it might be assumed that fourteen and fifteen would be the most usual years for entering apprenticeship. Actually, however, sixteen is the age at which most apprenticeships start. These figures support the implication of the over-all survey of absorption into employment—that a part of school-leaving youth either remains idle or engages in dead-end jobs for one or two years before starting systematic training.

In the building industry, including public works and construction, the picture is, on the whole, similar to that of the metal industry.[10] Total male employment in 1925–26 was estimated at 920,000, including 107,000 workers under twenty-one years of age. Of the latter, 76 per cent were either apprentices or learners, or so-called 'improvers' (a term also used to describe a young worker in his first year as a journeyman, but not yet receiving full compensation for his work). The number of apprentices and learners was therefore about 81,000. As in the metal industry, small shops employed a proportionately larger number of apprentices or trainees than the larger firms (Table 6). For the building industry, as a whole, the Ministry of Labour estimated that the journeyman-apprentice ratio was 4.4:1 and for a single trade, such as that of plumbers, even 2.2:1. These figures leave the impression that in the building industry systematic training was so widely expanded that it could more than supply the necessary replacements in the skilled labor force, and that in many cases apprenticeship was being used as a source of cheap juvenile labor.

In general, the length of training in the building industry was from five to seven years as in the metal trades. Among the reported apprentices, 42 per cent were serving a five-year term, 21 per cent six years, and 19 per cent seven years; the rest were not strictly classified. For cabinetmakers seven years was the most frequent term; for plumbers and painters, six. The age of entrance in these trades was rather equally distributed among fourteen, fifteen, and sixteen.

[10] British Ministry of Labour, op. cit. Part 2.

TABLE 6. RATIO OF TOTAL EMPLOYEES AND OF JOURNEYMEN TO
TRAINEES AND APPRENTICES IN THE BUILDING TRADES,
GREAT BRITAIN, 1925–26, BY SIZE OF FIRM [a]

Size of Firm (No. Employed)	Employees per Trainee	Employees per Apprentice	Journeymen per Trainee	Journeymen per Apprentice
1–4	2.0	2.4	.9	1.1
5–10	3.2	3.8	1.7	2.0
11–20	4.2	5.0	1.9	2.3
21–30	5.1	6.3	2.1	2.6
31–40	5.8	6.9	2.5	2.9
41–50	6.2	7.2	2.6	3.0
51–100	8.1	10.0	3.2	4.0
101–200	10.1	12.4	3.7	4.5
201–500	13.2	15.5	4.5	5.3
501–1,000	12.6	19.4	5.0	7.6
1,001–5,000	19.6	27.5	6.1	8.4

[a] British Ministry of Labour, *Report of an Enquiry into Apprenticeship and Training for the Skilled Occupations in Great Britain and Northern Ireland*, 1925–26, Part 2 (London, 1928).

The printing industry [11] offers another example of the customary method of recruitment through a well-developed system of apprenticeship and learnership. The entire industry employed 169,000 male, and 98,000 female, workers, but the Ministry's report was based on an investigation of firms employing 115,000 male workers or about two-thirds of all males employed in the industry. These firms reported 11,594 apprentices and learners, which suggests a total of about 18,000 male apprentices and learners in all printing trades.[12] In the reporting firms the worker-apprentice ratio was 9:1 and the worker-trainee (including learners) ratio, 8:1. The journeyman-apprentice ratio was 5.5:1, which would be too high for replacement requirements if four years were the prevailing apprentice term as it is in the United States, but which may not be excessive where seven years is the usual term. The percentage distribution according to the length of training may be seen in the

[11] British Ministry of Labour, op. cit. Part 1, p. 6.
[12] Female apprentices are rare in all trades.

following figures. Two-thirds of the apprentices enter the printing industry at fourteen years of age, rather than at fifteen or sixteen, which is common for the industries discussed.

Years	Per cent
4	2.0
5	15.2
5-7	5.6
6	6.8
7	70.4

In general, apprenticeship in Great Britain has ceased to be as strictly regulated an institution as it was in the past. Thus, the proportion of written apprentice agreements in England was relatively low. The highest rating was to be found in the printing industry, which made the best showing with 54 per cent of the agreements in writing; 12 per cent concerned learnerships, and 34 per cent of the apprenticeships were based on verbal agreements. In the building trades only 28 per cent of all trainees worked under written agreements, and 52 per cent under verbal agreements; the remaining 20 per cent were 'improvers.' The situation was about the same in the metal and machine industry.

The apprentices usually learned their trades by working either under or with journeymen, progressively acquiring skills while doing work of different kinds and at different machines. Occasionally they were under the direct supervision of foremen, but the employment of a special apprentice master was rare. Learning by working was therefore the chief feature; systematic and theoretical instruction played hardly any part in the apprentice program.

Technical instruction was apparently only slightly developed. Indeed, there was no general rule making technical instruction compulsory for all apprentices. The survey of the metal industry showed that compulsory evening classes were reported by only 62 firms, compulsory daytime classes by 19, and optional daytime classes by 78. Attendance at technical classes was nevertheless encouraged by most of the firms. Of those reporting, however, 111 firms stated that no opportunities were available for such studies, and 123 failed to answer the question, which may indicate a lack of interest in, or familiarity with, the subject.

Entering apprenticeship, as they do at fourteen to sixteen, apprentices do not obtain much compensation for their work. There are even instances in which apprentices pay a premium to the employer for being admitted to training.

In general, the scale of apprentice wages is indicated in the following standards developed by the Regional Joint Committee of the Building Industry,[13] which show what proportion of a journeyman's wage each age group of apprentices should receive.

Below 16	1/8
16 to 17	1/6
17 to 18	1/5
18 to 19	1/4
19 to 20	1/3
20 to 21	1/2

The future of apprenticeship in Great Britain is a controversial issue. There are those who, even before the war, said that apprenticeship was outmoded.[14] During the war it was felt that the 'force of change has been so overwhelming that a return to the former apprenticeship system would seem to have become impossible.'[15] Neither industry nor labor, however, expects any radical transformation in the system of absorbing youth into industry through apprentice training; reforms rather than an abandonment of the existing system of training are anticipated. A conference held under the auspices of Nuffield College in September 1942, in which representatives of management, labor, and education participated, categorically refused to accept the view that 'apprenticeship is obsolete, or in process of becoming so. On the contrary,' the report continued, 'we believe that in many industries the need for highly trained craftsmen is increasing, and certain to increase,

[13] British Ministry of Labour, op. cit. Part 2, p. 37.
[14] Gollan, op. cit. p. 231.
[15] C. A. Oakley, 'The Last Days of the Apprenticeship System?' in *Journal of the Industrial Welfare Society* (January–February 1943), p. 8.

and that even where the proportion of skilled workers in the total labour force is declining, the degree of skill required of the craftsmen is becoming definitely higher and more exacting; and we strongly urge in all appropriate industries the establishment of agreed National Apprenticeship Schemes under which the industry as a whole will accept responsibility for the training and welfare of apprentices, and for the necessary release to enable them to maintain their day-time studies.' [16] The conference also stressed that everything possible should be done to raise the quality of entrants to apprenticeship in the skilled crafts and that the bias of the educational system against manual occupations should be removed lest the development of industry be seriously prejudiced.[17]

In conclusion, the educational system and apprenticeship in Great Britain, both so deeply rooted in tradition, seem to supplement each other to such an extent that any great changes in the whole setup are hardly likely in the near future.

SWITZERLAND

With the great majority of children leaving school at the early age of fourteen, in Switzerland as in other European countries apprenticeship is the main source of skilled labor.

Prior to the French Revolution, the usual apprenticeship required the extremely long term of seven years; it then had to be followed by at least seven years of journeymanship before master status could be attained. Indeed, in the period of its decline, the corporate system virtually excluded all but a small group of the well-to-do from acquiring mastership. Thus, when this system was swept away at the end of the eighteenth century, vocational training was at an ebb. The matter, if considered at all, was held to be a private responsibility. For many years, the educator Fellenberg warned in vain that it was the duty of the state to make it possible for everyone, in his own interest and that of society, to recognize

---

[16] Nuffield College, Oxford, *Industry and Education* (Oxford and London, 1943), p. 12.
[17] Ibid. pp. 33–4.

and choose the vocation that offered the best prospect of success.

Individual craftsmen and industrialists with vision carried the burden of vocational training until an association of trade and industry representatives, created in 1879, took up the battle for improved apprenticeship, examination of apprentices, and compulsory attendance of continuation schools. The Swiss Commercial Association promoted comparable organization of the training of commercial employees. Shortly thereafter the cantons initiated legislation on apprenticeship, and finally, utilizing all the experience of the pioneers in the field, the federal government stepped in.

As early as 1884, the Federal Council decided to grant subsidies to institutions of vocational education for crafts and industry. In 1891, a similar step was taken to aid training for commercial pursuits, and four years later subsidies were granted for home economics and other vocational training for girls. With the creation of the office of a federal inspector for vocational education and training (1924), the Council took a step beyond the policy of simple subsidies. The inspector was assigned the task of reorganizing vocational training on a national scale, and the result of his work was the federal law on vocational training adopted by Parliament on 26 June 1930, and in force since 1 January 1933. Subsequently, the cantons adjusted their legislation to conform with federal law.[18]

The federal law carefully maintains decentralization, except where uniformity is required in the interest of the national economy and of more efficient training. Apprenticeship is under the general authority of the Federal Department of Economics, while direct supervision is exercised by cantonal governments. The Federal Departments of Economics and Labor, employer associations, and trade unions cooperate in laying down the rules of apprentice training in each trade with regard to terms of apprenticeship, training programs, examinations, and continuation school attendance. By 1938, 60 such apprentice regulations (*Lehrlings-*

---

[18] Emil Zucker, 'Berufsbildung und Berufsberatung in Handwerk, Landwirtschaft, Industrie und Handel,' in Walter Guyer, *Erziehungsgedanke und Bildungswesen in der Schweiz* (Frauenfeld and Leipzig, 1936), pp. 186-98.

reglemente) had been issued for 83 trades.[19] All of them stipulate written apprenticeship contracts. The examinations of apprentices, in which representatives of management and labor cooperate, are recognized for the whole of Switzerland. This is also true of the 'higher examinations' required of journeymen who wish to become masters. Journeymen must work for three years at that level before they are permitted to take the master's examination. The title of master is legally protected, and in certain trades designated by the Federal Council only masters are authorized to keep and train apprentices.

All regulations make theoretical instruction at continuation school a condition of apprenticeship. These schools are subsidized by the federal government; in 1938, 262 industrial, and 97 commercial, continuation schools received such grants. Regional and local apprentice training problems are dealt with by cantonal apprentice offices whose representatives hold frequent discussions among themselves in order to adjust the work in the cantons to the federal standards.

Although the enactment of federal law raised the standards of apprentice training appreciably, it contributed at the same time to a decrease in the number of apprentices. The new rules presupposed a certain knowledge of pedagogy which not all masters possessed. Thus many who had formerly trained apprentices withdrew from the field. Apprenticeship openings, especially in rural areas, declined with the suppression of small local vocational schools and the resulting necessity of sending the apprentices to more distant schools for theoretical instruction. The increase in apprenticeship fees, which was considered justified because of the improved training offered, made parents reluctant to enroll their children, particularly when the widespread unemployment that set in soon after the enactment of the federal laws aroused doubts whether even good training would offer better employment opportunities than no training at all. Since abnormal conditions prevailed during

[19] *Handbuch der Schweizerischen Volkswirtschaft*, vol. 1, s.v. 'Berufsbildung,' pp. 228–31.

the war years, it cannot yet be ascertained whether these unwelcome by-products of the federal law will be effectively eliminated.

The following figures show the number of apprentices in Switzerland in 1939.[20] The total number of trade apprentices represents a considerable decline: even in 1910 there were 46,000; in 1920

	Male	Female	Total
Trade apprentices	36,024	7,468	43,492
Commercial apprentices	8,022	5,450	13,472
TOTAL	44,046	12,918	56,964

there were 59,000, and in 1930, 61,000. Nevertheless, the 1939 figure was still remarkably high. The total of the gainfully occupied in industry, crafts, and construction was 781,581. Deducting about one-fourth for those who would profit more by preparation as commercial apprentices, there would remain about 600,000 positions for which trade apprenticeship could be considered adequate training. The 43,500 trade apprentices constitute 7.3 per cent of the entire technical and manual labor force in industry, crafts, and construction; this ratio of 1:14 would be too small for the replacements of skilled workers but is adequate in relation to the total labor force in these fields, which contains unskilled as well as skilled workers.

The term of apprenticeship averages three years for male, and two years for female, apprentices.[21] In 1939, 18,308 apprentice examinations were given, and 19,494 new contracts were drawn; in 1940, examinations totaled 18,531, and new contracts, 19,320.[22] Annually, from 18,000 to 19,000 apprentices, or about 95 per cent of all who enter apprenticeship, pass their examinations. Among these, there are about 14,000 trade apprentices who represent approximately 22 per cent of an average age group. Since 44.6 per cent of the gainfully occupied population worked in industry and

[20] *Statistisches Jahrbuch der Schweiz*, 1940, p. 144.
[21] Willi Luick, *Der berufliche Nachwuchs in der Schweiz* (Berne, 1929), p. 54.
[22] *Statistisches Jahrbuch*, 1940, pp. 382–3.

crafts,[23] trade apprentices are available for 50 per cent of all jobs in industry and crafts, and for much more than half of all those jobs for which trade apprenticeship provides adequate training. On the basis of the same computation made for the male employed alone, it is found that about 54 per cent of a male age group is occupied in industry and crafts, and that about 33 per cent of a male age group goes through trade apprenticeship; thus, for more than 60 per cent of all jobs in industry and crafts, there are trained trade apprentices. Considering the total number of the male trade and commercial apprentices, it may be presumed that annually about 15,000 complete their terms. This figure represents 46 per cent of a whole male age group and much more than half of all those gainfully occupied in the age groups fifteen to seventeen, which are the normal apprenticeship years. Thus, everything indicates a substantial systematic preparation for work through apprentice training.

There is no doubt that not all apprentices will do skilled work; many will work in semiskilled or unskilled jobs, at least during a part of their working lives. Although skilled work is a characteristic feature of the Swiss economy and an indispensable element for its successful operation, the trend toward mass production has made itself felt even here, and the proportion of skilled workers among the total has declined. The ranks of the metal workers showed rapid percentage increases of semiskilled and unskilled workers at the expense of skilled workers. According to reports of the Swiss Metal Workers Union, more than 50 per cent of its members are semiskilled or unskilled. The recent decline in the number of apprentices may therefore be not merely a temporary effect of the 1930 law but rather a permanent adjustment to changed conditions in the national economy.

The shifts among fields of activity and interest are suggested by the following figures on apprentice examinations given and new

[23] Figure for 1930, ibid. pp. 42, 46; only slight changes have occurred since.

contracts drawn in various trades, in 1939 and 1940.[24] In normal times, the trends of which are expressed in the number of examinations given in 1939, trade apprenticeship was highest in the field of clothing, cleaning, and dressmaking (with a majority of girl apprentices), and next highest in the machinists, metal, and electrical workers' group. High figures were also attained in construction,

	Examinations		New contracts	
	1939	1940	1939	1940
Machine, metal, & elec. work	3,618	3,874	4,771	5,035
Construction	1,321	1,214	1,076	792
Woodworking	980	930	906	810
Clothing, cleaning, dressmaking	4,457	3,903	3,712	3,542
Food, luxuries	1,551	1,482	1,575	1,754
Commerce	3,959	4,746	4,947	5,097
TOTAL	18,308	18,531	19,494	19,320

food and luxuries, and woodworking; the number of apprentices in any of the other trades did not exceed a few hundred. The figures on new contracts for 1939 and 1940 show the effects of the outbreak of the European war: an increase of apprenticeship in the metal trades, which rose to first place, and a decline in clothing and dressmaking, and especially in construction, the prospects for which were dark when manpower was being absorbed by military mobilization.

Interesting features of apprenticeship in Switzerland, which must be at least mentioned here, are the vocational guidance and welfare work set up for apprentices. At the end of World War I, several private organizations founded the Association for Vocational Guidance and Welfare Work for Apprentices (*Verband für Berufsberatung und Lehrlingsfürsorge*) in which all offices of vocational guidance cooperate with the great economic and vocational organizations, federal and cantonal departments, and welfare organizations. An intelligent distribution of the young people among the various vocations is thereby effected, and youth is af-

[24] *Statistisches Jahrbuch*, 1940, pp. 382-3.

forded a certain amount of protection, which is the more necessary since apprentices in Switzerland are not generally members of trade unions.[25]

There are 250 offices for vocational guidance spread over the country, which function as either cantonal or town units. Each is under the direction of one male and one female guidance counselor. Most of these counselors are teachers by profession, and on the strength of this background, they are equipped to obtain a good picture of the personality, inclinations, and aptitudes of the youngsters, and to give each one sound advice. Through circulars, courses, and other means, they are familiarized with the employment prospects in various trades and vocations, and they use this knowledge to modify their recommendations. The Association itself tries to influence public opinion by analyzing, through lectures, the press, and other media, the futures open to boys and girls in the various vocations.

The apprentice contracts contain clauses designed to avert any threat to the health and mental development of the apprentice. The Association goes further by recognizing that many youths who might usefully serve an apprenticeship are prevented from doing so by the immediate need to earn money. Thus, several organizations offer apprenticeship grants for children who could not otherwise afford to serve their term.

U.S.S.R.

Inasmuch as most of the available data on apprenticeship in the Soviet Union pertains to the institutions established for the schooling of the young workers rather than their actual in-employment training, the subject has been treated in Appendix II. There are, however, some figures on the number of apprentices which indicate the scope of the system prior to its abolition, as such, in October 1940.

[25] According to a report at the meeting of the Swiss trade unions in 1933, only 2,000 of the 230,000 members were in the usual apprentice age groups. See Schweizerischer Gewerkschaftsbund, *Protokoll des Gewerkschafts-Kongresses* (Zürich, 1933), p. 102.

When the first Five-Year Plan started in 1929, the number of apprentices was 133,200. The peak was reached in 1932 with 567,-900, but after the reorganization of the factory apprentice schools in 1933, the number dwindled to 269,200 in 1936 and 242,000 in 1938.[26] The number of apprentices produced by these schools *annually* remained about as high as it was before the restriction of training, but the quality of their training was, of course, considerably lower.

The proportion of apprentices to the number of workers in large-scale industries was 12.1 per cent in 1932 and 4.6 per cent in 1936. The highest percentage of apprentices was in printing and publishing with 17.8 per cent in 1932 and 11.8 per cent in 1936. In the machine, building, and metal working industries the percentage declined from 19.2 to 6.5 per cent; though the number of apprentices decreased only from 239,500 to 116,000, apprenticeship obviously did not keep pace with the expansion of the industries. The percentage of apprentices was lowest in the production of linen (1.7), food industry (2.3), coal mining (2.3), rubber industry (2.5), and fuel extraction (2.6).

Further analyses and comparisons are not possible, since the Statistical Abstract of the Soviet Union attempts no breakdown of the labor force according to skilled workers, operatives, and laborers. Moreover, on the basis of the brevity of training, if for no other reason, the term 'apprentice' can scarcely have the same connotations and significance that it does in other countries.

[26] *Socialist Construction in the USSR*, Statistical Abstract ed. by the State Planning Commission of the USSR, English translation (Moscow, 1936), pp. 378-9; *Socialist Construction . . .* , in Russian (Moscow and Leningrad, 1939), p. 116.

Distribution of the Labor Force, 1940, by Occupation[a]

Class 1: Professional (excl. Technical)	Male		Female	
	Employed	Unemployed	Employed	Unemployed
Actors & actresses	6,931	3,988	4,761	2,525
Artists & art teachers	34,478	4,364	17,507	2,231
Authors, editors, & reporters	51,523	3,809	18,536	1,135
Clergymen	133,449	1,641	3,148	——
College presidents, professors, etc.	55,123	407	19,884	203
Dentists	69,074	296	1,047	178 [b]
Lawyers & judges	173,456	1,805	4,187	106
Musicians & music teachers	69,800	15,286	59,456	4,267
Osteopaths	4,905	14	1,102	[c]
Pharmacists	76,131	2,577	3,216	[c]
Physicians & surgeons	157,041	607	7,608	107
Social & welfare workers	24,868	1,101	44,809	1,750
Teachers (n.e.c.)	247,716	6,763	772,044	15,935
Veterinarians	10,638	92	79	[c]
Other professional workers	68,803	2,845	57,556	1,422 [c]
TOTAL	1,183,936	45,595	1,014,940	29,859

[a] Compiled from Sixteenth Census of the United States, 1940, Population, vol. 3, *The Labor Force*, Part I, U.S. Summary (Washington, 1943), Tables 58 and 59. Figures do not include persons employed on public emergency work.

[b] Includes pharmacists, osteopaths, and veterinarians.

[c] *See* Dentists.

DISTRIBUTION OF LABOR FORCE, 1940 (*cont.*)

Class 2: Technical Professional	Male		Female	
	Employed	Unemployed	Employed	Unemployed
Architects	19,899	965	447	——
Chemists, assayers, & metallurgists	55,371	2,308	1,654	——
Civil engineers	80,171	4,245	191	——
Electrical engineers	53,103	1,628	164	——
Mechanical engineers	82,255	2,691	188	——
Other technical engineers	29,029	1,400	187	——
TOTAL	319,828	13,237	2,831	——

Class 3: Semiprofessional	Male		Female	
	Employed	Unemployed	Employed	Unemployed
County agents & farm demonstrators	5,845	4,577	4,396	——
Trained nurses & student nurses	7,509	563	348,277	12,938
Dancers, showmen, & athletes	31,147	——	13,927	——
Chiropractors	8,758	——	1,871	——
Funeral directors & embalmers	35,856	——	2,114	——
Healers & medical service workers	10,045	——	9,510	——
Optometrists	9,762	——	475	——
Religious workers	8,798	——	25,874	——
Semiprofessional workers	61,584	——	9,147	——
Postmasters, misc. govt. officials	198,377	3,531	33,896	——
Buyers & dept. heads, stores	51,935	——	17,581	——
Managers & superintendents, bldg.	40,394	——	28,488	——
Officials, lodge, soc., union, etc.	21,079	——	4,225	——

DISTRIBUTION OF LABOR FORCE, 1940 (*cont.*)

Class 3: Semiprofessional	Male		Female	
	Employed	Unemployed	Employed	Unemployed
Finance, insurance, & real estate	174,668	3,011	12,300	525
Personal services	91,572	2,219	31,655	——
Misc. industries & services	108,970	4,942	19,116	678
TOTAL	866,299	18,843	562,852	14,141

Class 4: Proprietors, Managers, & Officials (*n.e.c.*)	Male		Female	
	Employed	Unemployed	Employed	Unemployed
Mining	30,447	831	394	——
Construction	113,898	6,247	1,098	——
Manufacturing	402,506	6,843	17,862	289
Transportation, communications, & utilities	134,232	1,674	5,902	——
TOTAL	681,083	15,595	25,256	289

Class 5: Commercial Trades	Male		Female	
	Employed	Unemployed	Employed	Unemployed
Conductors, railroad	46,185	675	——	——
Advertising agents	30,110	——	3,602	——
Country buyers, shippers of livestock, etc.	38,007	——	509	——
Credit men	26,307	——	3,643	——
Floormen & floor mgrs., store	4,672	——	2,201	——
Purchasing agents & buyers (n.e.c.)	28,966	——	2,593	——
Proprietors, mgrs., & officials Wholesale trade	227,334	5,015	6,992	d

d Included in Retail trade, except eating and drinking places.

DISTRIBUTION OF LABOR FORCE, 1940 (*cont.*)

Class 5: Commercial Trades	Male		Female	
	Employed	Unemployed	Employed	Unemployed
Eating & drinking places	200,519	6,297	65,064	1,134
Retail trade, exc. eating & drinking places	1,242,323	24,277	161,999	1,701
Baggagemen, express messengers, etc.	27,759	357	117	——
Bookkeepers, accountants, etc.	447,606	31,178	448,359	24,438
Office machine operators	8,284	551	51,454	3,375
Shipping & receiving clerks	200,669	18,318	8,668	——
Stenographers, typists, & secretaries	68,805	5,252	988,081	67,582
Telegraph operators	31,554	1,644	8,228	220
Agents (n.e.c.)	80,040	——	8,601	——
Attendants & assistants, library	1,955	——	7,028	——
Attendants, physicians' & dentists' offices	1,387	——	27,922	——
Other clerical & kindred workers (n.e.c.)	1,134,933	86,670	630,471	46,499
Canvassers & solicitors	72,995	5,119	17,099	1,288
Insurance agents & brokers	226,061	8,020	13,081	284
Real estate agents & brokers	100,856	4,541	10,254	394
Salesmen, finance, brokerage & commission firms	18,327	——	380	——
Traveling salesmen & sales agents	579,423	——	12,904	——

DISTRIBUTION OF LABOR FORCE, 1940 (*cont.*)

Class 5:	Male		Female	
Commercial Trades	Employed	Unemployed	Employed	Unemployed
Other salesmen & saleswomen	1,021,329	105,186	724,223	74,931
Wholesale & retail trade services	28,422	——	2,509	——
Wholesale & retail trade inspectors	3,162	——	1,658	——
TOTAL	5,896,990	303,100	207,640	221,846

Class 6:	Male		Female	
Technical Trades	Employed	Unemployed	Employed	Unemployed
Designers & draftsmen	91,820	5,085	9,105	1,276
Surveyors	13,243	1,486	101	——
Aviators	5,828	——	51	——
Photographers	29,078	——	4,623	——
Radio & wireless operators	10,296	——	97	——
Technicians & assistants, lab.	41,487	——	21,511	——
Technicians, exc. lab.	6,567	——	781	——
Officers, pilots, pursers, & engineers, ship	30,978	——	97	——
Props., business & repair services	82,288	1,226	4,303	——
Foremen				
Construction	45,394	8,337	129	——
Manufacturing	262,851	5,816	27,126	1,829
Transportation, communication, & utilities	92,366	1,420	713	——
Mining	26,443	——	41	——
Business & repair services	5,892	——	212	——
Personal services	4,314	3,635	2,686	5,401

DISTRIBUTION OF LABOR FORCE, 1940 (*cont.*)

Class 6: Technical Trades	Male Employed	Unemployed	Female Employed	Unemployed
Government	9,411	—	398	—
Other industries & services	8,040	—	1,613	—
Industry, not reported	3,481	—	363	—
Inspectors				
Mining	6,954	—	19	—
Construction	4,336	—	114	—
Railroads (incl. repair shops)	28,261	—	75	—
Transportation (exc. railroads)	5,005	—	81	—
Communication & utilities	7,234	—	815	—
Misc. industries & services	11,173	—	1,707	—
Locomotive engineers	69,496	1,686	—	—
TOTAL	902,236	28,691	76,761	8,506

Class 7: Craft Trades	Male Employed	Unemployed	Female Employed	Unemployed
Bakers	119,039	11,025	10,017	—
Blacksmiths, forgemen, & hammermen	72,034	6,983	212	—
Boilermakers	27,589	3,278	73	—
Cabinetmakers & patternmakers	81,263	6,719	607	—
Carpenters	556,918	133,608	1,395	—
Compositors	150,647	11,598	7,425	382
Electricians	196,526	20,549	696	—
Locomotive firemen	43,851	3,559	—	—
Machinists, millwrights, & toolmakers	604,706	33,793	5,067	—

DISTRIBUTION OF LABOR FORCE, 1940 (*cont.*)

Class 7: Craft Trades	Male		Female	
	Employed	Unemployed	Employed	Unemployed
Masons, tile setters, & stonecutters	102,089	32,923	347	——
Mechanics & repairmen, & loom fixers	859,491	75,482	4,240	——
Molders, metal	75,559	7,542	345	——
Painters (construct.), paperhangers, & glaziers	350,372	89,100	3,849	——
Plasterers & cement finishers	51,926	16,824	214	——
Plumbers & gas & steam fitters	173,385	24,748	530	——
Printing craftsmen, excl. compositors & typesetters	60,830	3,810	1,019	——
Rollers & roll hands, metal	26,439	3,130	108	——
Roofers & sheet metal workers	103,715	14,857	420	——
Shoemakers & repairers (not in factory)	59,609	3,665	586	——
Stationary engineers, cranemen, & hoistmen	285,352	23,070	774	——
Struct. & orn. metal workers	27,769	6,893	182	——
Tailors & furriers	105,022	11,274	16,470	——
Other craftsmen & kindred workers	192,766	14,690	11,755	5,401
Apprentices	81,807	7,295	2,273	——
Dressmakers & seamstresses (not in factory)	2,324	259	133,627	12,146

Class 7:	Male		Female	
Craft Trades	Employed	Unemployed	Employed	Unemployed
Linemen & service-men, telegraph, telephone, & power	103,501	4,340	995	——
Barbers, beauticians, & manicurists	209,439	8,524	206,592	10,965
TOTAL	4,723,988	579,538	409,818	28,894

Class 8:	Male		Female	
Farmers and Farm Managers	Employed	Unemployed	Employed	Unemployed
Farmers (owners & tenants)	4,955,624	——	151,087	——
Farm managers	36,091	——	812	——
TOTAL	4,991,715	——	151,899	——

Class 9:	Male		Female	
Operatives	Employed	Unemployed	Employed	Unemployed
Telephone operators	10,697	488	189,002	6,646
Chauffeurs, truck drivers, & deliverymen	1,499,972	174,107	8,449	——
Mine operators & laborers	649,226	112,603	1,787	——
Painters, exc. construction & maintenance	82,768	8,550	6,258	——
Power station operators	21,285	311	620	——
Welders & flame cutters	122,688	10,061	2,053	——

DISTRIBUTION OF LABOR FORCE, 1940 (*cont.*)

Class 9: Operatives	Male		Female	
	Employed	Unemployed	Employed	Unemployed
Other specified operators & kindred workers	390,056	37,028	34,495	7,156
Operators & kindred workers (n.e.c.) by industry				
Manufacturing	2,303,054	229,578	1,596,579	154,331
Nonmanufacturing	366,175	45,120	86,509	11,022
TOTAL	5,445,921	617,846	1,925,752	179,155

Class 10: Laborers and kindred workers	Male		Female	
	Employed	Unemployed	Employed	Unemployed
Mail carriers	119,246	1,456	1,524	—
Messengers, exc. express	65,544	8,170	2,732	—
Collectors, bill & account	38,374	—	3,316	—
Hucksters & peddlers	48,357	—	2,338	—
Newsboys	53,313	—	1,057	1,288
Attendants, filling station, etc.	209,449	20,618	3,866	—
Brakemen & switchmen, railroad	107,432	6,304	—	—
Conductors, bus & street ry.	16,751	538	154	—
Firemen, exc. locomotive & fire dept.	112,612	9,889	383	—

DISTRIBUTION OF LABOR FORCE, 1940 (*cont.*)

Class 10: Laborers and kindred workers	Male		Female	
	Employed	Unemployed	Employed	Unemployed
Laundry operatives & laundresses (exc. private family)	48,296	4,457	167,967	10,362
Motormen, ry., mine, factory, etc.	53,281	1,907	227	——
Sailors, deck hands, exc. U.S. Navy	35,221	9,796	137	——
Domestic service workers	142,231	19,450	1,969,083	196,395
Protective service workers	677,213	24,557	4,321	214
Service workers, exc. domestic & protective	1,310,043	151,491	1,050,726	95,955
Farm laborers & foremen	2,770,005	300,566	320,005	20,730
Laborers, exc. farm & mine	2,965,693	828,557	98,435	17,578
TOTAL	8,773,061	1,387,756	3,626,271	342,522

APPENDIX B

Size of the Labor Force in Selected Technical and Manual Occupations, 1870–1940 (in thousands)[a]

Occupation	1870	1880	1890	1900	1910	1920	1930	1940
B.1: Technical Professional Occupations								
Technical engineers:								
Civil engineers & surveyors					52.0	64.7	102.1	105.5
Electrical engineers					15.3	27.1	57.8	55.7
Mechanical & industrial engineers					14.5	37.7	54.4	95.3
Chemical, mining, & metallurgical engineers					6.9	6.7	12.0	21.4
Total: technical engineers	7.1	7.1	28.2	43.2	88.8	136.1	226.1	277.9
Chemists, assayers, & metallurgists	.8	2.0	4.5	8.8	16.3	32.9	47.1	60.0
Architects	2.0	3.4	8.1	10.6	16.6	18.2	22.0	22.0
Designers, draftsmen, & inventors	1.3	2.8	9.4	18.9	47.4	70.7	102.7	111.8[b]
TOTAL	11.2	15.3	50.2	81.5	169.1	257.9	398.0	471.7

[a] Compiled from Sixteenth Census of the United States, 1940, Population, *Comparative Occupation Statistics for the United States, 1870–1940* (Washington, 1943), Tables 2 and 8. Figures for 1870–1930 pertain to workers 10 years old and over, while figures for 1940 refer to those 14 and over.
[b] Designers and draftsmen only.

Size of the Labor Force in Selected Technical and Manual Occupations (*cont.*)

Occupation	1870	1880	1890	1900	1910	1920	1930	1940
B.2: Metal and Allied Trades								
Blacksmiths								
Forgemen & hammermen	145.0	172.7	209.6	226.5	235.8	197.9	125.1 }	
Boilermakers					7.2	26.2	23.1 }	87.2
Plumbers & gas & steam fitters	7.0	12.8	21.3	33.0	44.8	76.1	50.5	32.9
Machinists	11.2	19.4	61.2	97.8	158.2	214.1	243.7	216.1
Mechanics	55.1	101.1	186.8	283.1	461.3	841.4	653.9	521.1 [c]
Loomfixers						281.7	638.3	949.7 [c]
Millwrights					13.3	16.0	19.2	24.7
Toolmakers, diemakers, & diesetters					17.4	37.7	42.0	43.6
Tinsmiths, coppersmiths, & sheet metal workers					9.3	55.1	78.8	96.9 [c]
workers					56.4	69.7	80.4	91.6 [c]
Molders, founders, & cutters					120.9	123.7	105.2	87.6
Electricians	.4	1.2	15.0	50.7	122.9	222.5	284.9	252.9 [d]
TOTAL	218.7	307.2	493.9	691.1	1,247.5	2,162.1	2,345.1	2,404.3
Locomotive engineers					96.2	109.9	101.2	72.4
Locomotive firemen					76.3	91.3	67.0	48.8
Stationary engineers	34.6	79.6	139.7	223.5	231.0 }	242.0 }	256.0	200.0
Cranemen, hoistmen, etc.						37.8	60.8	120.1
Firemen, exc. locomotive & fire dept.					111.2	143.8	127.3	127.4
Others, machinery					14.0	24.6	31.2	39.5
TOTAL	34.6	79.6	139.7	223.5	528.7	649.4	643.5	608.2

Size of the Labor Force in Selected Technical and Manual Occupations (*cont.*)

Occupation	1870	1880	1890	1900	1910	1920	1930	1940
Operatives:								
Automobile industry					21.0	121.1	161.9	219.0 [c]
Electrical industries					24.6	64.8	117.3	152.5 [c]
Other iron, steel, & mach. industries					451.7	694.1	633.8	733.5 [c]
Metal industries, exc. iron & steel					69.7	91.2	91.8	80.5 [c]
Total: operatives					567.0	971.2	1,004.8	1,185.5
Laborers:								
Automobile industry					15.7	83.3	123.7	69.5 [c]
Electrical industries					11.4	26.7	36.9	29.8 [c]
Other iron, steel, & mach. industries					466.8	648.4	538.3	408.5 [c]
Metal industries, exc. iron & steel					44.7	67.8	62.4	45.1 [c]
Total: laborers					538.6	826.2	761.3	552.9

[c] Not comparable with previous years.
[d] And power station operators.

SIZE OF THE LABOR FORCE IN SELECTED TECHNICAL AND MANUAL OCCUPATIONS (*cont.*)

Occupation	1870	1880	1890	1900	1910	1920	1930	1940
B.3: Building and Woodworking Trades								
Cabinetmakers	43.3	50.7	35.9	35.6	41.9	46.5	59.6	58.8
Laborers & operatives in furniture factories					68.3	91.0	115.0	109.0
Pattern & modelmakers	4.0	5.8	10.3	15.0	23.6	27.7	29.8	33.0
Carpenters	365.8	390.6	618.2	600.3	823.2	892.2	933.5	773.6
Brick & stone masons & tilesetters	90.8	102.5	160.8	160.8	171.5	136.5	173.3	141.7
Plasterers	23.9	22.1	39.0	35.7	48.3	38.8	70.7	52.9
Roofers & slaters	2.7	4.0	7.0	9.0	14.4	11.9	24.0	32.7
Painters, glaziers, etc.	87.5	130.3	222.2	277.5	340.0	327.1	531.6	450.3 [e]
Paperhangers	2.5	5.0	12.4	22.0	26.0	19.6	28.6	30.0
Structural iron workers					11.4	18.8	29.0	38.6 [e]
TOTAL	620.5	711.0	1,105.8	1,155.9	1,568.6	1,610.1	1,995.1	1,720.6

[e] Not fully comparable with other years.

Occupation	1870	1880	1890	1900	1910	1920	1930	1940
B.4: *Printing and Allied Trades*								
Compositors, linotypers, & typesetters					127.6	140.2	183.6	174.3
Electrotypers, lithographers, & stereotypers					12.5	13.7	16.7	
Engravers f					14.0	15.0	19.4	30.8
Pressmen & plate printers					20.1	18.7	31.2	35.8
Apprentice printers & bookbinders					12.4	16.6	10.9	10.0
Operatives & laborers					64.2	74.7	81.7	84.5
TOTAL	50.0	86.6	146.9	185.4	250.8	278.9	343.5	335.4
B.5: *Textile Industry*								
Operatives, exc. dyeing, finishing, & printing	244.4	352.9	454.1	559.1	670.2	774.7	818.7	937.7
Laborers, exc. dyeing, finishing, & printing					77.0	142.7	117.9	90.6
Dyers	8.7	13.6	20.9	28.3	14.1	15.1	17.7	24.9
Operatives, dyeing, finishing, & printing					16.4	17.7	19.6	26.1
Laborers, dyeing, finishing, & printing					9.9	10.6	7.6	5.9

f Includes engravers not working in the printing industry.

SIZE OF THE LABOR FORCE IN SELECTED TECHNICAL AND MANUAL OCCUPATIONS (*cont.*)

Occupation	1870	1880	1890	1900	1910	1920	1930	1940
B.6: Clothing Industry								
Dressmakers					455.3	238.5	160.0	165.0
Tailors & tailoresses					204.6	192.2	169.3	118.8
Operatives					340.6	409.4	534.5	690.5
Laborers					15.3	12.8	10.2	12.4
TOTAL	275.8	457.0	751.3	897.8	1,015.8	852.9	874.0	986.7
B.7: Occupations in Production of Shoes								
Shoemakers & repairers (not in factories)	172.8	194.0	214.5	208.0	69.5			
Operatives (in shoe factories)					181.0	206.2	209.9	221.8
Laborers					10.2	19.2	18.3	11.6
TOTAL	172.8	194.0	214.5	208.0	260.8	304.2	304.5	299.1
B.8: Beauty Industry								
Barbers, hairdressers, & manicurists:								
Male	23.1	41.9	82.1	125.5	172.9	182.9	261.0	221.1
Female	1.5	3.4	3.7	7.2	22.3	33.2	113.1	218.1
TOTAL	24.6	45.4	85.8	132.8	195.2	216.2	374.2	440.1
B.9: Drivers								
Chauffeurs, truck & tractor drivers					45.8	285.0	972.4	1,339.8
Draymen, teamsters, & carriage drivers	83.3	119.1	246.2	361.8	443.8	420.2	111.2	g

g Not classified.

Size of the Labor Force in Selected Technical and Manual Occupations (*cont.*)

Occupation	1870	1880	1890	1900	1910	1920	1930	1940
B.10: Clerical and Commercial Occupations								
Clerical:								
Bookkeepers, cashiers, accountants	38.8	74.9	159.4	254.9	486.7	734.7	930.6	931.3
Clerks, exc. in stores	29.8	59.8	188.0	248.3	720.5	1,487.9	1,997.0	2,037.8 [h]
Stenographers & typists	.2	5.0	33.4	112.4	316.7	615.2	811.2	1,174.9
Total: clerical	68.8	139.7	380.8	615.6	1,523.9	2,837.8	3,738.8	4,144.0
Commercial:								
Retail & wholesale dealers	440.2	602.5	853.2	1,022.8	1,251.2	1,410.7	1,796.5	1,927.0
Commercial travelers, traveling salesmen, sales agents	7.3	28.1	58.7	92.9	163.6	179.3	223.0	623.6 [i]
Salesmen, saleswomen, clerks in stores	240.8	385.7	614.8	970.4	1,264.3	1,539.7	2,390.3	2,174.4 [j]
Total: commercial	688.3	1,016.3	1,526.7	2,086.1	2,679.1	3,129.7	4,409.8	4,735.0
TOTAL: clerical and commercial	757.1	1,156.0	1,907.5	2,701.7	4,203.0	5,967.5	8,148.6	8,879.0

[h] Includes office machine operators (64.2) and clerical and kindred workers (2,037.8).
[i] Distinction between commercial travelers, traveling salesmen, and sales agents not fully comparable with previous years.
[j] Includes shipping clerks (229.7); salesmen and saleswomen, n.e.c., and commercial travelers (525.6); clerks in stores (1,402.1).

Index